VIETNAM: Some Basic Issues and Alternatives

VIETNAM: Some Basic Issues and Alternatives

edited by Walter Isard

Essays by:

Peter Archibald
Philip Brickman
Allan E. Goodman
Nigel Howard
Walter Isard
Solomon G. Jacobson
Jeffrey S. Milstein
William C. Mitchell
Ithiel de Sola Pool
Samuel L. Popkin
John P. Robinson
Thomas C. Schelling
David C. Schwartz
Phillip Shaver
Robert Strausz-Hupé
Ralph K. White

SCHENKMAN PUBLISHING COMPANY
Cambridge, Massachusetts
in collaboration with
Peace Research Society (International)

CONTENTS

PREFACE

These papers were presented at the June, 1968 conference of the Peace Research Society (International) in Cambridge, Massachusetts. They are being published jointly as Volume X, *Papers,* Peace Research Society (International) and in book form by the Schenkman Publishing Company.[1]

The Peace Research Society (International) has been primarily concerned with providing an arena at which scholars concerned with peace and world order can present their findings, methodology, and theory for critical comment and reaction. By its constitution the Society "is an international association for the advancement of peace research and related studies. The Society shall operate as an objective, scientific organization without political, social, financial, or nationalistic bias. Its main objectives shall be to foster exchange of ideas and promote studies focusing on peace analysis and utilizing tools, methods, and theoretical frameworks specifically designed for peace research as well as concepts, procedures, and analytical techniques of the various social and natural sciences, law, engineering, and other disciplines and professions. The Society shall support these objectives by promoting acquaintance and discussion among its members and with scholars from all fields and regions of the world, by stimulating research, by encouraging the publication of scholarly studies, and by performing services to aid the advancement of its members and peace research."

Until the holding of the Vietnam conference in June, 1968, all conferences of the Peace Research Society (International) had concentrated upon general empirical findings, methodology, analytical techniques and theories without reference to any specific conflict problem. However, it was felt, after the November, 1967 conference in Cambridge, Massachusetts, that the time was ripe for a conference at which the several papers might attempt to apply our findings and know-how to a particular, critical problem. It was against this background then that

In the preparation of the papers for publication the editor wishes to acknowledge the valuable assistance of Charles W. Hunt.
[1]Previous and forthcoming volumes of *Papers,* Peace Research Society (International) are available from the Peace Research Society (International), Department of Regional Science, Wharton School, University of Pennsylvania, Philadelphia, Pennsylvania, 19104, U.S.A.

the conference on *U.S.-Vietnam: Some Basic Issues* was called. In terms of the level, quality and intensity of verbal discussion, the conference was a real success.

It is to be observed that the papers of this volume cover contributions from several important disciplines. Yet, together, they cannot embody more than a small fraction of what is to be said about the Vietnam problem. Nevertheless, there is at least some insight and knowledge to be gained by the reading of this volume even by policy makers and scholars who are "fully informed" of the Vietnam problem.

For example, as one surveys the situation in early March, 1969— the time when the last changes to the manuscript of this book were possible—one may speculate on several key questions. One asks whether or not all the knowledge and negotiations know-how that lie behind and are contained in the various contributions of this book are being fully put to use by the State Department and the foreign affairs advisors of President Nixon. One wonders from the series of actions and reactions taken during and immediately after President Nixon's European trip, whether there is in Washington a positive, comprehensive approach and plan toward systematic disengagement—or at least a more comprehensive approach than characterized President Johnson's administration before his decision not to seek reelection. Were the State Department and President Nixon's foreign affairs advisors sufficiently aware of the full range of action-reaction possibilities that might be generated by his trip? One speculates whether Washington, through prior tacit understandings or agreements, took the necessary precautionary steps to confine any negative retaliatory propensities by North Vietnam and the Vietcong. The insights provided by the analyses in such papers as those by Howard, and Milstein and Mitchell are relevant to these questions. So also are the cooperative solution possibilities suggested by several papers dealing with coalition formation and the veto incremax procedure. Finally, one is forced to ask whether Washington is, in fact, aware of the urgent need for rigorous and thorough research to define policy alternatives and their implications, and to explore further the feasibility of cooperative approaches to reaching solutions.

These are just some of the questions the reader may have in mind as he studies the contributions to this volume.

Walter Isard
Philadelphia
March, 1969

INTRODUCTION AND OVERVIEW

CHAPTER 1. INTRODUCTION AND OVERVIEW

By Walter Isard*

This book is a collection of scientific papers by students of society.
They are concerned primarily with behavior in the international arena.
They focus on the selection of a best action or establishment of a viable
institution from among the alternatives available. The specific actors
are the participants in the United States-Vietnam conflict, and the institutions in question are primarily the social and political institutions relevant for both Vietnamese and U.S. society.

Though these papers are the work of scholars from several social science disciplines—economics, sociology, government, regional science,
psychology, operations research and applied mathematics—they nonetheless are easily woven into a fabric of interrelations which has considerable strength and flexibility for use by policy makers. In this sense,
the set of papers is viewed as making an important contribution. Yet,
it is fully recognized that not all factors and considerations that should
be woven into the warp of a better, or "improved", society can be cov-
ered in the brief span of this book. The contributions presented here
are to be supplemented by many other investigations.

The first paper of the series concerns the current and potential institutional structures in South Vietnam. Professor Pool, a leading expert
on this subject, throws considerable light on the current problems of orderly government within South Vietnam. He paints a most interesting
history of Vietnam to provide a better perspective on her contemporary

*The author is associated with the Department of Regional Science, University
of Pennsylvania.

problems.   The Vietnamese village was never a peaceful place.   Today, as with other peasant societies, Vietnam lacks the roads, the telephones and organized authorities to make possible the exercise of effective control of violent individuals.   Terrorists can operate in largely unrestricted fashion regardless of whether local population supports them.   These and other considerations lead Pool to advance the hypothesis: "the kind of organization that can successfully assert its claim to a monopoly of force is the one that at the same time has its roots right down at the village level, with members there and the physical ability to operate there, and at the same time extends itself upward well beyond the narrow arena of the village, establishing its management structure and legitimacy in the great society too."

At the end of his historical portrayal, Pool states: "Political organization, ideology and motives of self-interest for the underprivileged thus are all combined to make viable the Vietcong as a political movement aiming at improving its claim to the exercise of force over large stretches of the countryside.   The same thing can be said of the Hoa Hao.   But what of the government of South Vietnam?   Does it have any basis for establishing effective organization in the countryside?"   Or to avoid controversy, Pool asks: "If the government of South Vietnam wished to establish its legitimacy in the eyes of the villager, what practicable measure should it take?"

In answering this question Pool asserts that in both the village and Saigon there exist the bases for legitimate government; but the two bases must be linked.   In the former, the restoration of locally elected chiefs in a large part of the country has led villagers to feel that they are once more represented; and the Popular Force contingent in the villages if properly paid, armed and made responsible to authority could constitute a large power element available to the village officials.   In Saigon, itself, a stable government has been established in orderly legal fashion; and it embraces a representative cabinet and properly elected Senate and House.   But between these two, the beginnings of village self-government, and the beginnings of national responsible government, there is required an interface—namely, District Councils, bestowed with sufficient and proper kinds of power "so that the relationship of the District Chief to the elective village officials becomes much more that relationship of bargaining, tension, and responsibility which is normal between political executives and elective policy making bodies."

If Professor Pool has provided the proper prescription by way of an answer to the question he posed, it still may be claimed by some that his question is irrelevant to the existing situation. Professor Popkin, the author of the second paper, does seem to claim so. Popkin concludes, for example, that there is an "incompatibility of mass participation, local initiative, and consideration of local leaders with the values and attitudes of higher-ups having the two dominant voices of the Saigon government —Confucian sentimentalists and the military." He does, therefore, deny the relevance of Professor Pool's question. His paper almost by definition, makes an important contribution along another direction. He does indicate clearly how the past and current failures of the Saigon government can be attributed to its inabilities to effect at least a modest degree of local involvement and concern in the national government.

Before assessing the activities of the Vietcong, Popkin points out that traditionally the local villages have been the center of authority in Vietnam, but their viability declined rapidly under the French. Although many in Vietnam have conceived of pacification as a return to this pre-French village authority structure, it is clear that this structure is obsolete. Those areas which have been successfully pacified have moved in the other direction, surrendering more control to one of the forces from outside the local area. The village council, it appears, has lost its ability to create strong bonds, village unity, and a sense of urgency and dynamism.

While the power of the village council has significantly dwindled in modern times and while the Saigon government has failed miserably in making effective linkage with villagers, the Vietcong has been at least partly successful in amassing power—primarily because it has confronted the political problem head-on. For example, for the mass of villagers, it has provided a post-entry education system within which there is considerable upward mobility; hence, it was able to attract many young from the peasantry who lacked education and could not compete with the well-educated middle and upper classes. More important, the Vietcong did not pursue the traditional village system's inclination to avoid conflict; rather, it used conflict to create the politics of mass participation. It used, for instance, land reform as an effective issue around which to rally and involve villagers. As Popkin puts it:

> Diem's land reform distributed land to former tenants, leaving men who had been neither owners nor tenants landless. The Viet Cong appealed to the peasants' sense of justice to give some of the land to the poor, landless families, thus making them allies of the Viet Cong. This was by no means a simple matter. The Viet Cong land reform could only work if the villagers could be convinced

that justice had not prevailed under the Diem reform. This became possible precisely because justice means decisions at the village and not at the national level. Again, the reform was only workable if it could be implemented without making enemies of the men who were to lose some land. The Viet Cong were able to do this by open participation, putting men in the position of losing face if they were unwilling to go along with the new policy.

In these and many other ways, the Vietcong, letting local conditions guide them, have been able to begin to create mass participation and meet the needs of a post-village society. Thereby, it has catapulted its power resources.

In one sense Professors Pool and Popkin are at odds with each other. Pool puts forth a question which he considers basic and relevant. Popkin considers the question to be irrelevant. Therefore, the concerned reader is likely to want to have further evidence to indicate whether or not the question is relevant, or the extent to which the question is relevant. We cannot present in this volume all the additional evidence that is required. However, Professor White, the author of the third paper, does cast considerable light upon an important aspect of the debate between Popkin and Pool. He examines all the evidence available on attitudes of South Vietnamese. Although attitudes are clearly determined by past and present conditions and institutions, and not by future, they do reflect aspirations, hopes and wishful thinking. Hence, they can be taken to throw at least some light on the feasibility of the establishment by the South Vietnam government of a hierarchical structure whose "roots" might go right down to the village level.

White presents what he designates the dumbbell hypothesis. At one end of the dumbbell are those who are pro-Vietcong. At the other end are those who are anti-Vietcong. In the middle is the indifferent (ambivalent) population. Is the dumbbell balanced, with approximately the same percentage of population at the pro-Vietcong and anti-Vietcong ends? Or is it unbalanced, with a larger percentage of pro-Vietcong than anti-Vietcong? He cites five points to support the hypothesis that the South Vietnam population is anti-Vietcong: 1) The violence of the Vietcong. 2) The taxes imposed by the Vietcong. 3) The implications of the exodus from Vietcong-held areas. 4) The testimony of defectors, prisoners, and the like. 5) Improvement in South Vietnam since the death of Diem. However, he finds that only points one and two are strongly supported by the evidence. He lists five points on the pro-Vietcong side: 1) Violence by the South Vietnam government and the Americans. 2) Land reform by the Vietcong. 3) Unpatriotic connotation of the term "nationalism" which is associated with the South Vietnam government. 4) The record of Vietcong successes against odds. 5) The consensus of informed observers. White finds all these five pro-Vietcong points supported by the evidence. He therefore concludes that the dumbbell is unbalanced. He estimates 10% of the population as anti-Vietcong, 20% as pro-Vietcong, and 70% as indifferent. He closes his paper by questioning whether the U.S. support of 10% of the population against 20% is democratic, and whether in fact the U.S. can win against the large margin of superiority which the Vietcong has in number of dedicated men. He also suggests that in the future the U.S. ought to investigate whether the dumbbell is balanced or unbalanced before it becomes immersed in any more "democratic" involvements.

Thus, while White's paper does not resolve the specific question debated in the Pool and Popkin papers, it does effectively complement them. These three papers together provide the reader with some insight into the intricate, mutually-dependent structure of behavior within the South Vietnamese society, whose elements are difficult to unravel. Yet as Schwartz points up in his brief communication, all three of these papers are deficient in theory and theoretically-based policy. In his critique of Pool, Schwartz advocates (1) the development and testing of theories to explain revolutionary violence (and other revolutionary behavior which precede, cause or at least facilitate violence); and (2) the development of operational techniques based upon theory wherein relevant variables can be manipulated to project the implications of different policy alternatives. But while Schwartz's points are significant, realistically speaking, they do not constitute an immediate contribution to the Vietnam problem—except to make more explicit our inadequate ability to comprehend it fully. They do, however, expose the imperative need for investment by political scientists and others of many years of intense research on empirically-tested theory.

*　　　*　　　*

The Vietnam problem is not strictly a Vietnamese problem, or a problem that arises simply out of the behavior and attitudes of the South Vietnamese. It also arises out of the behavior and attitudes of a number of other societies and in particular those of the United States and the Soviet Union. While we do not have any papers on the attitudes of the Soviet people toward the major involvement in Vietnam, we do have papers on the attitudes of the United States population which we present in Part II of this book. That the attitudes of the U.S. population are relevant is without question, for they certainly determine the probability of reelection of political leaders who advocate different policy positions. They clearly affect the actions of different non-governmental and governmental organizations which in turn influence decisions by policymakers.

A first paper, by Robinson and Jacobson, examines the various surveys which have been conducted on public attitudes toward the war in Vietnam. For example, one survey concluded that the public attitude toward the war was complex and amorphous, that there was among the population no strict separation into "hawks" or "doves", and that public opinion failed to fulfill "rational" requirements. Further, clear attitudinal differences among the several social status categories were absent. The strongest background factor associated with differences in war attitudes was race. Black respondents were more opposed to escalation and more in support of deescalation than whites. Sex also was correlated with war attitudes; women are less pro-war than men.

Since the middle of 1965, Gallup polls have inquired into opinions about the Vietnam war. There has been a definite (though irregular) decrease in the public's approval of Johnson's Vietnam policy. His ratings appear to go up, however, whenever he does something one way or the other, either in the direction of escalation or deescalation. Gallup has not really queried *why* people disapprove of the war. One can only speculate, from the very limited data, that disapproval of Johnson's policy is just as likely to be on the basis of its being "too soft" as "too hard." Gallup also found that only about half the population claimed they had a clear idea of *why* we were in Vietnam.

There is recorded very little shift of opinion toward the war from November, 1964, to November, 1967, despite increased élite opposition in some quarters. While it appears (Spring, 1968) that the American public in general tends to favor escalation and victory, it also seems to favor negotiations with the NLF and to be willing to accept a Korean-type settlement.

Since frequently less than half the public is found to be informed on foreign affairs, investigators have judged it meaningful to survey only the well-educated segment of the population. Among the best educated, it is found that most are in favor of war, including college students. However, at the more prestigious educational institutions, "dovish" attitudes tend to be held by the majority of faculty and students who probably are the most articulate of those in university circles.

From all these surveys, however, it is clear that we have probed only one aspect of the problem. We have asked: *what* are the attitudes. We have failed to expose the factors which explain *why* current attitudes are what they are. We have failed to disentangle the ways in which the factors affecting attitudes do interplay, and to identify what changes in factors can be expected to lead to what changes in which attitudes. These questions then suggest new directions for attitudinal research. No doubt, once such research is conducted we will be in a better position to evaluate how different alternative policies may affect the Vietnam conflict not only directly but also indirectly through changes in attitudes in the population of the U.S., the Soviets, Vietnam, and the world in general.

A second paper on attitudes does provide more depth. This paper, by Brickman, Shaver, and Archibald, examines in some detail the attitudes prevalent among a rather select group of the American people. This group comprises the members of the Society for the Psychological Study of Social Issues. Recognizing at the start that this group is "liberal" and that a liberal bias would be contained in the sample, the authors nonetheless judged that certain kinds of questions could be validly posed. They found that the individuals surveyed did generally perceive a single "hawk-dove" dimension along which policy proposals might be ordered. Five subgroups of respondents were distinguished—those favoring: (1) immediate withdrawal, (2) phased withdrawal while seeking international guarantees for safety of all parties, (3) general de-escalation while seeking negotiations with Hanoi and the Vietcong, (4) limitation of military efforts to securing areas now held while offering to negotiate, (5) present policy of increasing military pressure while offering to negotiate. As could be expected, those favoring the two most "hawkish" policies—(6) general escalation of the war in both North and South, and (7) immediate all-out escalation using anything needed to win, including nuclear bombs—were too few in number to form meaningful subgroups for study.

There are many interesting findings in this inquiry. For example, all subgroups agree "that immediate withdrawal is very unlikely to lead to an anti-communist South Vietnam, and very likely to lead to a reunited Communist Vietnam." But "respondents preferring immediate withdrawal see a holding strategy and present policy as less likely to bring about an anti-communist South Vietnam than do other subgroups, while present policy advocates see this policy as much more likely to bring about an anti-communist South Vietnam. Estimates of how likely each of the various militant strategies is to achieve this outcome increase monotonically with militancy of preference. . . ."

A second type of finding relates to perceptions of U.S. control and U.S. choice in Vietnam. The authors reach the interesting conclusion that "people favoring immediate or phased withdrawal are more likely to say that the outcome in Vietnam will be mainly a result of factors beyond our control—a position that is consistent with their tendency to deny that even further escalation would succeed in bringing about an anti-communist South Vietnam."

In addition to these kinds of findings the authors examine the importance of other goals for the several subgroups, the impact of strategies on other goals, and the perceptions of Communist threat. Clearly, all these factors and many others are important. And without question, the skillful manner in which the authors conduct their survey and analyze their findings enhances our understanding of the structure of attitudes and their complex character within the United States society. From this and other studies of attitudes, which we know greatly influence actions, counteractions and outcomes, one thing is sure. The alternatives, and impacts of each, as presented by our military leaders and the Department of State, are not nearly as simple as they assert and as our newspapers lead us to believe.

As just indicated, Part II deals with the attitudes of the U.S. population with particular reference to the Communist world, in particular, the Soviets. There are, of course, attitudes within the Soviet Union which relate to the capitalist countries, in particular the United States. These attitudes are not only affected by, but lead to sequences of actions and reactions. And according to Professor Strausz-Hupé these sequences of actions and reactions take place in more than one place on this globe. Vietnam is only one such place. The social and institutional environment described in Part I represents only one such environment in which the United States-Soviet confrontation takes place. The Strausz-Hupé thesis is an incontrovertible thesis. The Middle East, Cuba, Czechoslovakia, Vietnam, and Korea are all interwoven into one world-encompassing fabric, at times tightly and at times only loosely. But the interdependencies are always there. No wishful thinking on the part of policy-makers, no simple mindedness, no inability to perceive these interdependencies, can deny their real existence and significance for world peace and order. Strausz-Hupé's contribution, the only paper in Part III, is a short one, but it is as forceful as it is short. It leads the thoughtful reader to recognize how changes in the social and institutional environment as suggested, projected, or regarded as potential by authors such as Pool, Popkin, White, and many others cannot be divorced from the bipolar confrontation. Nor can the attitudes and changes in attitudes as defined in the various attitude surveys summarized by Brickman, Shaver, and Archibald, and conducted by Jacobson and Robinson. Any marked change in the bipolar confrontation drastically changes and alters the attitudes of people and the potential for change in Vietnam and all the sore spots of the world as well. Moreover, we must recognize the non-static character of the bipolar confrontation. Other major poles, the Western European Community, Chinese East Asia, are tending to emerge, and their emergence is almost sure to alter the strategy of action of all nations and regional groupings, large and small.

It is the reality of the U.S.-Soviet confrontation that leads Strausz-Hupé to assert that "the evacuation by the U.S. of Vietnam would not have contributed anything—except negatively—to the making of a global settlement between the U.S. and the Soviet Union.

*   *   *

Against the background of mutual dependence and elaborate interconnection implicit in the brief statement in Part III and in previous papers, an analyst, or policy maker, or intelligent layman, who seeks a careful assessment of all relevant factors may throw up his hands in despair—particularly when faced with the choice of some alternative in the Vietnam conflict situation. Such a response, however, is simple, unjustified defeatism. It is true that we cannot anticipate all the implications of an action—all the possible outcomes and the probabilities to be attached to these—especially when the outcome depends on the choices of other participants in the game of world domination. Yet, we can do better than choosing actions randomly and throwing up our hands in despair. We can in specific situations attempt to define the critical factors at play. We can estimate, even though very crudely, the possible outcomes of the interplay of these factors when they take on different values, or when they correspond to different actions of participants. We can, by analysis and model building, discriminate between alternatives which are more likely to be bad alternatives, and alternatives which are more likely to be good alternatives—in terms of that general goal of peace and world order sought by both doves and hawks. It is just these considerations which motivate and make imperative such analyses as are presented in Part IV of this book.

We begin Part IV with a paper by Goodman. Following the traditional approach of political science, Goodman presents a set of key considerations which might be expected to guide discussions and negotiations for a Vietnam settlement. He tends to believe that the most probable outcome or solution to the war will be one that lies somewhere between defeat and victory; i.e., peace without victory. Limited wars, internal conflicts, and confrontations have often characterized the situation of powerful countries deciding to withdraw while in positions of strength without defeat or weakness. Such withdrawal has been regulated by explicit agreements, or effected in accord with the more informal rules of great-power diplomacy.

A "withdrawal in strength" tactic for the United States must, however, recognize several realities. First, the Vietcong "is in South Vietnam to stay. . . ." Second, any solution must fully protect members of all factions once an agreement has been reached. Third, the new government must involve and represent the spectrum of political, ethnic, and religious forces in Vietnam. Finally, in its diverse parts and as a whole, Southeast Asia today is a very different Southeast Asia than 10 or 15 years ago. Any solution must assess these changes and take them into account.

On the assumption that zones of Vietcong control and influence do exist, much as in 1954, and are part of the enduring landscape in South Vietnam, Goodman sketches three possible scenarios for peace. First, concurrent with a cease-fire declaration, regroupment zones, in accord with zones of influence, could be established with the population in the large contested areas assured regular election processes to determine their loyalties. Second, agreement would be reached, presumably with U.N. involvement, on peace-making machinery. Such machinery might be administered by the U.N.—to regulate foreign military withdrawal and to maintain a strategic presence to assure peace. Lastly, Thieu and Ky would be replaced by neutralist leaders capable of effecting coalition government fully involving the NLF. Through elections such a government would need to reflect diverse political elements in the South and be able to motivate villages and political groups alike to organize themselves. There would also have taken place the establishment of a permanent control and inspection commission, and demilitarization of foreign assistance in South Vietnam.

The Goodman contribution, as already indicated, represents a sound orthodox type of political analysis. However, as one surveys the historical record and observes the relative lack of success or inability of historians, political scientists, international lawyers and like scholars to prescribe solutions or steps towards solutions in conflict situations, one asks why. One possible answer is that these scholars have failed to narrow down sufficiently the several forces to be studied, to identify them precisely, and to focus intensely on their interplay. Here, perhaps, the approach of game theorists and similar model builders may have something to offer. As an example of this approach we have a paper by Howard. His work is some of the finest that has emerged out of the laborious efforts of many brilliant minds to develop game theory. Although ever since the end of World War II many have looked to game theory as a promising approach for cutting through the world impasse, they have been sorely disappointed. Embarrassingly little results have been achieved. Yet, some findings have emerged. Some worthwhile analysis is possible, and given the sorry state of the world, such analysis must be put to maximum use.

In a most ingenious manner, Howard has developed the concept of metagame and metarationality. He points out that when participants concentrate solely on the actions they can take, they frequently end up in an undesirable deadlock, or stalemate. Such a state of affairs may be said perhaps to characterize the Middle East situation and the Paris talks at the time of writing (January, 1969). However, if the point of concentration can be shifted from actions to policies, one can often achieve desirable results. One result may be the cooperative solution which one seeks. Also, from the standpoint of participants choosing policies rather than ultimate actions, the result can often be a stable equilibrium outcome.

To see this point, consider a simple Prisoners' Dilemma game.

Player 2

		c	d
Player	c	5,5	-10,12
1	d	12,-10	-2,-2

There are two participants: Players 1 and 2. Each player may choose one of the two actions, *c* and *d*. Player 1's actions correspond to the rows *c* and *d*. Player 2's actions correspond to the columns *c* and *d*. The numbers in the cells of the table (matrix) represent the payoffs of each player, when Player 1 chooses the action corresponding to the row of that cell, and when Player 2 chooses the action corresponding to the column of that cell. The first number in each cell is the payoff to Player 1; the second number is the payoff to Player 2.

It is clear that given the action of the other player, it is always best for a given player to choose *d*. For example, suppose Player 1 has chosen action *c*. Then Player 2 finds it better to choose *d* than *c*, for if he chooses *d* he gets a payoff of 12; if the choice had been *c*, he would get a payoff of only 5. Or suppose Player 1 has chosen action *d*. Then Player 2 still finds it better to choose *d* than *c*, for if he chooses *c* his payoff is -10, whereas if he chooses *d* his payoff is -2.

Since this payoff matrix is symmetric, it follows that it pays Player 1 always to choose *d* for any given action that Player 2 may take. Hence, in this game, each chooses *d*, and the equilibrium payoff to each is -2,-2. It does not pay for either to change his action unilaterally.

It should be clear to the reader that if by chance each of the two players had erroneously chosen action *c* at the start, so that their payoffs would be 5,5, this would not be an equilibrium outcome. For, where actions are independent, unrestricted and retractable, and when there is no opportunity to learn from playing the game many times, each player would then, out of pure self-interest, find it more profitable to switch to action *d*.

The rationale for choosing policies rather than ultimate actions (*c* and *d*) as strategies can be immediately seen. Suppose Player 2 is a bit more long-sighted than Player 1. After finding himself receiving a payoff of -2, and recognizing the stable equilibrium nature of the joint action (*d,d*) he may come to realize that there is a policy strategy that he might employ which will assure him the outcome 5, assuming Player 1's attitude and preferences do not change. He may, for example, publicly announce that henceforth, he will abide by a "tit for tat" policy; if Player 1 chooses *c*, he, Player 2, will choose *c*; if Player 1 chooses *d*, he will choose *d*. Furthermore, he may post a bond of $1 million with a third person who is instructed to give the $1 million to Player 1 if he, Player 2, does not abide by his publicly announced policy. It then is clear that it is to Player 1's best interest to choose action *c*, and the joint (*c,c*) becomes a stable equilibrium.

This oversimplified example suggests the rationale for *policy* rather than *action* strategies. However, the rationale developed by Howard is much more extensive and sophisticated; and the reader is urged to probe his paper intensively despite its use of some "new" but yet simple mathematics. Here, Howard does not view the Vietnam problem as one which involves only two participants. In the Vietnam conflict situations which he simulates, the United States, the South Vietnam government, the National Liberation Front, and the North Vietnam government are involved. (At Strausz-Hupé's suggestion, Howard would not hesitate also to involve the Soviets.) Howard is particularly concerned with the use of sanctions by one or more of the participants which lead some other participant to take a particular course of action because he prefers that one over all others, given these sanctions. Howard designates such sanctions as "inescapable sanctions." For example, he asks the question, "Do inescapable sanctions exist which would force the South Vietnamese to agree to a settlement?" He does find such inescapable sanctions against South Vietnam in his simulation model of the Vietnam conflict. These sanctions involve the choice by the United States of the action to withdraw (and thus, to stop both bombing and fighting), and the choice by both the NVN and NLF to continue to fight. Given such choices, the South Vietnamese cannot do anything which can yield an outcome which it prefers to a settlement.

In another simple model Howard asks whether there exist inescapable sanctions against each of the four participants which could induce all four to accept a settlement. Here he does not find inescapable sanctions which are at the same time credible. In still another model, Howard asks whether there are inescapable sanctions which would induce the coalition of the U.S. and North Vietnam to accept a cease-fire despite continued fighting by the South Vietnam government and the National Liberation Front. Here he does find inescapable sanctions which are credible, and concludes that if "levels of reduction could be agreed to by these players, the credible threat of a 'non-preferred' situation if the agreement were violated might be sufficient to keep it stable."

Schelling, in the paper which follows, continues the discussion. His first point is both brilliant and extremely important. He demonstrates that if *successive* rather than *simultaneous* credulity is permitted, a cease-fire by all four parties is potentially achievable in the Howard model. Step 1: "the US threatens to withdraw unconditionally unless South Vietnam (SVN) agrees to cease fighting conditionally, the condition being that both parties on the other side cease. . . . Step 2: having already used the credible threat of unconditional withdrawal, and the threat, having succeeded, being no longer necessary, the U.S. now threatens North Vietnam (NVN) that it will fight unless North Vietnam (NVN) and the National Liberation Front (NLF) accept a cease-fire. The credibility of the threat is no longer jeopardized by an outstanding contradictory threat to SVN because that one is no longer outstanding. Even if North Vietnam begs off, claiming it has no control over the National Liberation Front, U.S. can explain to North Vietnam the tactic it just used on South Vietnam and propose that North Vietnam similarly coerce the National Liberation Front into a coalition that is committed conditionally to a cease-fire. In effect, the number of participants has been reduced from four independent parties to two coalitions, and the conditional cease-fire may now be negotiated unembarrassed by the original credibility problem."

Schelling's comments penetrate other aspects of the problem. For example, he forcefully points out that in any real game the policy options are basic parts of the game and are there to be discovered and not invented by the analyst. Moreover, "there never is a unique metagame. There are as many metagames to be constructed as there are ways to specify the policy options and the sequences which can be adopted and made known. Not only is there no limit to this number, but the specification of a very few policy options to be taken in a specified short sequence of steps can generate an astronomical number of strategies."

The Howard model of cease-fire supplemented by Schelling's brilliant notion of successive rather than simultaneous credulity has considerable appeal. However, it still may be claimed by some to be subject to a major deficiency. This is the problem of how to get the participants moving in negotiations. For example, suppose à la Schelling, the South Vietnam and the National Liberation Front are committed conditionally to cease-fire, so that we have reduced the conflict to a two party (coalition) conflict, as in the diagram presented on p. 11. Suppose U.S. as leader of its coalition is Player 1 and North Vietnam as leader of its coalition is Player 2. Each player recognizes the possibilities of a (c,c) outcome but each may hesitate to move. Each may prefer to wait and see, a third alternative posed by Schelling. Further, each may have certain misgivings and feelings of insecurity about committing himself to the drastic change in strategy that would be involved by shifting from a choice of an action to a choice of a policy. What may then be needed may be a procedure that allows the participants to inch forward, more strictly to millimeter forward, so that possible error from a change can be viewed as possibly small and the risk worth taking. Further, each would like to be assured that he can return to the initial position without loss. It is in this respect that the "veto-incremax" procedures proposed in the Isard paper may prove of value.

There are several possible "veto-incremax" procedures. (Incremax is an abbreviation for incremental maximization, and involves a maximization process taken over each of a series of small steps.) They all have the following appealing features:

(1) each can be presented in a relatively simple form for a given situation, and can be rigorously defined mathematically;

(2) each gives each participant a full veto power which he may exercise at any time, and assures each participant that he will end no worse off than at the start if any participant does exercise his veto power;

(3) each clearly points up the inefficiency of the existing position (deadlock, threat point, current-stand point or prominent reference point) and identifies a common goal (the achievement of a mutually preferred outcome which is efficient);

(4) each requires that each participant be able to state consistently his preferences among outcomes. Thus, each does not depend on intercomparisons of utility and only requires the assumption of ordinal utility;

(5) each assures that no participant will ever be made worse off on any move, except by the exercise of the veto power;

(6) each allows each participant to be as conservative and cautious as he desires with respect to the amount of change in proposed actions on any move; that is, within extreme limits, each participant is allowed to make as small a commitment on change as he desires;

(7) provided the veto power is not exercised, each ensures that an efficient outcome will be reached, but that no participant is able beforehand to identify the specific set of changes in the joint proposals, or steps, required to achieve that outcome;

(8) each suggests a "fair compromise" or "equitable" procedure by which all participants may share in the gains from the gradual advancement to a mutually more efficient state of affairs;

(9) each allows the participants considerable flexibility in combining its appealing features with the appealing features of several other veto-incremax procedures into a single synthesized procedure.

The paper proceeds, step by step, to illustrate how Player 1 and Player 2 can move, bit by bit, in their negotiations toward the goal of, say, total disengagement. In the first move, each player proposes a joint action in an *improvement set,* which is the set of joint actions none of which involves the deterioration of the position of any player, and involves the improvement of at least one. In proposing a joint action, each player also selects a joint action from those in a *commitment set,* which is the set of all joint actions of which none exceeds the maximum change to which any party is willing to agree, that is, to commit himself. Finally, if the pair of joint actions proposed by the players are not identical, both agree to some equitable compromise. For example, both may agree to a "split-the-difference," a 50-50 compromise proposal. This compromise joint action then serves as a reference point for the next move. In this manner, a series of compromise joint actions are identified, each of which can involve an improvement in the position of each player. After a number of moves, the state of complete disengagement may be expected to be negotiated.

It is clear that the veto-incremax procedure by its various appealing features has a rationality of its own. When it can be combined with the metarationality, that is, the strategy policy rationality of Howard, it provides a double-edged tool to a mediator attempting to be useful in such a conflict situation as the U.S.-North Vietnam. It suggests that perhaps a quite new approach must be taken in the current Paris talks, and that the shifting of emphasis away from the conflict over solutions (outcomes) to the development and acceptance of a type of approach which cannot identify beforehand the set of compromise steps may, in fact, be able to help break the stalemate.

It is of course wishful thinking to hope that a combined veto-incremax metarational procedure can be effectively employed in the current negotiations. We do not know enough about the actions and strategies perceived by the participants. We do not know enough about the preferences that they have for different possible outcomes. We do not know enough about the aspects of outcomes which are significant for each. And so forth. Yet it is clear that this approach can be at least as useful as the approaches currently in use in Paris, the Middle East, and other conflict areas of the world.

The game analytic or cooperative procedure approach cannot stand on its own. It rests squarely upon the continuous output of information relating to the possible outcomes of the different alternatives. These outcomes in turn are related to our knowledge of behavior patterns of different actors. It is in this regard that the last paper is extremely important. Here we have a potential major breakthrough in the type of analysis that might be conducted by students of political science, international law, and history.

In their paper, Milstein and Mitchell present a quantitative analysis of the Vietnam War from January, 1965, through December, 1967. On the basis of this analysis, they develop and demonstrate a method of computer simulation for forecasting behavior in the war more than a year ahead. Models of the conflict held by policy makers in the United States, North Vietnam, South Vietnam, and the Vietcong are tested for their predictive adequacy. The authors employ standard statistical techniques involving correlation and regression analysis. Their data consist of: (1) *communications data* composed of publicly stated preferences and perceptions of national policy makers regarding the war; (2) *popular support data* such as domestic U.S. public opinion, Vietcong and North Vietnamese defectors, and the Black Market value of the South Vietnamese piastre; and (3) *military variables* such as force commitments, bombing, and casualties. The policy makers' models are then compared with empirically derived models where each variable is analyzed as being dependent upon present and past values of itself and of other variables in the system. Based on this analysis, a predictive computer simulation which allows forecasting more than a year into the future is developed and demonstrated.

The techniques explored in this study could make an important contribution to foreign policy making in two ways. First, they provide a means of evaluating the reliability and validity of the models upon which ongoing policy is based. Second, they provide a means of observing probable outcomes of *alternative* policies through computer simulation.

Examples of specific findings are: (1) The higher the level of U.S. bombing of North Vietnam, the lower the rate of Communist troop commitment, *but,* the more the *rate* of U.S. bombing is *escalated,* the more the Communists *counter-escalate* with their own troop commitments. ("This finding confirms the McNamara hypothesis that bombing will increase the cost of infiltration, but denies President Johnson's hypothesis that escalation of the bombing will reduce Communist commitment of troops." June, 1968.) (2) Battle outcomes advantageous to the Communists do not correlate significantly with U.S. preference for negotiations. (This finding does not confirm the public statements of Xuan Thuy and other North Vietnamese policy makers.)

The numerous empirical findings of Milstein and Mitchell are only as valid as the statistical techniques and data which they employ. Those familiar with these techniques and data are well aware of their limitations. At the same time it is clear that their analysis can be extremely valuable to policy makers who do make public statements on the basis of hypotheses they hold and act upon. Hence, to open-minded policy makers, findings of the sort that Milstein and Mitchell are able to develop can enhance their ability to project the impact of various alternatives and to select wiser policies. To this extent then, the new analytic tools for political analysis are valuable.

There were, however, at the Peace Research conference at which the Milstein-Mitchell paper was presented a number of scholars who were concerned with the possible application of the Milstein-Mitchell model by the Pentagon and other military groups. They were concerned that these groups might find in the Milstein-Mitchell development a means for the more efficient (optimal) use of their resources for destructive purposes. In a very real sense, the Milstein-Mitchell development posed a dilemma. Are advances in scientific analysis to be avoided particularly by scholars who designate themselves peace researchers because they increase the destructive potential of the military? This fundamental question often arises with the presentation of a finding or new methodology whose immediate impact upon the achievement of peace and world order appears to be negative. However, the philosophy of the Peace Research Society (International) is that through exchange of findings, methodology, theories and ideas we are able to chart out more thoroughly and systematically the alternatives which participants in conflict situations might adopt. Through such exchange we are able to spell out more comprehensively and accurately the implications of each alternative under different possible contingencies. Accordingly, we are able, certainly in the long-run, to decrease the probability that poor decisions by good-intentioned leaders and policy makers—as has characterized the foreign policy of U.S. and many other nations—will be avoided and increase the probability that wise actions will be taken. It is this long-run orientation involving the constant accumulation of knowledge, analytic technique and methodology, theory and ideas, which lies behind the conferences and activities of the Peace Research Society (International).

In conclusion, we have presented four sets of papers relating to the U.S.-Vietnam conflict. These papers cover contributions from several important disciplines—economics, political science, psychology, sociology, regional science, operations research and applied mathematics. Though many disciplines are represented it would be a mistake to think that these papers embody the essence of all that is to be said about the Vietnam problem—or 50%, or 25%, or even 10% of what is to be said. But it would also be a mistake for anyone to assert that he knows all that is to be said about the U.S.-Vietnam problem and has no need to go carefully through the contributions in this book. He may perhaps know a good deal of what is contained in the book. But he is unlikely to know all. For these papers represent both fresh contributions and reformulations.

It is in this spirit that the Peace Research Society (International) offers these papers for the enlightenment of either those with the curiosity to know more about the complicated behavior of world society, or, more important, those who must make decisions which affect the structure, function, and viability of this society.

PART I

VILLAGE AND SOCIAL-POLITICAL STRUCTURE: IMPLICATIONS FOR VIABLE GOVERNMENT IN SOUTH VIETNAM

CHAPTER 2. FURTHER THOUGHTS ON RURAL PACIFICATION AND INSURGENCY

By Ithiel de Sola Pool*

The author examines the history of Vietnamese villages to cast light on the problem of rural pacification and governmental structure in South Vietnam. An analysis of the reasons for the success of the Vietcong is made, and a question is asked: "If the government of South Vietnam wished to establish its legitimacy in the eyes of the villager, what practicable measure should it take?" Pool then proceeds to respond to this question. Ed.

Today's paper is a case study of inadvertant commitment to a situation and resulting escalation. Some months ago, at the last Peace Research Meeting, I gave a paper on Village Violence and International Violence.[1] It was a fairly controversial paper so when Walter Isard asked if I had any further thoughts as a result of the discussion that I might offer at the next meeting, I was flattered and said "yes". Thus I became committed to a course of action whose consequences I did not anticipate. The next thing I knew, the program appeared with this paper on it as a solo for a full morning session. That was escalation by the adversary if I ever saw it. Being thus trapped in a situation for which I am not prepared, I struggle on as best I can. To complete the analogy, I suppose you are the innocent victims caught in the cross-fire.

*The author is associated with the Department of Political Science at the Massachusetts Institute of Technology.
[1] Published in *Papers,* Peace Research Society (International) Volume IX.

At least we have learned one thing—how very general is the pattern of inadvertant commitment, escalation, and then involvement in a situation one would not have chosen. It is not Vietnam; it is the human condition, here simulated in a laboratory.

So now let me turn to where we left off six months ago.

In that paper I argued that throughout history intimidation, brutality, and violence have been endemic in peasant society. Such societies lack the roads, telephones, and organized authorities that make it possible most of the time to exercise effective control on violent individuals in modern society. Control is so lacking in peasant villages that terrorists can operate largely unmolested whether or not the local population supports them. When such men of violence organize into gangs the peasant must usually acquiesce. Some such gangs gain legitimacy if they offer moderate treatment and effective protection against worse oppressors. No great distinction exists in peasant eyes between that exercise of force to tax and to keep the peace, which we would call government, and that which we would call a protection racket.

The examples I used for evidence were drawn from Turkey, India, and contemporary Vietnam.

Regarding the last of these situations, I argued that neither the government nor the Vietcong could as yet assure enough security against the other side to establish their claim to monopolistic legitimacy in the eyes of the peasants. While the government has been gaining significantly in the contest for legitimacy since 1964, the Vietcong have still succeeded in maintaining for themselves the aura, in the eyes of the peasant, of a brutal and tyrannical dual government, rather than that of mere thugs.

I then concluded by stating some conditions for the control of such village violence. One conclusion was that the control of such violence and the channeling of it, if it is to be achieved at all, must take place through organization. It cannot occur by the sheer weight of superior force on the rival side. Under the conditions of a rural peasant society the facilities do not exist for routing out all the armed men from the jungles, mountain fastnesses, or swamplands.

The kind of organization that can successfully assert its claim to a monopoly of force is one that at the same time has its roots right down at the village level, with members there and the physical ability to operate there, and at the same time extends itself upward well beyond the narrow arena of the village, establishing its management structure and legitimacy in the great society too.

It is these conclusions on which I should like to expand today, and with particular reference to Vietnam. An historical view might help put some of the contemporary phenomena in perspective.

The Vietnamese village was never a peaceful place. For 900 years, from the 10th to the 18th centuries, the Vietnamese pressed by conquest ever southward, driving the Chams and Khmers back into the hills and jungles, until finally about the time of the French Revolution, they reached the end of the Ca Mau Peninsula. As Paul Mus, the great French authority on Vietnam puts it,

> Viet Nam did not just happen; she occupied her territory only at the price of incessant wars. . . . The army did not merely defend the country . . . but it also organized the territory behind the front of its advances. As it conquered the land, it established a network of military villages, or villages of veterans, then a penal colony, especially suitable for political exiles, and finally a solid blanket of free villages of the ordinary sort.

These ordinary villages were usually ruled by a council of elders whose formal purpose was religious, but who were also the leading citizens and most prosperous farmers of the village. They dealt with the mandarins from the Court in a way that has often been described in perhaps the most quoted single proverb about Vietnamese society: "the Emperor's writ stops at the village gate."

To quote Mus again, "the state's power extended only to the imposition of the tax or other obligation on the village as a whole. Central authority did not deal with the individual . . . except when criminal matters were brought before it."

Even water works, which in more complex systems of irrigation required central control, were handled in the Delta of Vietnam in a largely decentralized manner.

But decentralization did not imply that the villages were left in peace. Does the following quotation sound familiar?

> This country once so rich and fertile is now almost totally ruined and lacks everything. . . . War and famine have caused such ravages that half the inhabitants of the country have perished.

That was written by a French priest in 1776, when conditions were even worse than now, for he continues,

> Whole families take poison in order to die immediately and to

avoid slow death by starvation. Mothers eat their babies. One often sees human flesh sold in the market.[1]

Out of these conditions, grew a massive peasant rebellion headed by the three Tay Son brothers who succeeded in controlling part or all of the country for about three decades. These revolutionists with their red flag described by their opponents as "malcontents, smugglers, bandits" were expected by the peasants, as Buttinger tells us, to reduce taxes and forced labor and to redistribute rice fields concentrated in the hands of the landlords. But like every rebellion since, including the Vietcong rebellion, the peasants were disappointed. As has happened in every instance, the taxes were increased and the rebellion lost its voluntary support. Nonetheless, like some of their successors, the Tay Son rulers retained their power for a while by military force, and by the claim to be nationalist opponents of the foreign invaders, in this instance the Chinese.

> When they entered Saigon in March 1782, they burned and pil-
> laged the Chinese shops of Cholon and massacred more than
> 10,000 Chinese of that city.[2]

All of that happened even before the French occupation. The years from then on continued to be punctuated by innumerable guerrilla movements.

The bases for these uprisings were problems in the villages, but the revolts that showed the greatest viability were ones that unified the discontent from village to village, by providing an ideology. Such as the Bu Son Ky Huong, the Hoa Hao, the Cao Dai, and the Communists.

The first three of these movements were all religious. The Bu Son Ky Huong was founded in 1849 by a young man who came to be known as the Tay An Buddha. In the midst of an epidemic of the plague, one day after being seized by a vision, he proclaimed that one could be safe from the disease if one truly had faith in the Buddha and carried a yellow piece of paper with four Chinese symbols. Within months he had gathered hundreds of thousands of followers in the Delta. This new sect was anti-clerical, opposing worship in the temples and opposing the power of the Buddhist priesthood. They favored simple home worship. Their communities as observed in the decades following, were cleaner

---

[1] Joseph Buttinger, *The Smaller Dragon,* Frederick A. Praeger, Inc., New York, 1958, pp. 264-5.

[2] *Ibid.*

than those of their neighbors, their adherents worked harder. I suggest a comparison with Max Weber's description of the Puritan sects in Europe in the 17th and 18th centuries. The Bu Son Ky Huong sect gradually turned into a guerilla movement against the French and by about 1916 they were destroyed by the French.

The Cao Dai sect was founded in 1926 and was also a combination of religion, political reform, and an army. The three principal gods that they worship from the present era are a Vietnamese poet born in 1492, who represents the nationalist strain in their thinking, Sun Yet-Sen, who represents the modernizing movement in the developing countries, and Victor Hugo who represents for them the French radical tradition. They, too, became an armed guerrilla nationalist and reform movement.

The Hoa Hao were founded in 1939. As in the case of the Tay An Buddha, Huynh Phu So, their founder, was also a young man seized by visions. He prophesied in 1939 that a great nation would conquer Vietnam, driving the French out, and that they, in turn, would be defeated, leaving Vietnam finally free and happy. When World War II broke out, So's prophesies seemed confirmed and within a few months he, too, had hundreds of thousands of followers in the Delta. His preachings, too, were anti-clerical, advocating simple worship in the home. He, too, founded a movement that was religious, political and was also a guerrilla army. Today the Hoa Hao are next to the Vietcong the most successful political organization in Vietnam. They have a million and a half followers. The province that they control is fully pacified. There are no Vietcong operations in it. Of their villages, too, one can say that they are cleaner, and that the members work harder than the neighboring peasants. These results have been achieved even though there has been no land reform among them. The Hoa Hao ideology is not equalitarian. However, the peasants are not cheated and grievances are heard through the channels of the Hoa Hao organization. The Popular Forces in the Hoa Hao villages are well organized to keep the peace.

In each of the above three cases a mystical religion has provided some organization extending above the village level and permitting villagers with arms in their hands to organize their own communities.

This is the pattern in which the Communists also found that they could succeed in Asia. In China, in the 1920's and early 1930's, the more orthodox Communists (such as Li Li San) tried to build an urban proletarian Marxist movement; it failed. The urban workers in the developing countries have seldom been Communists. In Vietnam today the labor union movement is one of the strongest bulwarks against the Vietcong. Mao Tse-Tung discovered a new formula for Communist organization, and in Vietnam Ho Chi Minh followed the Chinese model. The peasant guerrilla movement is a traditional mould into which the Communists can readily fit.

Organization is not easy in Vietnam. Douglas Pike has vividly described the personal factionalism that rends every organization in the country.

> A strong sense of associational linkages combined with feelings of racial superiority and manifest destiny and nourished in the setting of a foreign-power occupation usually yield a collection of blood brotherhoods, militant nationalist organizations, general-purpose clandestine associations, or some combination of all of these. Such was the case in Vietnam. Many of the traditional village groups were, if not clandestine, at least *sub rosa,* the result of native caution. Unless an organization had some reason to be public . . . it remained inconspicuous . . . the less anyone knew of a group's existence and purpose the better. . . .
>
> The basis of the Vietnamese clandestine organization . . . rested on the Vietnamese assumption that society consisted of a host of dangerous and conflicting social forces with which only enigmatic organization and secret "inness" could cope. . . .
>
> Today Vietnamese politics still bear the mark of the clandestine organization. The organization, clandestine and otherwise, is the arena in which the struggle for power takes place. . . . The world of organizational infighting is fluid and dynamic, in constant flux. One must keep running simply to hold his own. Daily activity involves negotiation and bargaining, sincere or otherwise, partially or completely in secret, and usually through third parties. The world should never know precisely where one stands; not only should the organization be clandestine but so should its membership. Constantly there are realignments, or revelations as to one's true colors. No position is ever irretrievable, no commitment ever final. It is a system of centrifugal force always tending to fly apart, only to form again. The rule is: Be flexible, be changeable, adapt. No organization is ever completely undisguised. All consist of at least two parts, the overt face and the secret apparatus; but the best, in addition to the covert leadership that "clever" Vietnamese eventually penetrate, has a third layer, which is reality. However, because it is a system of mutation, the reality, even if you discover it, does not last long; soon new alliances outdate your discovery. Sometimes an organization is within an

organization, with one organization evincing great hostility for a second when actually both are controlled by a third. Most have false patrons; almost certainly the proclaimed leader is not the wielder of maximum influence. Proselyting is common, and no opprobrium is placed on one who changes sides, providing he observes a decent interval. . . . Members assemble around individual leaders rather than around an ideology or a political platform. The best leader is paternalistic, sly, skilled at intrigue, master of the deceptive move, possessor of untold layers of duplicity, highly effective in the world in which he moves.[3]

This divisiveness plagues even the successful organizations. There are two rival Cao Dai Popes. There are four factions of the Hoa Hao. The Lao Dong Party (the Communist Party of North Vietnam) and the Vietcong like all Communist organizations, suffer from fierce factional struggles too. Right now the issue in the North seems to be between a technocratic wing whose pet phrase is construction and reconstruction and which seems to want to negotiate an agreement that would stop the bombing and the fierce manpower drain and allow them to start economic reconstruction, versus a militant military wing that wants to fight on.

Nonetheless, in the successful organizations such as the Communists and the Hoa Hao, the factions co-exist in a structure of mutual negotiation and accommodation. The structure recognizes the localism of the villages, but also unites them.

The constitutional structure of the Hoa Hao illustrates a number of the problems and strengths of such Vietnamese modes of organization.

The Hoa Hao church is essentially congregational.

The lowest level is the Branch Association, consisting of 15 families in a hamlet. The members who pay dues of two piastres (2 cents) a month elect their officers. The hamlet committee is also elected by the members.

At the next higher level is the Village Board. The Village Board of 9 members is elected by the members of the previous Village Board, plus delegates from each Hamlet Board. (Under the new constitution, 3 from each Hamlet Board and one from each Branch Association.)

The next level is a 9 member District Board elected by the members of the previous District Board plus 5 delegates from each Village Board in the District. Next comes the Provincial Board of 11 members elected in parallel fashion by the members of the previous Provincial

---

[3] Douglas Pike, *Viet Cong*, pp. 8-10.

Board and 5 delegates from each District Board and 3 from each Village Board. At the top of this structure is a 17 member Central Board for the whole country.

The Social Democratic Party, the Hoa Hao political party, has a similar structure and earlier there was also a parallel military structure. Factionalism is promoted by a prohibition on dual office holding. Party officials may not be members of the Church Boards.

Let me carry this description of the Hoa Hao organization a bit further to demonstrate the handling of factions, the linking of participant village organizations, and some of the commonalities between the Hoa Hao and Vietcong and indeed among all the successful rural organizations in Vietnam. Let me quote some passages from the original 1945 Hoa Hao Constitution.

The membership will be divided into two classes.

I.   Active Members
II. Support Members

a. Active members—includes all clergy, laymen, or intellectuals who are willing to sacrifice their lives and property in the hope of developing moral principles and helping mankind while it is in its wretched state.

b. Support members—includes all people who are philanthropic of heart but due to their family and occupations can't completely sacrifice themselves, but who praise and support the undertakings of the Association spiritually and materially.

DUTIES OF THE MEMBERS

(1) They must explain the policy of the Association so that the masses clearly understand it, and rapidly expand the Association.

This reminds one of the distinction between the Party and the Front. Then there is criticism, self-criticism and discipline.

It is required to denounce all unrighteous behavior before the Board of Directors; concealment due to a personal affection is prohibited.

It is required to admit one's errors and to express regret and repentance when the Board of Directors has judged that one has erred.

It is required to accept the control of one's local Board of Directors.

Finally, there are a whole series of provisions designed to keep factional conflict within bounds.

"Each faction will have a representative on the Board of Directors."

"Any clergyman, layman, intellectual or common person with clear Buddhist tendencies . . . may become a member of the Association. Even though they have joined the Association all sects may follow the . . . ceremonies of their teachers or sects."

DISCIPLINE OF THE ASSOCIATION

A. Jealousy, hate, and mockery of each other because of different teachers or religions is prohibited.

B. Exhorting followers of other clergy or sects to abandon their teachers or sects to follow one's teacher or sect is prohibited. . . .

D. Mocking other sects is prohibited.

E. It is required to be peaceful toward all other religions and towards the people.

F. It is required to sincerely love unity and look for ways for mutual instruction.

G. It is required to be loyal to the Policy of the Association.

These structures and the analogous ones in every partly successful guerrilla and political movement in Vietnam tell us something about how a village society can become organized on a broader than single village basis. It will do so, however, only if there is some strong motivating force attracting villagers to the movement. That motivation is often religious. It can also be ideological. It can be ethnic prejudice or nationalism. It can be a combination of all of these. A successful movement must also tap crasser motives of self-interest.

Let us consider the Vietcong. It taps both ideological and nationalistic motivation. I know I will start an argument if I add what must be obvious to anyone who has interviewed many ex-members of the Vietcong, namely that Communist ideology is a much more important factor in the combination than is nationalism. But since the issue of relative weight is irrelevant to today's subject, let me not start that argument and simply concede that both factors enter in.

In addition, there are what Max Weber called robust motives of interest. One of these is land, and I am not talking of land reform. I am talking of patronage. It is the exceptional Communist Party secretary whose family has not gained land in the land redistribution that goes under the misnomer of land reform. These exceptions are singled out for praise by the villagers, but as being exceptions. Even more important, however, is the opportunity the Vietcong gives the peasant boy to become a bureaucrat. For the ambitious peasant boy, the Vietcong offers a kind of middle-class existence in the sense that he no longer has to be a farmer with the sweat and toil entailed. He is now a politician, a "cadre" to use their own word, a kind of lower level local bureaucrat, who administered and organized things rather than worked. This, indeed, was one of the great attractions of the Vietcong for an uneducated peasant boy who couldn't make it up the ladder on the government's side. Vietcong politics offered the way out of peasant life, the way to become a minor official.

Finally, but probably last in importance is the element of excitement that has attracted a few young men to every guerrilla movement since Robin Hood. Guerrilla life, by peasant standards, is not too bad. Until the Americans took the initiative and started attacking in 1966, the average guerrilla fought only about one day a month. The rest of the time he spent in his jungle hideout in training, preparatory activity and planning. The few fights they had were carefully planned attacks on points where they would have the predominance of strength and where casualties could be expected to be low. There were, of course, hardships to the guerrilla life in the jungle, but to a peasant for whom the alternative is to dig in the fields in the tropical sun, the hardships were not so striking.

Political organization, ideology, and motives of self-interest for the underprivileged thus are all combined to make viable the Vietcong as a political movement aiming at imposing its claim to the exercise of force over large stretches of the countryside. The same thing can be said of the Hoa Hao. But what of the government of South Vietnam? Does it have any basis for establishing effective organization in the countryside?

While it is far from clear that the Government will seize its opportunity, the answer to the question of feasibility must be in the affirmative. There does exist a basis for political organization that would link self-determined villages into a broader national entity. This prospect is the result of rather remarkable political development in South Vietnam since 1964.

Once again I realize I am heading straight into an irrelevant controversy. The unmitigatedly hostile attitude of many American intellectuals towards the present government of South Vietnam would probably lead many persons present to the conviction that that government neither seeks to represent its people not does so in any way. I would rather avoid arguing that question today for it is not our subject. Let me pose the question in this form, which might avoid some arguments: If the government of South Vietnam wished to establish its legitimacy in the eyes of the villager, what practicable measure should it take?

The usual American answer is to say: 1. Get yourself an honest, idealistic government in Saigon and 2. Win the hearts and minds of the people by making them better off. That is not an adequate answer because it disregards the irrelevancy of Saigon and the government there to the villager in the countryside. It fails to answer the need for a structure of organization based in the village itself but also reaching up to Saigon.

Both in the village and in Saigon the bases for legitimate government now exist but linkage between them does not.

In the village the basis for stable political organization lies in the elective village and hamlet chiefs and in the Popular Force troops. The reinstitution of elective village and hamlet chiefs just over a year ago was a major step forward in political development in Vietnam and very meaningful to the villagers themselves. In 1956 the Diem regime striving to achieve greater unity in the country replaced the system of elective chiefs by ones appointed from above. No single measure of that dictatorship was more of a favor to the Vietcong.

With the restoration of locally elected chiefs in a large part of the country, the villagers came to feel once more that their officials represented them. That the elections were for the most part genuine is attested to by the fact that about a third of the encumbants failed to be reelected.

The largest element of power potentially available to the village officials is the Popular Force contingent, averaging 60 men per village in Vietnam. Paid barely enough to survive, not issued uniforms, armed with old M2's or less, given little or no compensation if wounded or killed, they nonetheless have a better record in casualties inflicted on the enemy than the Army of the Republic of Vietnam. Although a start has been made now, they are still seldom trained beyond the most casual introduction on the job.

Most of these 150,000 to 175,000 men are poorly led. There is no higher organic level above the platoon, offering jobs to which a good leader can be promoted. Being platoon leader is a dead end. Most platoons are not aggressive against the Vietcong, usually confining themselves to defending their own post and therefore not inhibiting Vietcong infiltration even in their own village; but some platoons patrol and ambush aggressively.

Popular Forces unlike the Army of the Republic of Vietnam seldom abuse the villagers. They are living in their own home village, which is why they joined Popular Forces rather than the regular Army, and their basic relations with their fellow villagers are good. On the other hand, in insecure areas they and their fellow villagers tend to avoid close contact with each other because the Vietcong may penalize someone who associates too closely with the Popular Forces.

To make them the backbone of the local government structure they should be better paid and armed and made directly responsible to the village chief who should be encouraged to use them as his political machine for civic action, local administration and various functions in addition to defense.

At the national level too, there has been great progress towards legitimacy. After a period of repeated coups, a stable government has existed since 1965, changing in an orderly legal fashion. A Constituent Assembly was elected and adopted a Constitution not very much liked by the military authorities, but forced upon them. Last fall, elections were held under this Constitution. In the Senate elections the military government backed three slates, all of which were defeated. The House elections especially resulted in a remarkably representative body. The first cabinet was a weak one but now a widely representative cabinet has been installed headed by one of the leading opposition candidates. The extraordinary inadequacy of American reporting on these matters is illustrated by the fact that the *New York Times* did not bother to carry the list of new cabinet members. They did not regard it as news, for example, that the Minister of Information is Ton That Thien whose excellent and outspoken newspaper was closed down by the military regime less than two years ago. His first act was to abolish censorship which had been reinstituted at the time of the Tet offensive after having been abolished during the elections. Candor compels recognition that for a country in civil war there is a remarkable amount of civil representative politics at the Saigon level.

But between the beginnings of village self-government and the beginnings of national responsible government there is no interface. Between these two levels is a structure of appointive province chiefs and district chiefs who are virtually all army officers. The elective village chief sees the Government of Vietnam in the form of a Captain or a Major who calls him in from time to time to issue orders, to whom he addresses requests for money, cement, fertilizer or forces in case of attack. It is a master-client relation, sometimes good, sometimes bad, depending on personalities, but still master and client.

The next needed step, in what has been a rapid progress of Vietnam towards representative government, is the establishment of District Councils with power so that the relationship of the District Chief to the elective village officials becomes much more that relationship of bargaining, tension, and responsibility which is normal between political executives and elective policy making bodies.

I present this proposition not because it represents our American democratic political bias, as indeed it does, but because it is relevant to our topic today, which is how pacification can be achieved in turbulent village societies.

The requirement for pacification is that the villagers and the authorities have shared notions about the legitimate exercise of force. Another requirement is that the villagers have available at their call when needed, a modern technology of force to supplement that which they can provide themselves out of their meager resources. Such requirements can be met if, but only if, there exists the kind of organization that we have been describing, representatively rooted in the village but fanning out to higher levels.

CHAPTER 3. VILLAGE AUTHORITY PATTERNS IN VIETNAM

By Samuel L. Popkin*

The author denies the validity of Pool's question and the validity of any proposal which would couple mass participation and local initiative with the present leadership in the South Vietnam national government. Sentiments toward restoration of the old village structure must also yield to the crucial political *problem of the development of an effective hierarchical system of government which serves the needs of the overall society and still legitimatizes itself within the villages and districts. Ed.*

> Those who are ignorant about government say: 'Win the hearts of the people.' If order could be procured by winning the hearts of the people, then even the wise ministers . . . would be of no use. For all the ruler would need to do would be just to listen to the people. . . .
>
> —Han Fei Tzu

The United States has brought an extraordinary amount of military power and economic resources to bear in the problem of rural security and pacification in Vietnam. The payoff has been negligible. Pacification has been a failure.

The central problem of pacification is how to translate economic resources and military power into village control. It must be emphasized that this is a political and not a technical problem. The problem is polit-

*The author is associated with the Department of Government, Harvard University.

ical because it concerns the distribution of political power and control between various elements of society. Specifically, it is the problem of linking the central government and the army to the demands the state places upon the village in such a way as to obtain reasonable success. More specifically, it is the problem, never successfully resolved by the Saigon government, of replacing the traditional model of village authority with a system that can serve the needs of the overall society and still legitimatize itself within the village.

If pacification is defined militarily as the development of total security and the ability to resist outside forces, then pacification is clearly a goal that no group in Vietnam can achieve. The United States has an Air Force and the Vietcong has long range rockets. But success can be measured in less ambitious terms: the development in a village of the will and means to defend itself against outside attack and subversion, or the creation of a situation where the security of a locality can only be improved through an increased level of military power, because existing human resources are already optimally employed.

By these criteria, there are large areas of rural Vietnam that can be called "pacified". The areas dominated by the Cambodians, the Hoa Hao, Cao Dai and Catholic areas, and of course the areas controlled by the Vietcong themselves are relatively stable, secure and able to resist subversion by outside forces. But most of the war for the villages has been fought over control of that fraction of the population (some 35%) living in places never converted to the Catholic, Cao Dai or Hoa Hao religions. In these villages, where the belief system is the traditional mixture of Confucianism, Animism and Mahayana Buddhism, the struggle for power has been in effect directly between the Government of Vietnam (GVN) and the Vietcong. Here I think it is fair to say that by almost any standard, the Vietcong have been more successful.

Before the French colonization, the villages of Vietnam were autonomous and viable. There was a weak central state which served mainly as a coordinator with the right of verification and oppression but not of execution. Taxation, welfare and public works were the affair of the village and were well-handled by the traditional village elite. Pierre Gourou described the operation of the traditional commune thus:

> . . .The Annamese commune has settled institutions, which bind the inhabitants in a close-knit system of fiscal, religious, and civic obligations. This commune well represents the collective wishes of its members and, strong in the cohesion and obedience of its citizens, is really capable of performing administrative functions, that

is, attending to public rights of way, public buildings, the distribution of communal land, renting of land allocated to the support of religion, planning irrigation if this necessitates a collective plan, putting rice in reserve in a commune granary against a period of want, and many other tasks of common interest.[1]

Under French rule, the traditional viability of the villages declined drastically, largely because of the development of a stronger central government and the creation of urban areas. Yet there is a great deal of Mandarin sentimentality among the Vietnamese and many of them have attributed the decline of the traditional commune to the corruption of the French and the rise of the cities, rather than blaming the changing scope and pattern of central government.

The 'last Confucian' Ngo Dinh Diem had faith that "village traditions, if once reinstated, would of themselves expel the Vietcong . . . like natural antibiotics."[2] Many prominent Vietnamese still hold these views, although all the evidence contradicts them. Less than a year ago, Ton That Thien, the new South Vietnamese Minister of Information, wrote that before his plan of pacification could work in the provinces, ". . . these provinces should be all but cut off from the rest of the country to avoid the corrupting influence of the cities."[3]

The fundamental error of this analysis is its assumption that pacification means a return to the pre-French situation in the villages. In these traditional village areas, for which Sam Huntington has coined the term CRABVN (Confucianist Rural Animist Buddhist Vietnamese), security and stability for the Saigon government has not come from resisting progress or turning back history. A country which has started to modernize cannot be pacified by a return to the past. As Paul Mus noted nearly twenty years ago, it is necessary

> to desist from efforts to pacify the country by re-establishing traditional village institutions as part of a political and military security network—a concept which . . . is economically and socially obsolete.[4]

In fact, the successfully pacified areas have been able to transform themselves to meet the demands of a Hobbesian world by utilizing the

[1] Pierre Gourou, *Land Utilization in French Indochina,* Institute of Pacific Relations, 1945, p. 218.

[2] Dennis Duncanson, *Government and Revolution in Vietnam,* New York, 1968, p. 259.

[3] Ton That Thien, "Town and Country," *Saigon,* 1967, n.p.

[4] Paul Mus, "The Role of the Village in Vietnamese Politics," *Pacific Affairs,* September, 1949, p. 271.

human resources necessary to develop the viability demanded for security. The failure of pacification in the other areas has been the inability to develop the kinds of communications, institutions and patterns of coercion within and among villages appropriate to the twentieth century.

The point may be clarified by a review of what happened to the traditional villages under the colonial rule of the French. Under the French colonial system, the introduction of urbanism, stronger central government, absentee landlords and usury changed the life of the Vietnamese considerably. At the village level, there were, according to Paul Mus, three major points of French impact:

1. the creation of a proper system of registering births and deaths
2. control by the French administration over the village budget
3. an attempt to replace the traditional village council system of cooption by introduction of elections[5]

About the only thing the French could not change was the traditional village council system of cooption from among holders of traditional status, based on age, knowledge and wealth. French legislation changed the size, scope and manner of selection of the village government, but in the end, the same people held power in the villages.

As village birth and death lists came under scrutiny and control from the outside, village councils had less leeway and power. Traditionally it was their skill and machinations that determined the extent of the taxes levied upon the village. Now the total village levy and the formulas for individual assessment were no longer in council hands. Again, increased outside control of the budget took leeway from the village council, whose traditional role of buffer protecting the village or at least some strata of it was thereby reduced. The effect of elections was not to change the power structure, but to increase opposition to the French among the notables, whom forced elections degraded. Still, it seems that the notables retained the role of legitimators of action within the village.

Because he abolished this elective system of village government, substituting appointive officials, Diem has often been accused of destroying the ancient traditions of village democracy. In villages not yet scarred by war, however, the change was relatively insignificant. The traditional village oligarchy still held sway as a moral arbiter over the conduct of village affairs, as they had held sway under the electoral system.

---

[5] Paul Mus, *Sociologie d'une Guerre,* Paris: Editions du Seuil, 1952, Chapter 2.

Khanh Hau, one village studied extensively during the Diem era, is revealing of the limitations on Diem's system of village government. Khanh Hau was the site of an historic shrine with a large impact on village pride and it was the site of a new school built as part of a special pilot project. Still all was not well in Khanh Hau. There were no strong bonds among members of the society and no sense of village solidarity. Nor was the village council motivated to, or perhaps even capable of, developing cohesion, national allegiance or a sense of urgency or dynamism.[6]

Positions on the village council were almost purely bureaucratic, involving a staggering amount of paper work and carrying little financial reward. A conversation in Khanh Hau, reported by Gerald Hickey, gives the "mandarin" view of the increasing bureaucratization of the councils.

> A group of older men, many of whom had served on the council, laughed heartily when one noted that "the people used to be the servants of the Village Council, now the Village Council is the servant of the people."[7]

Though council positions were appointive, the pay was minimal. The financial demands of the position were much higher, in general, than the pay. Village positions required conspicuous consumption in the form of banquets, for example. A council position could only be held by an upper status villager, with both the time and the money to participate actively in the political life of the village.

Why then did anyone allow himself to become placed on the Village Council? The answer lies with the existence of a still functioning cult committee. Upward mobility in the oligarchy meant a place in the Cult Committee and the road to the Cult Committee was through the Village Council.

Village councils had been stripped of their religious aspects by the French in 1904 in an attempt to streamline village government. The traditional village oligarchy thereafter kept the cult committee going on their own. This committee, responsible for infrequent rituals held at the village *dinh* or communal temple, provided the legitimization and moral justification for government, where it still existed. And to join the cult committee, with its concomitant status, a man had first to serve

---

[6] Gerald Hickey, *Village in Vietnam,* New Haven, 1964 and James Hendry, *The Small World of Khanh Hau,* Chicago, 1966.

[7] Hickey, *op. cit.,* p. 185.

a term on the village council, an almost totally menial and bureaucratic task.

In Khanh Hau, at least, Diem did little to change the village or develop its viability. A point to note is the role of the young in village affairs: *they had none*. The village council was the route to traditional village status. Age, education and wealth determined the membership of the upper class and among this group the most revered were those on the Cult Committee. Diem's penetration of Khanh Hau consisted of introducing more paperwork for those aspiring to become a venerable one. The only young person who had anything to do with the council, in fact, was a twenty-one year old boy who served as clerk for the council members, who were becoming increasingly irritated at the demands on their time, and eventually, at the possible dangers in their job. Anyone young and ambitious for a career with a chance of advancement had two choices: Saigon or the Vietcong.

It has become fashionable to talk of the breakdown of the village and the loss of qualities and virtues it once possessed. To a certain extent this is romanticism, what I like to call the "myth of the village". In this mode of thinking, patterns that may have only existed for lack of alternatives are raised to the level of virtues. Peasants who have no material rewards are assumed to have spiritual rewards. When a son sticks to his father perhaps only for the sake of survival, it is called filial piety. When one village doesn't talk to another, it is called village solidarity. Somehow what may have been no more than the necessities and/or oppressions of one era seem to have become the traditional values of the next.

The traditional system as it existed in Khanh Hau was based upon cushioning the village from outside demands and powers. It was a system for avoiding rather than resolving conflict and that depended upon intravillage considerations for legitimacy. Most important, the system could only work if everyone placed the preservation of the village above the interests of any single faction. Under the traditional system, a village that caused trouble or didn't pay its taxes or that harbored a single dead body was subject to destruction. With no cities and without the privilege of entering other villages, village destruction meant a long trek to new lands and starting life all over again for everyone, including those who had started the trouble. This was an effective sanction in the days before French rule.

The same attitude of "punishing the village", however, works against the interests of the state when any group or person owes his primary allegiance to a group beyond the village, or more precisely, if there is a group willing to let the village be destroyed rather than compromise its aims. It makes it possible for the Vietcong to use "political judo", turning outside power to their own ends. This is why, once the Vietcong can demonstrate with high credibility a determination to stay in a village no matter what, the bombing of such a village is to their advantage. First, it means that it is to the peasant's interest to keep knowledge of the Vietcong presence from outsiders to prevent bombing. Second, when bombings happen anyway, even without Vietcong presence, something that can easily happen when intelligence is poor and/or the village council is not consulted, it decreases the legitimacy of the village council, making it irrelevant to a major problem of the peasants. Of course, if the Vietcong help with the construction of shelters and repair work and if they can give the peasants advance warning on bombings, it makes them very useful to the peasant, even if he considers them the cause of the bombing. Similarly, when government soldiers loot and plunder the villages, it makes sense for peasants to help the Vietcong build punji traps around the villages. While the Army of the Republic of Vietnam steps around the traps, the peasants have time to hide their chickens.

At the same time, a system legitimized on the basis of the moral sanctions of elders and the face-to-face social pressures of village life does not work well when the village chief is an outsider who doesn't care about the village. When the village chief is indifferent to the attitude of the villagers and when villagers have no channels or redress to grievances outside the village, corruption can reach very high levels.

These failings of the traditional system, which has changed little since Diem, can best be shown by looking at some features common to the Hoa Hao and the Vietcong (I use these two groups as I know them best) that are in sharp contrast to the GVN system. This comparison will, I hope, also show why I feel it so important to emphasize that the problem of pacification is political and not technical.

In both Hoa Hao and Vietcong operations, local officials have the ability to control outside forces and to use them as a rationale or an excuse for much of the coercion they must exercise if they are to control their areas. In contrast, if a GVN official tries to intervene to prevent a rampaging ARVN (Army of Republic of Vietnam) soldier from stealing something, he is likely to be putting himself in danger. Not only does the ARVN not coordinate with or work with local officials: the urban officer corps tends to scorn them as "mere peasants".

The relationship with outside power is terribly crucial to the ability of the Vietcong, for example, to use attentism to their advantage in contested areas. The local Vietcong cadre has a say with outside recruiters, tax collectors and military units. This means that if he is captured or killed by the GVN, many peasants who had complied with him out of self-interest lose a "voice at city hall" which would be a useful voucher if the Vietcong were to win. There is no such institutional memory in the GVN.

There is similar problem with the 59-man Revolutionary Development teams (RD), who are under the control of district and provincial officials and not village chiefs or councils. RD presence has nearly always been popular with villagers because it means a temporary beefing up of local security and a decreased possibility of local fighting. Village officials, however, have gained nothing from the cadres in the long or the short run. That the cadres have had so much better access to supplies and materials, in fact, has actually decreased the legitimacy of local officials.

In the Hoa Hao province of AnGiang, the GVN teams were no better coordinated with local officials than elsewhere. However, the judicious use of propaganda still turned the RD presence to Hoa Hao advantage. Before the team arrived in one village, the district chief and village chief went around together telling the peasants, "We're bringing an RD team here. They won't work well with us, but we don't mind, because they will be bringing lots of building materials and benefits to you." In another Hoa Hao village, the official waited until the team was nearly done working, then took and hid their rifles, which the cadres had carelessly left aside one day. After the cadres had spent several hours frantically worrying about what had happened, the officials "found" their guns. Within a few days, the story had been spread by the officials throughout the area.

For both the Hoa Hao and the Vietcong, village government and military service is part of a career system that emphasizes post-entry education and social mobility. The fact that positions are a career rung with a chance for advancement is important because it is an incentive to high performance standards. In addition, belonging to an organization that reaches beyond the village is a vitally necessary source of social support and rationale for necessary but unpopular acts at the local level. Outside pressure is especially important for local soldiers. In the CRABVN areas, where the village soldiers are not part of a larger organization, it is very hard for a local platoon leader to exact risky strategies from his men. Without effective outside pressure and encouragement, a dedicated platoon leader has to be ready to accept the role of a pariah, in case of failure.

That post-entry education is possible also means the ability to attract and motivate ambitious but uneducated young peasants. In both the Hoa Hao and the Vietcong, a peasant can progress as far as his abilities will take him. If he wants to learn to read, he will be taught. In ARVN, by contrast, military rank is almost completely a function of education. Without a baccalaureat—held only by city-dwellers or upper class rural gentry—there is no way to attend officer training school or to become a bureaucrat.

At the same time, the career system of the Hoa Hao and Vietcong makes it easier for them to substitute outsiders for village level cadres lost through assassination or defection. When you depend on local status and the traditional oligarchy for legitimacy, however, the replacement problem is much more difficult.

Finally, the emphasis on mobility and career opportunities recruits younger and more energetic men than does a system based on a council of elders.

Perhaps the most glaring difference between the effective political systems and the traditional system lies in the realm of mass participation and its role in creating legitimacy and commitment. The traditional village system was based on avoiding conflict while the Vietcong in particular used participation and conflict to reach a more durable and viable consensus.

Because there was no real mass politics worthy of the name in villages ruled in the traditional manner it is often said that the Vietcong filled a vacuum. The idea of vacuum does not do justice to their particular skills, for creating politics of participation in Vietnam was by no means an easy task. Before the Vietcong could fill a vacuum, they had to create one.

To involve the villagers in mass politics was a job for skilled and dedicated cadres and could not be done instantly. Land reform is a good illustration. The simplified view of Diem's land reform was that it was conservative and did little for the peasantry. The main reason, however, that the Vietcong were able to use the land problem as an effective issue was more due to the fact that it was a centralized program and not one in which decisions were made at the village level.

Land is a scarce commodity. No matter how it is distributed among villagers, no peasant can have all the land he could possibly till and any scheme of distribution leaves alternate formulas that are equally plausible. (Thus if every man were given a plot of identical size, one could argue for distribution by family size, by age, or by status.) Diem's land reform distributed land to former tenants, leaving men who had been neither owners or tenants landless. The Vietcong appealed to the peasants' sense of justice to give some of the land to the poor, landless families, thus making them allies of the Vietcong. This was by no means a simple matter. The Vietcong land reform could only work if the villagers could be convinced that justice had not prevailed under the Diem reform. This became possible precisely because justice means decisions at the village and not at the national level. Again, the reform was only workable if it could be implemented without making enemies of the men who were to lose some land. The Vietcong were able to do this by open participation, putting men in the position of losing face if they were unwilling to go along with the new policy.

While it may have taken long and hard labor to create mass participation in the villages, the issues which the Vietcong seized upon for this purpose were sometimes relatively trivial from an outsider's point of view. Land reform was certainly of no use in some areas, but there was very often some other issue that could be used to legitimize the Vietcong and discredit the traditional, mandarin-style village politics. The Vietcong success was due to their ability to let local conditions guide them, especially before their control was solidly established, at which point they often became oppressive, but with a minimal loss of effectiveness.

What is important to note is that the Vietcong were virtually the only group in the Buddhist areas seeking to develop participation and a following. This is because political parties and mass movements have never found favor with the Saigon government, precisely because there is no way to induce a mass following from the top in a village society.

Why, then, is the myth of the village *still* the panacea of the Saigon government, while the Vietcong and the Hoa Hao have transcended the old forms with a system of mass participation that meets the needs of a post-village society? The answer, I would suggest, lies in the incompatibility of mass participation, local initiative, and consideraton of local leaders with the values and attitudes of higher-ups with the two dominant voices of the Saigon government—Confucian sentimentalists and the military.

CHAPTER 4. ATTITUDES OF THE SOUTH VIETNAMESE

By Ralph K. White*

With significance for the Pool-Popkin debate, the author investigates the attitudes of the South Vietnamese in an attempt to estimate the level of opposition to and support of the Vietcong, and also asks whether U.S. involvement in Vietnam can be termed "democratic." Accepted throughout this analysis is a pluralistic, minorities-in-conflict, conception of government in a society wherein a majority of the popu-lation is apathetic to any government. The findings suggest that the pro-Vietcong population outnumbers the anti-Vietcong. These findings also have a bearing on the relevance and potential success of major power involvements in small nations with guerrilla capabilities. Ed.

In this paper, I shall attempt to present my present thinking on attitudes of the South Vietnamese. This thinking is based upon the few empirical studies already conducted, which unfortunately could not obtain as reliable data as we would like, and on my own observations.

I shall begin with two simple diagrams. Each represents along a straight line an estimated percentage distribution of attitudes of South Vietnamese. These diagrams necessarily underestimate the complexity of attitude identification, but nonetheless they can be useful for guiding our thinking. As I see it, these two diagrams represent the two major hypotheses regarding attitudes among the South Vietnamese.

*The author is associated with the Institute for Sino-Soviet Studies and the Department of Psychology, George Washington University.

These hypotheses are both "major" in the sense that they are seriously held by intelligent, well-informed, responsible people, including people in decision-making positions in our government. The first is more often held by "hawks," though it is not confined to them, and the second is more often held by "doves," though it is not confined to them.

Attitudes of South Vietnamese: Their Relative Distribution

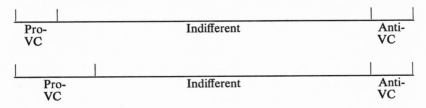

The hypotheses have a good deal in common. Each recognizes a very large intermediate group that can be called "indifferent" for practical purposes. Perhaps "ambivalent" would be a better name, because a great many of those in the group certainly have mixed feelings. But they are overtly indifferent in that they let their personal self-interest override any ideological preferences they may have. The two diagrams are in agreement that most of the people want most to be left alone to pursue their own safety and economic self-interest.

Another thing which those who advance these two hypotheses have in common is a primary emphasis on the people at the two ends, who do have strong ideological preferences and commitments. Both doves and hawks tend to accept the near-axiom of political science which says that in politics the people who count are the people who care. What matters most, they would agree, is the balance of feeling among the politically-involved people who really care about the outcome of the war. Both the informed, responsible hawks and the informed, responsible doves would accept what might be called a "dumb-bell" picture of the situation in South Vietnam, with heavy weights at each end and a much thinner part in the middle.

But they differ as to the relative weights of the two ends. The hawks tend to think, at least implicitly, that there is no significant difference; theirs is a balanced-dumbbell hypothesis. Many doves tend to think that the number of dedicated people at the pro-VC end is much greater than the number of dedicated people at the anti-VC end. Theirs, typically, is an unbalanced-dumbbell hypothesis.

Which one is closer to the truth is a question with important implications. It has a bearing, for instance, on the question of which side is
"the aggressor" in this war (if either side is). If the situation is a balanced dumbbell, this is not inconsistent with the assumption that the
North Vietnamese are aggressors, at least by one definition of aggression. The world would certainly be in trouble if every country went
around interfering violently in the internal affairs of its neighbors, with
no more basis for doing so than an evenly balanced equilibrium between
the government faction and an anti-government faction. By the same
token what we (the U.S.) are doing could be justified, not exactly on the
basis of democracy but on the basis that we are not going *against* the
preponderance of opinion in South Vietnam, and are therefore free to
decide what is good on the basis of other considerations, such as the
domino theory. But if the unbalanced dumbbell hypothesis is closer to
the truth, there is a real question whether we ourselves (the U.S.) are
more appropriately described as aggressors than the North Vietnamese.
Without realizing it, we may have been intervening against one minority
on behalf of an even smaller minority, and by any definition of democracy that is undemocratic. Also, by one definition of aggression, it
is aggression.

The question of which hypothesis is closer to the truth also has some
important practical implications. For instance, it has a bearing on the
question of whether we can win the war. If the psychological situation
in South Vietnam were evenly balanced, as the hawks tend to assume,
one would think that our piling in there with our thirty billion dollars
and our half-million men (balanced, Mr. Strausz-Hupé said yesterday,
by only one or two billions in Soviet military aid on the other side)
could certainly tip the balance in favor of our side. But if not—if the
side we are against is much stronger in number of dedicated men—the
chances of our victory are much more dubious.

So the task I am going to set myself in the rest of this talk is simply
to survey the evidence on which hypothesis does come closer to the
truth. It will be a very sketchy survey, hitting only highspots, since
there is far more to be said than I have time to cover.[1]

Naturally we social scientists, confronting a problem of this sort, ask
first: "What studies are there? Who has done a thorough, careful, empirical study of the problem—particularly a quantitative study?" When

---

[1]For a much more detailed statement, see Ralph K. White, *NOBODY
WANTED WAR: Misperception in Vietnam and Other Wars,* Doubleday, New
York, 1968, pp. 29-84.

we do that in this case we are sure to be disappointed, because there are in my judgment only two studies that seriously claim our attention: the CBS survey of attitudes in South Vietnam,[2] and Douglas Pike's book on the Vietcong.[3] And neither really hits the mark.

The CBS study is a good study in a number of ways. It was done through the Opinion Research Corporation (ORC), working with a Vietnamese research organization and a Vietnamese team of interviewers in late 1966 and early 1967. The sample was quite adequate as to size —1,545 people—and it was a good probability sample of the population of South Vietnam living in "secure" areas, which for the purposes of this study were defined in a way that included about 80% of the population. But it did run into the great problem of frankness. While the study is useful in a number of ways, it can hardly be taken at face value when it says, for instance, that 83% of the respondents were on our side, against the Vietcong, and 0% were for the Vietcong. In Vietnam peasants who oppose the government and favor the Vietcong are not likely to say so to a strange middle-class interviewer coming from the big city. I was very skeptical about this point before I went to Vietnam last summer, and became more so on the basis of my experience with a team of middle-class Vietnamese interviewers very similar to the team used in the CBS survey. To that kind of interviewer the peasants just do not open up, on sensitive subjects.

Pike's book is excellent in a number of ways: intelligent, thorough, scholarly. And his estimate that "no more than 10% of the people are really for the Vietcong" has been taken seriously in high places, by people like Walt Rostow, because of Pike's reputation as the outstanding authority on the Vietcong. But I am skeptical of his conclusion for three reasons. In the first place, Pike is not an authority, and I do not think he ever really claimed to be an authority, on peasant attitudes. What he has done is to cover certain kinds of documents very thoroughly, including interviews with Vietcong defectors, prisoners and so on. But his knowledge does not include much first-hand contact with ordinary peasants or any direct, systematic study of their attitudes. He is not a public-opinion specialist. Second, a good deal depends on what we mean by "really" on the Vietcong side. Perhaps he is thinking of a degree of dedication that would represent a pretty stringent criterion of

[2] *The People of South Vietnam: How They Feel about the War; A CBS News Public Opinion Survey*, Princeton, Opinion Research Corporation, 1967.
[3] Douglas Pike, *Viet Cong: The Organization and Techniques of the National Liberation Front of South Vietnam*, M.I.T. Press, Cambridge, 1966.

"realness" and by the same criterion there might be a good deal less than 10% of the people feeling equally strongly and equally dedicated on the other side. The dumbell might still be unbalanced, with perhaps only 10% at the pro-VC end and 5% or so at the anti-VC end. Third, the picture has changed since he first made that estimate. He made it before the Tet offensive, and before the new evidence of a certain kind of support for the Vietcong—even in the cities—shown by the high degree of surprise achieved, with the implication that very few of the people even in the cities were willing to inform on the Vietcong. I just do not know whether Pike would make the same estimate now.

So we have to turn to other kinds of evidence. I am going to list five points that are commonly made on the "anti-VC" side—i.e. they are reasons to think that the strongly anti-VC people in South Vietnam are at least as numerous as the strongly pro-VC people. I shall also list five points commonly made on the other side, which we can call "pro-VC."

ON THE ANTI-VC SIDE:

1. *The violence of the VC*—throwing of grenades, mining of roads, assassination of village leaders, and so on. In the CBS survey two of the questions were "What do you think is bad about the Vietcong?" and "What do you think is good about it?" At the top of the list of bad things, by a sizable margin, was violence. This is a rather elemental emotion—physical fear—and I think it should be given more weight than a good many Americans, especially opponents of our involvement in the war, realize.

2. *Taxes imposed by the VC.* They have been heavy, at least since 1964 when the VC shifted from primarily political to primarily military actions, and the bill fell chiefly on the peasants. The taxes were often collected by strong-arm methods. It has been estimated that they amounted to as much as the rent that the peasants formerly paid for their land; the piasters that would have gone to absentee landlords went to the VC instead. This too is a very tangible thing, and represents in my judgment a stronger factor on the anti-VC side than most of the opponents of the war in the United States realize.

3. *The exodus from VC-held areas.* There has been far more migration out of VC areas than into them. The people, it is often said, have been "voting with their feet" against Communism, in much the same way they did in 1954 when nearly 900,000 came down from the North to the South and only a small fraction of that number went

the other way. But there is an ambiguity here. These VC-held areas and hamlets are at the same time the ones that have suffered most from what our side has done—the bombing, the shelling, sometimes the napalm, the poisoning of crops. That could be the big reason for it. So I would be inclined to give only a little weight to this point.

4. *The testimony of defectors, prisoners and the like.* This is the kind of evidence Pike was presumably relying on most. In many cases such interviews show more internal evidence of validity than the CBS survey did, for example, since the peasants who are talking are telling concrete things about what happened to them and to others in their villages. These peasants often give an impression of considerable frankness, since they tell about good as well as bad things done by the VC, and bad as well as good things done by government officials or government troops. But here too there is room for skepticism. Apart from the question of how representative these people are, there is still the question of frankness. Granted that they are probably telling the truth, on the whole, are they telling the whole truth? Could they be trying to give an impression of neutrality by holding back on some of the things they might be saying against the government, and holding back, in many cases, on expression of an overall pro-VC judgment if that is what is in their minds? They know they are talking to an anti-Communist interviewer, and they know they will now have to get along in a society controlled by anti-Communists. So it seems to me that this point too should be given only a very moderate amount of weight.

5. *Improvement since the death of Diem, 1963-67.* There is little doubt that in several ways there was improvement during that time. I wrote a book in 1966, called *Misperception and the Vietnam War,*[4] that emphasized mainly the "pro-VC" points on this question, the pessimistic side of the picture. I was told by some well-informed persons that while my pessimistic picture would have been essentially correct as a picture of how things were under Diem, things have changed since then and the picture is no longer accurate. I am sure there was an element of truth in what these informed persons said. But, they were talking before the Tet offensive, before the recent demoralization of the cities, and the recent falling apart of the pacification program, and so on. I am not at all sure that *now* the situation is better from our standpoint than it was in 1963. So I would be inclined to give this point, too, only a very slight amount of emphasis.

[4] Ralph K. White, "Misperception and the Vietnam War," *The Journal of Social Issues,* XXII (July, 1966), 3, entire issue.

Hence, we are left with only two clearly strong arguments on the anti-VC side: violence and taxes.

ON THE PRO-VC SIDE:

1. *Violence by the government and the Americans.* At least equal in total amount to the violence of the VC is the violence on the other side, including bombing, shelling, poisoning of crops, torturing of prisoners. We Americans are still handing over to the Vietnamese troops the prisoners we capture, knowing that in many cases this means handing them over to be tortured. As a basis for sheer anger this seems as potent as the violence perpetrated by the VC, and should be given as much weight.

2. *Land reform.* As Ithiel Pool said this morning, there is some question about the genuineness of VC land "reform," since much of it has been appropriation of land by the VC cadres themselves. Probably more important has been the support given by the VC, even in contested areas, to the non-payment of rent by peasants on land owned by absentee landlords. This has made a very substantial difference, at least in the Delta area, probably comparable to the difference made by the taxes imposed by the VC, and should be given as much weight.

3. *Nationalism.* There is not much question that up to now nationalism has been mobilized much more effectively on the VC side than on the government side. Ho Chi Minh is the hero of the struggle for independence against the French, in South Vietnam as well as North Vietnam. As we were saying this morning, the words used by the peasants illustrate this asset of the Vietcong. The peasants habitually use the term "liberation forces" when referring to the Vietcong, and "nationalist forces" when referring to the government troops. You might think, from this, that the powerful force of nationalism was on the side of the government. But that would be a mistake. The same two terms were used during the glorious, heart-breaking years of struggle for independence. During those years the term "liberation forces" was applied to the Viet Minh, led by Ho Chi Minh, while the term "nationalist forces" was applied to the troops of Bao Dai, who was generally regarded as a stooge of the French. The great majority of the people then supported Ho Chi Minh. By their usage, the term "nationalist" therefore has strong connotations of "taking the side of the foreign overlord, against our own people." By a curious semantic reversal, "nationalist" has apparently come to mean almost *un*patriotic. The factor of nationalism,

then, should probably be given heavy emphasis as a factor on the pro-VC side.

4. *Success against odds.* The success of the Vietcong, always against a very great superiority of its opponents in the weapons of modern war, has been extraordinary. Many Americans do not fully realize the nature of the odds against the Vietcong. In the beginning, for instance, the VC got almost no material help from the North. Its first big success was in 1959 (there was no substantial material help from the North at least until the end of 1960). Also, the big success at first was mainly in the Delta area, so far from the North that the VC could hardly have gotten much of any help even if the North had then been willing to supply it. The relatively primitive weapons of the guerrillas had to be constructed or captured, when Diem was already drawing heavily on the enormous technical superiority of the United States. Even if we attribute a considerable share of the Vietcong's early success to its ability to assassinate village leaders and intimidate the rest of the villagers, it looks as if they must have also had a very large amount of voluntary support by the rank-and-file peasantry—feeding them, helping them to conceal themselves, telling them about government troop movements—in order to establish this kind of record. I would be inclined to give this evidence more weight than any other item in either of the two lists. Actions do speak louder than words.

5. *Consensus of informed observers.* I have been quite surprised by the degree of agreement on this point between well-informed Vietnamese observers. After I had been there a little over a month I arrived at a formula representing the unbalanced dumbbell hypothesis. It seemed to me that the strongly motivated pro-Vietcong element in the South Vietnamese population represented something like 20%, and the strongly motivated anti-VC element perhaps 10%, while something like 70% were, for most practical purposes, indifferent. I tried out that formula on eight particularly well-informed anti-Communist Vietnamese —and seven and one-half of them bought it. (The half represents one of the eight who wavered; first he agreed with the formula and then said that he thought "maybe there are more than 10% on the anti-VC side.") Eight people are not very many, but I would still give a good deal of weight to this evidence, since they were all unusually intelligent and politically alert, and for all of them the judgment as to the greater size of the pro-VC group must have been *in spite of* their general anti-Communist bias and the natural direction of their wishful thinking. It could not have been because of it.

So my own adding up of the two sides is that there are five points on the pro-VC side, all of them fairly strong, and only two equally strong points, or two and a few fractions, on the anti-VC side. The unbalanced dumbbell hypothesis seems to be closer to the truth.

As for the particular figures in my 20-10-70 formula, they do not have any solid basis; what is relatively solid is only the conclusion that the dumbbell is unbalanced, with the pro-VC end heavier. But I can tell you why I estimate 20% pro-VC rather than, say, 15% or 25%. It starts with the finding of the CBS survey people that they could do their interviewing in localities representing about 80% of the South Vietnamese population. That leaves about 20% in localities so much under VC control that interviewing could not be attempted even in the daytime, when the hamlets were relatively "secure." Another line of evidence comes from the official American estimates that came out last November. You may remember that at that time Bunker and Bundy and others publicized the estimate that two-thirds of the population were living in localities under a "reasonable" degree of government control, one sixth in disputed areas and one-sixth under VC control. A sixth is not much less than 20%, and if you regard our own official estimate as probably somewhat on the optimistic side—which seemed likely at the time and seems much more likely now, after the Tet offensive—you are brought back to something like 20%.

Of course not all the people in VC-controlled hamlets are strongly in favor of the VC. We have good reason, on the basis of interviews, to think that a good many of them are now disillusioned. But the skill of the VC cadres in both organization and propaganda, in the places where their methods of organization and of propaganda have had a chance to be fully effective, are generally regarded as so very great that I think it would be fair to say that probably a half to three quarters of the population in these hamlets are strongly on their side. This would constitute 10 or 15 of the 20% we have estimated to be living in such hamlets. If we then estimate that as many as 5 or 10% of the total population are pro-VC although they do not live in hamlets now under VC control—a figure that seems conservative in the light of all the evidence we have just reviewed—it brings the estimate again back up to 20%. This is not "science", but as an educated guess, taking into account all the various kinds of evidence available to us, it seems respectable enough.

What about the other estimate that not more than 10% of the population are equally dedicated, equally strongly motivated on the anti-VC side? Here too the evidence is non-quantitative, but there seems to be just about universal agreement that the Vietnamese on the government side are mainly motivated by personal self-interest rather than ideological conviction, that the government side is riddled with corruption and factionalism, and that most of the government troops are perfunctory in their attitude toward the war. To estimate as many as 10% with a degree of conviction comparable to that of the Vietcong seems quite liberal. It may be a good deal less.

We are left, then, with strong evidence favoring the unbalanced dumbbell hypothesis.

If this hypothesis is at all close to the truth, it has some possible implications which ought to be looked at. Two of them I have already mentioned. One is that we have little right to talk about "aggression" on the part of the North Vietnamese because of their intervention on the side of the pro-VC 20%, when we ourselves have been intervening on behalf of a much smaller minority—10% or so. This has a bearing on what we should regard as an "honorable" peace. To help 10% to dominate 20% is not necessarily any more honorable than it is democratic. The other implication already mentioned is that we are likely to continue to have great difficulty in winning the war. If the balance were equal our intervention surely could tip the balance toward the anti-Communist side, but if the other side has a large margin of superiority in number of dedicated men, which now seems to be the case, winning the war may be literally impossible.

There is also a third possible implication, much broader in scope, that calls for some consideration: should not this kind of evidence be given a good deal of weight when we are tempted to intervene somewhere else? There are perhaps sixty other countries in which we might conceivably be tempted to intervene, as we have already been, not only in Vietnam but also in Laos, Cuba, the Dominican Republic, Lebanon, Guatemala, Iran and elsewhere. In Vietnam, the evidence suggests we became involved in a mess partly because we did not bother to look hard at the evidence on whether the dumbbell of political attitudes was balanced or unbalanced against our side. Perhaps out of the whole Vietnam mess we can salvage one lesson that will contribute to peace in other situations—the proposition that *unless* we have evidence suggesting that the majority of the politically involved people in a given country are on the anti-Communist side and wanting our intervention in order to prevent a takeover by a Communist minority, we had better not intervene. Ignorance on this point is not a good enough basis for intervention. We should have at least a fair amount of evidence, and it seems to me the evidence should really point toward a majority being on the anti-Communist side before we undertake the costs and the very great risks that intervention involves.

CHAPTER 5. A CRITIQUE OF POOL'S: "FURTHER THOUGHTS ON RURAL PACIFICATION AND INSURGENCY"

By David C. Schwartz*

The author, in his critique of Pool and political science analysts in general, urges development of more adequate theories of revolution which can be both tested and made operational in terms of manipulatable policy variables. Ed.

To attain pacification in Vietnam would: (1) require a predictive theory of the revolutionary violence which is to be pacified; and (2) consist of a manipulation, through policy programs, of the variables in that theory. My critique of Pool's paper will follow this theory and theory-to-policy dichotomy. On the theoretical or explanatory side, I will: 1) show how Pool's assertions do fit with certain conventional wisdoms regarding revolutionary behavior; 2) evaluate his assertions in their own terms and 3) discuss some newer conceptualizations, theory and research on revolutionary behavior which may shed light on the validity and utility of Pool's formulations. On the policy side, I will: 1) evaluate Pool's suggestions in their own terms and 2) indicate how the newer thinking on revolution might be brought to bear on policy-derivation.

*The author is Assistant Professor of Political Science and is associated with the Foreign Policy Research Institute, University of Pennsylvania.

ON THEORY

Initially, Pool's identification of criminal elements in the Vietcong, his attribution of social striving motives to Vietcong administrative cadres and his recognition of the linkage between traditional village violence and contemporary revolutionary violence—all fit well into our conventional understanding of revolutionary behavior. All revolutionary movements recruit from among previously criminal and/or other deviant groupings; indeed, at some stages and/or places, most such movements disproportionately recruit from among such elements. That rebellious and other deviant behaviors tend to be exhibited when legitimate means of upward mobility are inaccessible is not unique to the Vietcong administrative cadres; it is rather a ubiquitous fact of social life— much discussed by Durkheim, Merton and the neo-Mertonian sociologists. So, too, with the ever-present link between pre-extant social structure and political violence. We have in Pool's paper, then, a nice application sketch of some generalizations about revolutionary behavior.

When we seek something more specific, some weighting of factors or some distinctions among competing theories, however, we are somewhat less satisfied. Whatever motivation for revolutionary behavior you happen to prefer—alienation, frustration, threat, organizational loyalty, ideological commitment—you can find it in abundance in Vietnam and listed, or at least implicitly alluded to, in Pool's paper.

Pool sees the peasant's support for the Vietcong as basically fear-motivated. Protect him more cheaply than the Vietcong protects him against Saigon and his loyalty can be won. If the motivation for supporting revolutionary movements were simple fear-motives, we should expect a rapid extinction of this response tendency when fear was reduced. Is this really our experience or do we rather find the impact of, say, counter-attitudinal dissonance whereby peasants come to support the Vietcong in order to have a consistent attitude-behavior set, after having been forced to pay taxes, etc. to the Vietcong?

Why do peasants actually join the Vietcong? Surely it begs the question to say that they let themselves be drafted by the Army of their choice! Why do they choose the Vietcong? If guerrilla life were really more desirable than farming in the tropical sun, why does it appeal only to some peasants? Again, Pool's assertions that Vietcong participation satisfies one's violent impulses do not discriminate for so would joining the Army of the Republic of Vietnam.

Some newer thinking on revolution sees revolutionary behavior as a process whereby initial alienation (withdrawal of attention, affection and legitimacy) from the government becomes radicalized and a predisposition to revolutionary support becomes activated through revolutionary symbology, ideology and propaganda-indoctrination.

Alienation creates perception blockages and distortions which government messages must "penetrate." Alienation, radicalization, and revolutionary support must be reversed if pacification is to take place. We are beginning to have effective theorizing on these phenomena and so, we can begin to have theoretically guided policy-derivation.

ON POLICY

Pool's policy recommendations do fit with some of his theoretical assumptions. Effective organizational infra-structure is required to develop a competing social movement by which the government of South Vietnam might attain legitimacy. But what of the motivational problems which Pool himself raises? Decentralized organization will not be used if men are "tuned out, turned off" from each other by being alienated from each other. Without effective national symbology, decentralization becomes just another gap between the center and the village.

We need, then, not merely better and more comprehensive theory but some explicit analytic techniques for turning that theory into action. The intuitive "touch," "feel," etc. of the policy-maker may be indispensable but it can certainly be aided by theory-to-policy routines. What variables in our theories are manipulatable, by what actions, over what time frames, with what costs, to achieve what utilities? These are the tough but omni-relevant questions. Until we ask them, we shall not answer them. Until we answer them, we shall not develop effective social policies to attain social peace—whether in Vietnam or at home.

PART II

ATTITUDES OF THE UNITED STATES PUBLIC: SIGNIFICANCE FOR U.S. STRATEGIES AND ALTERNATIVES

CHAPTER 6. AMERICAN PUBLIC OPINION ABOUT VIETNAM

By John P. Robinson and Solomon G. Jacobson*

Recognizing the major impact of American public opinion on U.S. policy in the Vietnam conflict, the authors summarize the results of surveys which have been conducted. They observe among other interesting findings that public attitudes toward the war are complex and amorphous and, in fact, not strictly "rational." The authors go on to stress the still greater importance of studies which would investigate why current attitudes are what they are. Ed.

In this review of public opinion about the war in Vietnam, we conclude that more probing into the psychological supports for war is vitally important. The surveys, which we summarize in this paper, do provide an understanding of the structure and distribution of public opinion on the war in Vietnam. However, the closed-ended questions asked in the typical surveys supply only the most indirect information on *why* people feel the way they do about the war. We could not locate any surveys utilizing a series of open-ended questions—invaluable for understanding into the structure of attitudes. The answer to "why" is necessary in order to both understand public attitudes towards war and the dynamics of possible changes in public opinion.

We first review what is probably the most comprehensive of these survey studies and the conclusions it reached. We then proceed to ex-

*The authors are associated, respectively, with the Survey Research Center, University of Michigan, and the Center for Research on Conflict Resolution, University of Michigan.

amine some general trend data on Vietnam attitudes from other survey organizations. Next, we pay special attention to the important college-educated segment of the population. We conclude with some specula-tions about the psychological reasons for public attitudes about the war.

I. THE VERBA ET AL. STUDY

The most authoritative study on public attitudes toward the Vietnam war was conducted by Sidney Verba and associates,[1] mainly at Stanford University. Field work and interviewing was done by the National Opinion Research Center at the University of Chicago in the early spring of 1966. A national probability sample of about 1500 adults, a typical size for surveys done by academic institutions, took part in the survey.

The most interesting conclusion of this intensive survey, for our pur-poses, was the complex and amorphous nature of public attitudes about the war. A person might endorse a belligerent position on one aspect of the war, while on the next aspect, a very neutral or pacifistic position.[2] In other words the correlations between the items were not high enough to clearly separate the public into the two camps of hawks and doves. That public attitudes fail to follow what we in academia might consider "rational" criteria in forming opinions about political issues merely reaf-firms previous research perspectives about public attitudes.[3]

Another finding of interest from the Verba et al. study was the lack of attitudinal differences between social status categories. As expected,

[1]S. Verba et al., "Public Opinion and the War in Vietnam", *American Political Science Review,* June 1967, pp. 317-333. This study is often referred to as the "Stanford Poll".

[2]The correlation between an escalation scale and a deescalation scale (each composed of eight separate questions) was $-.37$, far below what one would expect for scales presumably measuring different ends of the same continuum. The find-ing of contradictory attitudes was also noted in detailed interviews done by poll-ster Sam Lubell, whose in-depth studies are unfortunately not conducted on repre-sentative samples.

[3]Reasons that American voters have given for voting for certain political candi-dates provide abundant evidence for "irrational" attitudes in the public. Thus people have told interviewers from the Survey Research Center that they voted for Eisenhower because he was the first American president who went to church, or that they didn't like Nixon because of his eyes (especially his left one) or because he was a foreigner. For several further examples see Converse, P., "The Ideological Character of Mass Participation in American Business" in Govert Van den Bosch (ed.), *Political Issues and Business in 1964,* Ann Arbor, Michi-gan: Foundation for Research on Human Behavior, 1964, pp. 11-19. In the 1968 election a large proportion of Wallace supporters said they would have voted Democratic if McCarthy or Robert Kennedy had been the Democratic candidate.

level of information increased with more educational background, but respondents' attitudes toward the war differed little according to educational level. This finding refutes the common assumption that the college population is the vocal anti-war group in the country. (We will have more to say about this later.) Indeed, the Verba et al. study found those most informed (and educated) were slightly more likely to support escalation and slightly more consistent than those who had less knowledge about the war.[4] In short, the Verba study showed that the structure of attitudes on the Vietnam war was quite similar throughout all strata of society (and was paralleled in Congress as well) and few of the traditional background factors could explain such diversity as did exist. The complexity of the war had its parallel in a complex public opinion.

A nationwide Harris survey conducted for *Newsweek,* on the other hand, characterized certain types of respondents as holding positions on the war as shown in Table 1. Many of these relationships were noted by Verba et al., but these authors did not consider them as well-defined as Table 1 would suggest.

The strongest background variable associated with differences in war attitudes discovered by Verba et al. (a difference also noted by Harris in Table 1) was race. The black respondents were significantly more opposed to escalation and were more willing to support deescalation than whites. Among possible explanations for the dovish tendency among blacks, the most obvious one—a feeling of disaffection from white society and its wars—is indirectly supported by findings from studies of black residents in areas where civil disorders took place. In a survey administered in Detroit[5] and later in Newark[6] after the riots of 1967, respondents were asked "If the United States got into a big World War

---

[4]Furthermore that small subset of persons in the Verba et al. sample who volunteered their opinions through letters—the "articulate public"—was virtually no different in their attitudes from the rest of the general public. In addition the authors found the "letter writers are not more likely to take extreme positions". At the same time as the less affluent were more likely to oppose the war, paradoxically, they were completely out of sentiment with civil demonstrations against the war. A Harris survey (done before the Harris poll reported below) found 81% of the most affluent and educated backing the right to demonstrate vs. only 40% of the nonaffluent. This result is consistent with earlier survey results reported in Samuel Stouffer's classic *Communism, Conformity and Civil Liberties* (Garden City, New York: Doubleday 1955).

[5]Meyer, P., "A Survey of Attitudes of Detroit Negroes after the Riot of 1967," Detroit: *The Detroit Free Press,* 1967. (Also cited in the *Report of the National Advisory Commission on Civil Disorders.*)

[6]*Report of the National Advisory Commission on Civil Disorders,* New York: Bantam Books, 1968, p. 178.

TABLE 1. Differences in Background Characteristics of Respondents with Various Orientations Toward the Vietnam War

Category	Agrees with:	Description	Percentage in June, 1967
Extreme Hawk	All out military effort	Lives in West Suburban resident Voted for Barry Goldwater	18%
Moderate Hawk	Administration's policy, but wants escalation to force negotiations	Lives in South People over 50 Income under $5000	40%
Moderate Dove	Administration's policy, but wants reduction in escalation to encourage negotiations	Lives in East People under 35 Jews	36%
Extreme Doves	Unconditional halt to bombing and withdrawal of American troops from South Vietnam	Negroes The poor Women City residents	6%

Source: Louis Harris as reported in *Newsweek,* July 10, 1967.

today, would you personally feel this country was worth fighting for?" The question did not mention Vietnam nor did it specify who we might be fighting, but it is worth noting that 40% of those involved in rioting in Detroit and over 50% of those in Newark felt that the country was *not* worth fighting for.[7]

Verba et al. dismissed the notion that white-black differences, which parallel social status differences, were in fact attributable to social class. Their main argument was the finding that war attitudes and race were

---

[7] Comments such as, "I am not a true citizen, so why should I?" and "My husband came back from Vietnam and nothing has changed!" illustrate some of the reasoning behind these responses. Among a sample of respondents who did not participate in the rioting, 15% in Detroit and 30% in Newark also felt the country was not worth fighting for in the event of war. These attitudes were in sharp contrast with the responses of "counter-rioters"—those who attempted to persuade rioters to "cool it." This group, which the Kerner Commission *Report* portrayed as active supporters of existing social institutions, were far less willing to be non-supportive and only 3% of these citizens with a stake in their community would fail to fight for their country in the event of war. To anticipate differences discussed later, (see p. M51) only 18% of a group of University of Michigan students, 3% of teachers enrolled in a University of Michigan extension service course in Public Opinion, and 1% of a group of students at Adrian College said that the country was not worth fighting for.

even more strongly related when controls were made for level of information.

The other main correlate of war attitudes—sex—was not as strongly associated as race with attitudes. The finding that women are less pro-war (also noted in Table 1) is consistent with expectations related to women's role in society and with findings from a great body of survey data which reveal sex differences in aggressive or belligerent attitudes toward political issues.

Verba and certain of his associates have completed two further surveys since the one reported here, but neither is close to the scope of this initial study. One of these was conducted in February 1967, the other in February 1968.[8] Only the sketchiest of information is currently available from the two surveys. The data suggest a hardening of opinion against a coalition government and greater desire for military escalation between 1966 and 1967. The 1968 survey shows little further hardening of opinion but does indicate surprisingly (in view of increased civil disturbances) that Americans continue to consider Vietnam, far and away, the most serious problem facing the U.S.[9] As before, blacks and women showed up most opposed to war policies but differences by social status and age also seem more visible, with those of higher status and middle age most in favor of war policies.

While these latter surveys promise some time perspective on the study of war attitudes, there are better sources for trend data. Unfortunately, these sources provide very little understanding of *why* attitudes have changed over time.

II. TRENDS IN SUPPORT FOR THE WAR

The most complete set of trend data is available from the Gallup Poll. Two questions have been asked frequently enough to chart how public reaction has varied over time. These questions are:

---

[8]This latter survey is one of five that Verba, along with Richard Brody and Jerome Laulicht, plan to carry out during this election year repeating the same questions on candidates and parties vis-a-vis Vietnam. The major intent of these studies is to clearly indicate how public opinion on foreign policy becomes related to voting behavior.

[9]In early May, 1968, after the murder of Rev. Martin Luther King, and the start of negotiations, Gallup found that 42% of the respondents cited Vietnam as "the most important problem facing the nation today", while 25% found race relations, and 15% cited crime and lawlessness as the major problem. (*New York Times,* May 26, 1968). In terms of other priorities, there has been a shift which has seen concern about "cost-of-living" reduced and concern for race relations increased since 1966.

1) Do you approve or disapprove of the way President Johnson is handling the situation in Vietnam?
2) In view of the developments since we entered the fighting in Vietnam, do you think the U.S. made a mistake sending troops to fight in Vietnam?

Public response to these two questions is graphed in Figure 1 and shows a definite (although irregular) decrease in percentages approving of Johnson's policy over the last three years, while the percentage feeling the U.S. made a mistake in getting involved in Vietnam has doubled. Gallup's figure on approval of Johnson's job as President declines at much the same tempo as his ratings on Vietnam. It also appears, as Verba et al. noted, that approval ratings go up as long as Johnson does something, whether it be more militaristic or more pacifistic.

Gallup, however, has paid little subsequent attention to the important question of why people disapprove of Johnson policies. Only twice, when the "approve-disapprove" question was asked, did Gallup follow with an open-ended question asking why people said they disapproved. The reasons given had only a slightly more dovish than hawkish ring to them, so that disapproval of Johnson's policy is just about as likely to be based on feelings that his policy was "too soft" as "too hard".[10] Undoubtedly, the same sort of split opinion underlies positive response to the question asking whether it was a mistake getting involved in the war.

Two other survey questions asked by Gallup about Vietnam merit attention. In one 1967 survey, Gallup asked his respondents if they had a clear idea of why the U.S. was fighting in Vietnam. Only about half of the population said that they had.[11] The majority of those gave a general "stopping Communism" response, with little apparent thought to the problems peculiar to Vietnam itself. Only a quarter of those replying referred to the conflict specifically in terms of problems in Vietnam.

---

[10]Brody reports the following interesting finding in relation to the standard Gallup question about approval or disapproval of President Johnson's handling of Vietnam. In the 1966 Verba et al. study, those who disapproved of Johnson's policies favored deescalation policies over escalation policies. In 1967, the disapprovers (now 50% more numerous than in 1966) *favored* our bombing policy, although still tending to be opposed to more troops and still more in favor of a coalition government than approvers. In at least one sense, then, the mounting disapproval of Johnson's policies appeared not motivated by pacifistic motives. See R. Brody "Vietnam and the 1968 Election: A Preview", *Trans-action* (in press for September 1968).

[11]*Gallup Opinion Index,* Princeton, New Jersey: Gallup International, Inc., Report 25, July 1967. At the height of World War II, 83% had a clear idea of what we were fighting for.

FIGURE 1. Trends on Gallup Questions Regarding Vietnam

Later in 1967, Gallup conducted an 11 nation comparison of a single policy question about Vietnam:[12]

Just from what you have heard or read, which of the statements (LISTED ON CARD) comes closest to the way you, yourself, feel about the war in Vietnam?

A. The U.S. should begin to withdraw its troops
B. The U.S. should carry on its present level of fighting
C. The U.S. should increase the strength of its attacks against North Vietnam.

The responses are compared in Table 2 and show the Scandinavian people by far the most opposed to the war. The greatest support for increasing the war, not surprisingly, comes from U.S. citizens, although Australians were less in favor of a withdrawal of troops than were Americans.

TABLE 2. Comparison of the Popularity of Vietnam Policy Alternatives Across 11 Countries

	Begin to Withdraw	Carry on Present Level	Increase Attacks	No Opinion	
Finland	81	4	5	10	= 100%
Sweden	79	10	4	7	= 100%
Brazil	76	5	5	14	= 100%
France	72	8	5	15	= 100%
India	66	4	8	22	= 100%
Uruguay	62	10	5	23	= 100%
West Germany	58	11	14	17	= 100%
Argentina	57	6	6	31	= 100%
England	45	15	15	25	= 100%
Canada	41	16	23	20	= 100%
Australia	29	18	37	16	= 100%
United States	31	10	53	6	= 100%

We have also examined some limited data on Vietnam attitudes collected by the Survey Research Center at the University of Michigan. Unfortunately, we have only three[13] national readings of a single SRC

[12] *Gallup Opinion Index,* Princeton, New Jersey: Gallup International, Inc., Report 29, November 1967.
[13] The question in 1964 and 1966 was asked as part of the election studies. In 1967, the question was part of a study of economic behavior. Vietnam has been

question dealing with Vietnam policy. This question is very similar to that charted in Table 2:

Which of the following do you think we should do now in Vietnam?
1. Pull out of Vietnam entirely
2. Keep our soldiers in Vietnam but try to end the fighting
3. Take a stronger stand even if it means invading North Vietnam.

Percentages of the population endorsing each of these alternatives between 1964 and 1967 are listed in the left hand columns in Table 3. In both the Gallup and the SRC question, the most hawkish stand remains the most popular.[14] In 1966 nearly four times as many people endorsed the "stronger stand" as the "pull out" proposition in the SRC poll. While we expected increased support for the pull out proposition in 1967 as a result of reported increased elite opposition to the war, such a shift was hardly noticeable in the general public.[15]

An interesting policy dilemma arises if we must draw conclusions from survey data—an often dangerous occupation. We see the Ameri-

---

found to be a most relevant variable in the regular series of SRC surveys done to predict economic behavior. When asked the open question "What would you say are the most important things that may influence business conditions during the next 12 months?", 60% of respondents in a February 1968 national sample said Vietnam; no other factor was mentioned by more than 25% of the population, including such important economic variables as taxes, balance of payments, the stock market or unemployment. There is little doubt that Vietnam has had a depressive effect on consumers' willingness to buy, be the consumers hawks or doves. Vietnam dampens consumer enthusiasm by increasing uncertainty and worry about the future. There is one further intriguing piece of information from these studies of economic behavior and attitudes. When asked whether Vietnam financially makes for "good times" or "bad times", over twice as many respondents (54% in the last survey of February 1968) say good times as say bad times (26%). In each of the ten surveys in which the question has been asked between 1965 and 1968 the most affluent (those with income over $7500 per year) have been three to four times more likely to choose the good times than the bad times alternative. How much this reflects reality (the more affluent have had proportionately greater income increases in the last few years) and how much this may underlie greater support of the war by the more affluent is a moot point. Data are reported in G. Katona et al., *1967 Survey of Consumer Finances,* Ann Arbor, Michigan: Survey Research Center 1968, and G. Katona and J. Schmiedeskamp, *The Outlook for Consumer Demand,* Ann Arbor, Michigan: Survey Research Center, March 1968. Further studies of the effect of Vietnam on consumer attitudes are currently underway.

[14] With a more extreme dove position in the SRC question than in the Gallup question, it is seen that the middle status quo position becomes the most popular in contrast to its extreme unpopularity among the three alternatives offered by Gallup.

[15] Harris found that 48% of his respondents favored ground invasion of North Vietnam (*Newsweek,* July 10, 1967). Support for invasion decreased only slightly to 44% (*New York Times,* March 26, 1968) after more than a year of opposition to the war by some leading clergy, politicians, business leaders, and military men.

TABLE 3. Distribution of Opinions About Vietnam (and Korea)
Using Survey Research Center Question

	National Samples				University of Michigan Psychology Students		Adrian College Students
	Nov 1964	*Nov 1966*	*Nov 1967*	*Korea (Nov 1952)*	*Sept 1967*	*Jan 1968*	*March 1968*
Pull out	11%	10%	13%	(11%)	47%	41%	7%
Keep soldiers there	30	39	34	(45)	38	50	47
Take stronger stand	39	39	42	(39)	15	9	46
Other	*	2	1	(*)	—	—	—
Don't know	20	10	10	(5)	—	—	—
	100%	100%	100%	(100%)	100%	100%	100%

can public as strongly favoring escalation and victory, yet the official policy is leaning towards a negotiated settlement. There are no polls to date which indicate public reaction to current negotiations, but we would expect the public to be mistrustful and cynical—yet hopeful— about the outcome. The policy dilemma, therefore, revolves about the public's willingness to accept a Korea-type settlement. In Table 3 we find that public opinion on Korea before negotiations was amazingly similar to that on Vietnam before negotiation. One can recall that Americans managed to accept a settlement in Korea without great resentment.[16] We suspect that there are clues in the original Verba et al. survey which indicate that the public is willing to accept a Korea type settlement. In 1966, 88% were willing to negotiate directly with the

---

[16]We would also expect future polls to indicate an increasing acceptance of a Korean type settlement. In a recent "survey" (actually, a series of interviews), done by the National Staff of the *U. S. News and World Report,* there were both unfavorable and favorable comparisons with Korea. According to a Chicago salesman, "The peace overture will be a farce. I just know nothing is going to happen. At the time of Korean peace talks, we were slaughtered." But a Baltimore restaurant manager was more optimistic, "I am very happy about Hanoi's offer to talk, I am hopeful. Even if all we get out of it is a standoff like Korea, it will be better than we have now." This information was given in the article "At Grass Roots: A Nationwide Survey", *U. S. News and World Report,* May 13, 1968, p. 41.

Vietcong—a remarkably strong showing for a nation which views itself as more hawk than dove. The study concluded[17] that, "our data suggested a higher permissiveness for reduction of the war but evidence from other polls since then suggests that the President's support increases no matter what he does—increase the war or talk of negotiations —as long as he does something."[18] Thus the strong support for military escalation (i.e., bombing) in this country may not include increased use of U.S. troops in Vietnam. The President could make a negotiated settlement sound somewhat like a victory. He could claim to have obtained major policy objectives, making further loss of U.S. soldiers unnecessary. While public acceptance of negotiations may be highly conditional, indications are that the public will follow the President's lead and endorse nearly any agreement given his approval. Interestingly enough, after the negotiated settlement in Korea, there was a dramatic drop in the proportion of the population who said that we had made a mistake getting involved in Korea.

III. ATTITUDES OF COLLEGE GRADUATES AND COLLEGE STUDENTS

Those familiar with survey or poll data realize that clear gaps exist in the information structure of large majorities of the population. In 1964, for example, less than half of the population were aware that there were two Chinese governments, one Communist on the Mainland the other non-Communist on Taiwan.[19] This leads one to question the meaningfulness of survey results from mass populations on foreign affairs attitudes. It might even be argued that a high level of education and training is required before a person can adequately understand the complexities and subtleties of foreign policy. For this reason, we devote special attention to the most-educated 10% of our population.

How is it possible for the best-educated segment of the population to be most in favor of the war when its members usually embody the most vocal anti-war sentiment encountered in the public debates? To explain such a paradox, the college population in the United States might be profitably differentiated according to two characteristics: (1) the

---

[17] Verba, 1967, op. cit. p. 333.

[18] The latest Gallup poll we have available shows that 65% approved, 26% disapproved and 10% had no opinion of the President's March 31 "decision to stop bombing North Vietnam" ("How Young People Will Vote", *U. S. News and World Report*, April 29, 1968, pp. 32-33).

[19] See J. Robinson, *Public Information about World Affairs,* Ann Arbor, Michigan: Survey Research Center, 1967.

"quality" of the school which the person attends, and (2) the person's academic field of interest.

(1) Survey analysts are becoming more aware of the differences between individuals from different kinds of institutions of higher learning. Wilensky found that exposure to high brow material in the mass media was far more dependent on the "quality" of the college attended than on college attendance *per se*.[20] In similar fashion, Converse found that while 9% of college graduates from institutions rated A or B by the American Association of University Professors were happy to see Goldwater nominated in 1964, 57% of those who graduated from colleges rated E, F, or G were enthusiastic for Goldwater.[21] In both instances, ideas and perceptions that are fashionable among graduates of the leading "prestige" educational institutions may be completely alien to the bulk of college graduates in this country.

With this orientation, it is less surprising that Armor et al. found 60% of faculty members of large public universities in the Boston area opposed to the war in Vietnam vs. 45% of faculty members at large private universities vs. 33% at small private colleges vs. 17% at Catholic universities.[22] Parallel differences can be found in the right hand columns of Table 3, where close to half of the students in an advanced undergraduate social psychology class at the University of Michigan endorse the withdraw policy on the SRC question as opposed to only 7% of an "opportunity sample" of students at Adrian College, a small school located about 40 miles south of Ann Arbor. Neither the sample at Michigan nor at Adrian comes close to being a definitive representation of students at either school, but the dramatic differences are in line with expectations from the previous discussion. They are also in line with other polls of college students which report more hawkish than dovish sentiment on college campuses. Thus, that vocal minority most opposed to Vietnam—probably the most articulate segment of today's university students—has probably created the misimpression that the majority of college students share their feelings.

(2) In terms of a person's academic field of interest, the differences between departments appear not as pronounced as those that exist between alma maters. Armor et al., for example, find 49% of those in the

---

[20] Wilensky, H. "Mass Society and Mass Culture: Independence or Interdependence", *American Sociological Review*, 1964, *29*, pp. 173-197.
[21] Converse, P., "Social Cleavages in the 1964 Election", paper read at the Annual Meetings of the American Sociological Association in Chicago, August, 1965.
[22] Armor, J. et al., "Professors' Attitudes toward the Vietnam War", *Public Opinion Quarterly*, 1967, *XXXI*, pp. 159-175.

humanities faculty opposed to the war vs. 45% of social scientists and 36% of natural scientists.[23] Somewhat larger, but still moderate, differences were found between faculty members in the humanities, social sciences and natural sciences by Schuman and Laumann in a Vietnam survey at the University of Michigan.[24]

It would not be surprising to find parallel divisions of opinion between students majoring in these fields or between individuals employed in "people-oriented" professions (e.g., social workers, school teachers, clergymen) and those in "object-oriented" professions (e.g., engineering, business, medicine). To our knowledge, no study of Vietnam attitudes has documented the effects of such sources of variance to date. This only illustrates one aspect of the huge research gap that remains about attitudes toward the Vietnam war—namely the reason *why* people hold the attitudes that they do.

IV. PSYCHOLOGICAL ORIENTATION TOWARDS WAR— A RESEARCH GAP

In attempting to explain attitudes regarding the war, we are hampered by lack of in-depth descriptive probes into the public's cognitive orientations toward organized violence. In spite of increasing inquiry and speculation about the psychological basis of war,[25] we have few theories and fewer empirical studies of public support for any war—let alone the war in Vietnam.

In urging more in-depth analysis, we realize that this is a costly, time-consuming, and complex task. It took several years of research by three senior authors, four well-qualified associates, and several graduate students to produce *Opinions and Personality*,[26] an in-depth study of the attitudes of ten Boston males towards Russia. This study takes nearly three hundred pages to describe the opinions of these ten men toward the single object of Russia, an attitude object about which these men cared little. The authors' findings caution against simplistic interpretations of public attitudes. They found little in the way of either

---

[23] Armor et al., *op. cit.*
[24] Schuman, H. and Laumann, E., "Do Most Professors *Support* the War?", *Transaction*, November 1967, pp. 32-35. At Michigan, it was the social scientists who most opposed the war, then humanists, with natural scientists again most in favor of current or stronger war policies.
[25] An excellent summary of this literature appears in Jerome D. Frank, *Sanity and Survival: Psychological Aspects of War and Peace*, New York: Vintage Books, 1968.
[26] M. Brewster Smith, Jerome S. Bruner, Robert W. White, *Opinions and Personality*, New York: John Wiley, 1956.

"unalloyed hostile orientation" toward Russia or in the way of abstract thinking about Russia. Thus individuals arrived at similar policy orientations from vastly different motivational bases. The study concludes that opinions are a complex product of "reality demands, social demands, and inner psychological demands". These three demands are closely interdependent and a change dictated by one factor (reality demands, for example) will not ensure that the person's opinion will change accordingly. The complex of determinants which shape an individual's opinion cannot be easily discovered, nor may they be simply assumed as we are so often forced to do when interpreting public opinion polls.

The Verba et al. study concludes that policy preference in terms of the war in Vietnam may be patterned by the respondent's attitude to the war itself. Instead of drawing clues about their attitudes from social sources, people are tending to think, react, and respond directly to the object itself—the war in Vietnam.[27] If attitudes regarding the war are specific and situational, as Verba and his colleagues suggest, then we need to devote attention to study into the complexities of individual attitudes. Again underscored is the desirability of in-depth and open-ended interviews as a fruitful way of developing working hypotheses on attitudes concerning war.

It seems reasonable to conclude that further surveys using the conventional demographic approach will not add much more to our understanding of the basic structure of opinion regarding the war. We must probe deeper into the process of attitude formation than is possible in the usual one-shot national survey. We now need to know: what justifications people give for the policy stands that they take,[28] what factors

---

[27] Verba, et al., *op. cit.*, p. 331.

[28] We suggest that two justifications dominate grass roots public acceptance of the war:
1. Containment of Communism—in which Communism is seen as an immoral force and essentially evil. Any differences between types and aims of Communist governments are neither relevant nor important. Any action to stop Communism is seen as justified.
2. Meeting our Commitments—which has both internally- and externally-oriented elements. A major internal theme is the feeling that if America gets involved in a conflict, we ought to win, combined with an outlook that our sacrifices of men and money shall not have been in vain. Two externally-directed elements can also be isolated: America's obligation to help those we have promised to help, and the maintenance of our international prestige as a defender of freedom.

To be sure, citizens vary widely in the degree to which they knowingly accept these reasons or consciously advance them as justification for the war. But we would not be surprised to find them emerging as central factors when people are asked to explain their Vietnam policy stands. Our remarks should not be construed as

work to condone the systematic brutality of modern warfare,[29] what information is sought in order to decide on support or opposition to the war,[30] how internal contradictions are compartmentalized or rationalized,[31] and many further questions along this line of inquiry.

A comparison of the conclusions reached in the Verba et al. survey in 1966, a modest "poll" done on one street in Jeffersonville, Indiana by *Parade* magazine, the Harris poll of 1967, and recent reaction to the situation in Vietnam indicates an interesting trend as shown in Table 4.

TABLE 4. Some Survey Conclusions—U.S. Attitudes Towards the War, 1966-1968

Our first finding is that public opinion is relatively orderly. The public expressed concern about the war and was relatively in-

---

evidence that justifications against the war are by nature superior to arguments for the war. Moreover, we would be interested in finding that war justifications are considerably more sophisticated than indicated in this and the following footnote.

[29] In our estimate, Ralph White has done a very comprehensive job in this direction. His monograph constitutes a suitable hypothetical framework to begin research into the possible distortions which occur within an individual's perception of the world. White identifies seven misperceptions which may support aggression. These misperceptions are:

1. The diabolical enemy-image—'*they* are evil'
2. The moral self-image—'*we* are good'
3. The virile self-image—'we are also strong'
4. Military overconfidence
5. Absence of empathy
6. Selective inattention
7. Conflicting territorial self-images

Ralph K. White, "Misperception and the Vietnam War," *The Journal of Social Issues*, July 1966, 22, entire issue.

[30] In gaming simulations, we are beginning to discover what type of information is sought by players for decision-making in a conflict situation. In a review of these experiments, it was found that those individuals who were inclined to think in abstractions tended to search for information along all categories of a problem. Those individuals who were more concrete tended to explore one category in great depth and detail. Under conditions of stress, decision making followed a normal curve: (1) at low levels of stress and information—decisions are relatively simplistic; (2) at "optimal" levels—(a) abstract persons make more complex decisions with reference to past decisions, (b) concrete persons make relatively simple decisions in spite of increased information, and (3) at "super-optimal" levels of stress and under conditions of information overload—all players tend to make simple decisions, with concrete individuals actually being more effective at filtering out bits of information which the abstract individual tries (unsuccessfully) to relate to his complex decision making pattern. These findings relate to decision making in conflict situations, but experiments could be adopted to discover the information patterns behind both "grass roots" and "elite" decision making in terms of foreign policy. See Schroder, H. M., Driver, M. J. and Streufert, S., *Human Information Processing*, New York: Holt, Reinhart and Winston, 1967.

[31] Some processes relevant in this context are presented in D. Katz and E. Stotland "A Preliminary Statement of a Theory of Attitudes" in S. Koch (ed.) *Psychology: A Study of a Science*, vol. 3, New York: McGraw-Hill, 1959.

formed about it. The correlational analysis among scales shows patterns of consistency among the population; and many of the inconsistencies can be interpreted as more apparent than real. An overwhelming majority (88%) expressed willingness to negotiate with the Viet Cong and a similar majority (81%) would oppose withdrawal of our troops "tomorrow." One can argue that many respondents are taking positions at the opposite ends of the spectrum at the same time; but this is not necessarily the case since the two policies are not in conflict. Negotiations do not necessarily imply precipitate withdrawal.

But though the preferences we found among the population were patterned, they were patterned in a more complex way than would be suggested by the summaries of public attitudes found in the standard surveys based upon one, two or three questions. Despite the consistency found, few respondents could be called "hawks" or "doves"; rather, they took more moderate positions somewhere nearer the center of the spectrum.

> Sidney Verba et al., *op. cit.*
> March, 1966

But, bewildered by the spate of information and debate that seems to add up in no clear way, many Chestnut Streeters have simply "turned off" the war. They are troubled but detached from it—they admit it sheepishly—despite the fact that fellow Americans are fighting and dying in Vietnam. The matters of policy that rouse intellectuals and cause debate on Capitol Hill—escalation, the bombing of Hanoi, who should sit at the peace table— are greeted with a shrug. Like many Americans, they wish they could see the matter more clearly, and feel more patriotic about it, but they can't. They wish there was a simple way out.

> J. Rogers "How the Vietnam War
> Affects Chestnut Street, U.S.A."
> *Parade,* February 19, 1967

In essence, the *Newsweek* survey pictures a nation determined to persevere in what it believes is a grimly distasteful but altogether necessary struggle for national security. Confronted by a conflict without glory and seemingly without end, Americans seek not an old-fashioned kind of total victory, but a new kind of compromise peace.

> Louis Harris survey in *Newsweek*
> July 10, 1967, p. 22

Cautious optimism is the attitude of most Americans on the possibilities of negotiations leading to ending the war in Vietnam. Most applaud President Johnson's moves, but are convinced there is no easy road to a settlement.

National Staff of *U.S. News and World Report,* May 13, 1968, p. 41

The nation has few illusions about the technical nature (if not the justifications) of the war, but accepts it as a necessary evil which may be with us for a long time. As a nation, we have shown ourselves to be willing to follow the lead of three Presidents in pursuing our Vietnam policy and to react favorably to any positive action. The present dissatisfaction with the war, its overwhelming unpopularity, should not be interpreted as a rejection of war in general or of our foreign policy.

If current negotiations are successful, it will be interesting to see how the public rationalizes the heavy price our country has paid for what may be an undistinguished (if not unfavorable) settlement. Even more interesting will be its effect on the public's willingness or reluctance to support similar "limited" military actions which will undoubtedly face our country again in the near future.

In the absence of in-depth studies, we would speculate that little reaction to the war is based on humanitarian or moral considerations.[32] Americans are not now rejecting "war," they merely wish to see this current conflict ended. To achieve this goal, most Americans would pursue a more militant policy and ignore resultant atrocities. The psychological supports for war in this nation run far too deeply to allow anything other than a major defeat or a major victory to alter attitudes. If the public opinion polls show anything, they indicate that this nation tolerates war and war-like conditions with extended patience and unquestioning complacency, but not for indefinite periods with little visible progress.

---

[32] While 62% of respondents to the Harris poll in 1967 replied that it was wrong to kill innocent civilians, 72% supported continued bombing of North Vietnam. While 41% believed wars are morally wrong and 34% felt it was especially wrong to intervene in civil wars, 48% actually favored ground invasion of North Vietnam. Harris *Newsweek* survey, op. cit.

CHAPTER 7. AMERICAN TACTICS AND AMERICAN GOALS IN VIETNAM AS PERCEIVED BY SOCIAL SCIENTISTS

By Philip Brickman, Phillip Shaver and Peter Archibald*

Since most of the American public is not well-informed on foreign relations, authors find it meaningful to confine their attention to the attitudes of a sample that could be presumed to be concerned and informed. They survey the members of the Society for the Psychological Study of Social Issues, a group with a liberal bias. They are able to penetrate more deeply into attitudes than the previous paper and most surveys. One of their interesting findings is that while all respondents agree that immediate withdrawal of the U.S. is very likely to lead to a reunited Communist Vietnam, respondents preferring immediate withdrawal see a holding strategy and present policy as less likely to bring about an anti-Communist South Vietnam than do other subgroups while present policy advocates see this policy as much more likely to bring about an anti-Communist South Vietnam. Ed.

INTRODUCTION

The dilemma the United States has faced in Vietnam has been as

*The first author is at Northwestern University, while the others are associated with the University of Michigan. Their research was partially supported by a grant from the Society for the Psychological Study of Social Issues. The authors are grateful to Ralph White, Herbert Kelman, Reiner von Konigslow and Sharon Rosen for help in designing the questionnaire, and to Terry Gleason and Keith Smith for suggestions concerning the data analysis.

painful and as difficult to resolve as any in recent times, and differences of opinion within this country over the Vietnam conflict have been serious and intense. This study explores the understanding of this dilemma and the nature of differences of opinion about it in a sample that could be presumed to be both concerned and informed.

First of all, what do people see as the nature of the choice available to the U.S. in Vietnam? Sometimes the press and the Administration have implied that, apart from the Administration's policy, there are only the equally reprehensible alternatives of abandoning the South Vietnamese or waging unlimited war. The popular debate has seemed to be seriously weakened by the fact that other alternatives, despite the efforts of people like General Gavin, were not very well differentiated or understood. We were interested in finding out what people would see as meaningfully different strategies in Vietnam, and further, in just what ways these alternatives would be differentiated. To do this, we designed a survey that would allow us to scale the psychological distance between alternatives. Knowing how far apart different Vietnam strategies were in some psychological space would tell us something about how psychologically far apart people were who favored different strategies. In addition to asking for preferences among possible strategies the U.S. might adopt, we asked respondents what they thought would happen in Vietnam—what a likely outcome would be—if the U.S. adopted each of the strategies; and we also asked them what the impact of adopting these strategies would be on American goals in political spheres other than Vietnam.

Secondly, what is the nature of the difference between people who advocate different strategies in Vietnam? If there is a dimension (such as "hawk-dove") along which strategy choices can be placed, do people who disagree still see this dimension in the same way, or do they actually use different dimensions in ordering their choices? Do they share a frame of reference in making their choices, or do they employ different ones? If their understanding of the alternatives *is* similar, what about their perceptions of what is at stake? Has the Vietnam war exposed a genuine value conflict among Americans, such that those who favor varying strategies actually want to implement different goals? Or is there still some common conception of what American goals are, of what a desirable outcome would be, such that the conflict is of the more benign sort in which people disagree only about the best means to reach essentially shared ends?

In recent years social psychologists have demonstrated that the tendency to achieve and maintain "cognitive consistency" is an important mechanism for organizing beliefs and attitudes, and a significant factor in predicting attitude changes.[1] We are exploring the various ways in which people with different positions achieve consistency between their important values and their beliefs and attitudes about the war in Vietnam. In future work we hope to use this case study to shed light on some of the unresolved issues in the study of cognitive structures. Here, however, we shall focus mainly on the nature of differences in opinion regarding the war and on some of their implications.

THE SAMPLE

The present survey had the official purpose of conveying the views of the membership of the Society for the Psychological Study of Social Issues (SPSSI) on the Vietnam war to its Executive Committee. The questionnaire itself was accompanied by a covering letter from members of a special SPSSI committee appointed to coordinate the project. In return for doing the polling, we gained access to a well-educated, concerned sample.

The questionnaire was mailed in late November, 1967, and most returns were received in early December. The date of the survey should be kept in mind in examining the results, since Johnson's resignation and the opening of the Paris talks have changed the situation considerably. In particular, the definition of "present policy" in this survey ("increasing military pressure while offering to negotiate") may no longer be applicable.

Of 2326 questionnaires sent out, a total of 835 (about 35%) were returned. More than 90% of our respondents favored strategies that were milder than the Administration's policy, i.e., there was a strong skewness of the returns toward non-militant positions. The strategy options considered in the survey, and the percentage of the sample that favored each of them above all others, are presented in Table 1.

In the entire sample, there were only four people favoring further escalation beyond present policy (three of these advocated "immediate all-out escalation, using everything needed to win, including nuclear

---

[1] L. Festinger, *A Theory of Cognitive Dissonance,* Evanston, Illinois: Row, Peterson, 1957: M. J. Rosenberg, C. I. Hovland, W. J. McGuire, R. P. Abelson, and J. W. Brehm, *Attitude Organization and Change: An Analysis of Consistency Among Attitude Components,* New Haven: Yale University Press, 1960; M. Rokeach, "A Theory of Organization and Change within Value—Attitude Systems," *Journal of Social Issues,* Vol. 24 (1968), pp. 13-33.

TABLE 1. Strategy Choices and the Distribution of Opinion

Strategy Choice	Percentage Favoring
1. Immediate withdrawal	21.0
2. Phased withdrawal while seeking international guarantees for safety of all parties	40.1
3. General de-escalation while seeking negotiations with Hanoi and the Vietcong	16.0
4. Limitation of military efforts to securing areas now held while offering to negotiate	11.3
5. Present policy of increasing military pressure while offering to negotiate	7.7
6. General escalation of the war in both South and North	0.1
7. Immediate all-out escalation using anything needed to win, including nuclear bombs	0.4
Other or multiple choice	3.5
	100.1

Number of respondents = 835

bombs"). Thus, for purposes of analysis, we have no extreme militants in our sample. We do, however, have a substantial number of people (61) who favored the present policy of increasing military pressure while offering to negotiate. Furthermore, there was considerable diversity of opinion about which of the various strategies involving de-escalation would be best.

Clearly, SPSSI as a group was not representative of the American people in December, 1967, for the Gallup polls reported a majority of the people at this time favoring a policy at least as militant as the Administration's.[2] It might be questioned whether our returns are even representative of SPSSI opinion, since the rate of return (35%) obviously involved considerable self-selection. The questionnaire was long (ten pages) and complex, probably requiring at least a half-hour for a reasonably careful respondent. It happens, fortunately, that we were in a position to assess the representativeness of the returns, since a postcard follow-up was carried out in March, 1968. Over 70% of the members returned the postcard, on which they indicated not only their strategy choice, but also whether or not they had returned the earlier, de-

[2]J. P. Robinson and S. Jacobson, "American Public Opinion about Vietnam," Chapter 7, this book.

tailed questionnaire. The overall distributions of opinion among initial respondents and non-respondents were very similar.

SCALING VIETNAM STRATEGIES ALONG A "HAWK-DOVE" DIMENSION

We wanted to know whether all of the various policy proposals which have been advanced were perceived by all respondents as falling along a single dimension. Perhaps one of our options would be seen as different in kind from all others, or the preference structures of one group of respondents might be different in kind from all others. If a single dimension were implicitly used by all respondents, regardless of their specific policy preferences, then their policy orderings should be transitive and consistent with such a dimension.

On the first page of the questionnaire respondents were asked to compare each of the seven strategies with each other using the method of triads. If there is a dimension strongly ordering the alternatives, people should be able to rank order the alternatives without intransitivities; i.e., they should be consistent, in the sense that if a person prefers A to B and B to C, he will also prefer A to C. The results are presented in Table 2, with each column representing a different group of respondents —the group whose most preferred strategy is indicated by the number at the head of the column. As can be seen from the first row of Table 2, one group—those who favored "present policy"—were more likely to have intransitive preference structures. This suggests that people preferring "present policy" may be less likely than others to make clear, consistent distinctions among a set of alternatives to that policy.

TABLE 2. Scalability of Respondents with Different Strategy Choices

	Strategy Choice				
Scale Type	1	2	3	4	5
Transitive	86.8%	90.8	89.6	91.4	68.9
Fit qualitative J-scale	79.2	80.3	74.4	84.4	49.3
Fit quantitative J-scale	79.2	73.0	36.8	72.8	36.1

Each number in this table represents the percentage of respondents in that column who meet the condition at the left of that row.

Strategies might have been ordered, say, by the extent to which they promised a quick end to the war. However, we anticipated that some version of the popular "hawk-dove" dimension would be the dominant one for our sample. If this were true, and if our perceptions of the degree of escalation implied by each item were accurate, then we should observe rank orderings such as 1234567 or 4321567, but never 1235674 (number 4 is out of order) or 4732156 (number 7 is out of order). For the entire sample, 75% expressed preferences that were transitive and compatible with this dominant rank ordering. (See the second row of Table 2.) In this technique, the "unfolding" of preference orders developed by Coombs,[3] is employed. This is called a qualitative J-scale.

Finally, one can go further and consider not only the ordering of preferences but also the distances between various alternatives. Using the technique of unfolding, one gains information about distances between alternatives by observing which rank orderings do not appear. For example, if the true dimension is such that alternative 1 is widely separated from 2, 3 and 4, while these three are all close together (i.e., 1---234), then we should not find people whose preferences are *321*4567, though we may find *324*1567. In this case, if the person's "ideal point" is between 2 and 3, he cannot prefer 1 to 4. The object of this scaling is to find numerical values compatible with the preference structures of as large a percentage of the sample as possible. The scale values that account for the largest percentage of our sample, 63% at a conservative estimate, are listed next to the alternatives in Table 3. It can be seen that the three strategies in between immediate withdrawal and present policy do fall quite close together. Since they were so close, we felt it was appropriate (taking into account random errors as the person responded to the items) to count those individuals who permuted only 2, 3, or 4 as fitting our scale.

TABLE 3. Numerical Values Assigned to Strategies
Along the Dominant Militancy Scale

Strategy	Scale Value
1. Immediate withdrawal	1.00
2. Phased withdrawal	2.10
3. General de-escalation	2.25
4. Enclave holding	2.62
5. Present policy	4.84
6. General escalation	5.61
7. All-out escalation	7.00

[3]C. H. Coombs, *A Theory of Data,* New York, Wiley, 1964.

Those favoring present policy are fit less well by our scaling than any of the other groups, though now, somewhat mysteriously, we find that those preferring general de-escalation are not very well fitted either (see the third row of Table 2). About 37% of the latter, although they order the items from 1 to 7, do not fit our quantitative scaling. Examining these cases, we found that most of them differed only in seeing number three (their choice) as closer to number one (immediate withdrawal) than to number four (enclave holding)—i.e., unlike most people favoring general de-escalation, this subgroup would prefer immediate withdrawal to the "limited de-escalation" involved in the holding strategy.

There are no well-worked-out statistical techniques for evaluating the significance level or the goodness of a scaling effort, but the probability of fitting this large a proportion of our sample with a single scale by chance is extremely small. On the other hand, as regards our question of dimensionality, there is some indication that fives may not dimensionalize the strategies in the same way as the less militant remainder of the sample. The scale that fits the sample best is one that clearly separates immediate withdrawal from phased withdrawal, general de-escalation, or enclave holding, and in turn separates each of these from the present policy of increasing military pressure and also from any further escalation. For our sample, the different alternatives in between immediate withdrawal and present policy were not clearly distinguished.

In the rest of this paper, we shall not consider differences between people with the same first choice among strategies. Respondents with preferences 4321567 will be grouped with others who prefer 4532167, since both prefer strategy four to all others. With this simplification, we found that there were no significant differences between respondents who fit our dominant scale and others; i.e., between the two individuals mentioned above and a third who preferred the nonscalable 4321675. The latter is treated as someone who simply "made a mistake" in his ordering of the alternatives.

We have, then, a group whose most preferred strategy is immediate withdrawal; another which prefers phased withdrawal above all others; a third group preferring general de-escalation; a fourth group that prefers the holding strategy; and a fifth advocating increased military pressure. We shall sometimes refer to these groups by the *number* of the strategy its members favor, one through five, as these strategies are numbered in Table 1. The column headings in Table 2 and in all subsequent tables refer to the groups favoring strategies one through five, respectively.

In his analysis of perceptions of the Vietnam war, Ralph White (1966) distinguished four positions: escalators (who call for expanding the war); reclaimers (who want to regain all of South Vietnam); holders (who want to secure those parts of South Vietnam now held); and withdrawers (who are ready to give up Vietnam). He labelled the first two of these groups "militants" and the last two "non-miliants." These positions seem to correspond reasonably well to the spacings of strategies we obtained. As mentioned earlier, we have no escalators in our sample. However, supporters of the Administration's strategy, number five, would seem to be reclaimers; and those favoring immediate withdrawal, strategy one, are clearly withdrawers. The holding strategy (number four) proved to be not very distant, in terms of psychological preference, from either general de-escalation or phased withdrawal. We shall adopt a modification of White's terminology and occasionally refer to those favoring strategy five as militants; those favoring strategies four, three or two as non-militants; and those favoring strategy one—to indicate their extremity—as anti-militants. In general, the dimension we have isolated is considered to represent *degree of militancy*.[4]

Interestingly enough, even though most of our respondents are non-militants, they draw clear distinctions among the various militant alternatives: present policy, general escalation, and use of "anything needed to win." To establish this, however, further analysis would have to show that intransitive preferences were no more likely among rejected militant alternatives than among preferred non-militant ones.

ACCEPTABLE VS. UNACCEPTABLE OUTCOMES

Respondents rated each of seven possible outcomes in Vietnam as either "ideal," "desirable," "acceptable if necessary," or "unacceptable." We assigned the numbers 400, 300, 200, and 100 to these categories, respectively. Thus, a mean rating of 250 or better indicates that an outcome is seen as desirable by the group in question, while a mean rating of 150 or less indicates that it is rejected as unacceptable; ratings between 150 and 250 indicate that the outcome is, on the whole, acceptable if necessary. The outcomes and their evaluation by people favoring different strategies are presented in Table 4.

The groups differ significantly in their evaluation of every outcome,

---

[4] By "militancy" we mean the use of military force, not the intensity with which a preference for any particular strategy is held. Recently it has become common to speak of "militant non-violence," but as we employ the term here this would be a contradiction.

and these differences have a significant linear component (by a non-parametric analysis) in every case, except for the highly desirable outcome of a reunited, neutralized Vietnam and the highly undesirable one of a partitioned South Vietnam with Communist and anti-Communist sectors. The greatest differences, which are perfectly monotonic, appear in the ratings of a reunited Communist Vietnam, a Communist South Vietnam, and an anti-Communist South Vietnam (rows three, four, and five of Table 4). Advocating a more militant strategy is accompanied by stronger rejection of Communism for Vietnam (rows three and four), and by a more favorable evaluation of an anti-Communist South Vietnam (row five). Moreover, a neutral South Vietnam with a coalition government including the Vietcong is less acceptable to fours and fives than to others.

TABLE 4. Desirability of Various Outcomes in Vietnam

Outcomes	Strategy Choice				
	1	2	3	4	5
A reunited, neutralized Vietnam	342	359	349	373	313
A neutral South Vietnam, with a coalition government, including Vietcong	289	286	287	259	215
A reunited, Communist Vietnam	228	201	189	175	130
A Communist South Vietnam	207	189	184	179	125
An anti-Communist South Vietnam	169	212	220	253	284
A partitioned South Vietnam, with Communist and anti-Communist sectors	157	173	169	189	157
A military stalemate in South Vietnam without a peace settlement	125	144	138	160	157

Those for immediate withdrawal differ from all the others in that they rate a Communist Vietnam and a Communist South Vietnam as more desirable outcomes than an *anti*-Communist South Vietnam.

Groups one and two differ from the more militant fours and fives in that the former find a Communist Vietnam *more* acceptable than either a partitioned South Vietnam or a military stalemate. Fours prefer a partitioned South Vietnam to a Communist one, while the fives prefer even a military stalemate without a peace settlement to a Communist Vietnam.

Fives differ from all the others in that for them the outcomes are best ordered by a dimension which has Communism at the rejected extreme; while for the other groups the inconclusive outcomes (a partitioned South Vietnam and a military stalemate) appear at the rejected extreme.

Nevertheless, all groups agree that a reunited, neutralized Vietnam is more desirable than any other outcome, though this is rated somewhat less favorably by fives. Alongside the powerful disagreement about Communism and about appropriate strategies, this agreement is perhaps encouraging. It may in part be produced by the "social desirability" of the words "reunited and neutralized," however, and be more spurious than real—each group defining these desirable terms to mean something congruent with its evaluation of Communism.

LIKELY VS. UNLIKELY OUTCOMES

We selected four of the outcomes—an anti-Communist Vietnam; a reunited, neutralized Vietnam; a reunited, Communist Vietnam; and a partitioned South Vietnam—and listed them at the heads of four columns. As rows, we listed each of the seven strategies in a random order. Respondents indicated for each strategy how likely each outcome would be, using a four-point scale of "very likely," "likely," "unlikely," "very unlikely." We coded these scale points, as 400, 300, 200 and 100, respectively. Thus, a mean rating above 250, indicates that the outcome in question is considered relatively likely, while a rating below 250 indicates that it is considered relatively unlikely. In this analysis only those people who filled out every cell in both this matrix and a subsequent one to be considered shortly are included, giving us 96, 216, 88, 59, and 43 respondents favoring strategies one through five, respectively.

We wanted to be able to make many different kinds of comparisons —to test both whether one group found a given outcome more probable for strategy A than strategy B, and whether one group found a strategy more likely to lead to a given outcome than another group. In order to do this in a statistically meaningful way, we decided to treat these probability estimates as a series of repeated measures and to perform an analysis of variance on the entire matrix. The overall analysis of variance indicated that there were highly significant interactions between strategy choice and the perceived probability of outcomes given various strategies. Many of the differences among strategies are perceived by all groups, a fact indicated by the very large F-ratios for the effects obtained by collapsing over all preference groups. In analyzing the results, all differences were tested against the appropriate error terms derived from this analysis of variance.[5,6] The analysis of variance summary tables are omitted here in order to proceed directly to individual mean comparisons, based on the results in Table 5.

All groups agree that immediate withdrawal is very unlikely to lead to an anti-Communist South Vietnam, and very likely to lead to a re-united, Communist Vietnam. The differences between groups appear in rows four and five of Table 5a. Respondents preferring immediate withdrawal see a holding strategy and present policy as less likely to bring about an anti-Communist South Vietnam than do other groups, while present policy advocates see this policy as much more likely to bring about an anti-Communist South Vietnam. Estimates of how likely each of the various militant strategies is to achieve this outcome increase monotonically with militancy of preference, with only those favoring strategies two and three not differing from one another. On the whole, those favoring strategies one, two, or three do not distinguish among the various militant strategies as being more or less likely to secure an anti-Communist Vietnam, though they see all of the militant strategies as slightly more likely to do so than any of the non-militant alternatives. Those who prefer strategies four or five draw distinctions between strategies four, five, six, and seven. Notice that here fours are more similar to militants than to twos or threes.

The striking fact in Table 5b is that the diagonal entries of the first five rows are always the largest numbers in their rows, and in three of the five cases, also the largest numbers in their columns; that is, each group sees its favorite strategy as more likely to lead to this desirable outcome than does any other group. The differences between groups for all strategies are all large and significant. While we saw in Table 5a that anti-militants refused to concede that militant strategies had any great chance for success in achieving an anti-Communist South Vietnam, we see in Table 5b that militants deny that non-militant strategies have any chance of succeeding in bringing about the desirable goal of a re-united, neutralized Vietnam.

One may also note that *all* outcomes are seen as less likely given

[5]In both this analysis of variance and in the following one, we made the highly conservative assumption that the number of degrees of freedom for the repeated factors was 1, rather than J-1. Collier, R. O., Jr., Baker, F. B., Mandeville, G. K. and Hayes, T. F. "Estimates of Test Size for Several Test Procedures Based on Conventional Variance Ratios in the Repeated Measures Design," *Psychometricka,* Vol. 32 (1967), pp. 339-353.

[6]B. J. Winer, *Statistical Principles in Experimental Design,* New York, McGraw-Hill, 1962, pp. 319-337.

TABLE 5. Probability of Various Outcomes in Vietnam for Different Strategies

Table 5a: Probability of an Anti-Communist South Vietnam

	Strategy Choice				
	1	2	3	4	5
1. Immediate withdrawal	134	136	131	119	144
2. Phased withdrawal	177	203	202	209	193
3. General de-escalation	176	194	217	214	179
4. Enclave holding	199	227	234	246	261
5. Present policy	198	237	231	259	326
6. General escalation	202	234	236	270	319
7. All-out escalation	196	224	228	246	286

Table 5b: Probability of a Reunited, Neutralized Vietnam

	1	2	3	4	5
1. Immediate withdrawal	242	185	183	163	135
2. Phased withdrawal	260	274	242	242	191
3. General de-escalation	246	249	261	232	167
4. Enclave holding	205	224	219	236	191
5. Present policy	175	176	183	197	226
6. General escalation	157	162	161	176	212
7. All-out escalation	145	154	157	159	195

Table 5c: Probability of a Reunited, Communist Vietnam

	1	2	3	4	5
1. Immediate withdrawal	320	331	330	342	330
2. Phased withdrawal	275	265	251	259	277
3. General de-escalation	242	247	225	234	261
4. Enclave holding	224	205	208	198	198
5. Present policy	208	198	185	176	154
6. General escalation	200	198	182	185	149
7. All-out escalation	190	188	167	151	137

Table 5d: Probability of a Partitioned South Vietnam

	1	2	3	4	5
1. Immediate withdrawal	195	210	209	192	205
2. Phased withdrawal	233	257	253	256	254
3. General de-escalation	251	268	271	259	267
4. Enclave holding	275	309	305	298	291
5. Present policy	233	248	257	249	230
6. General escalation	210	221	242	225	216
7. All-out escalation	183	194	194	192	186

drastic escalation. This might be interpreted as indicating that respondents see such actions as essentially making the issue of the specific outcome in Vietnam irrelevant by expanding the area of conflict. It would be interesting to know whether people who favored such escalation also believed this to be the case. This is one point at which the absence of extreme militants in our sample limits our ability to make statements about the grounds for escalation. However, the trend of our present sample, and White's discussion of "underestimation of an enemy's will to resist" as a cause of two world wars, suggest that people favoring rapid escalation would see this as a good means to end the conflict rather than expand it.

Table 5c, representing the perceived probability of a reunited, Communist Vietnam, is in many ways a mirror image of Table 5a. With one or two exceptions, the more militant the strategy (looking down columns), the less likely this outcome is rated by all groups. Here people favoring immediate withdrawal make considerably sharper and more regular distinctions between strategies regarding their likelihood of producing a Communist Vietnam (Table 5c) than they do in comparing them with respect to the establishment of an anti-Communist Vietnam (Table 5a).

In Table 5d, all groups see that an enclave holding strategy is more likely than any other to produce a partitioned South Vietnam. The range of probability estimates in this table is somewhat smaller than in the others, suggesting that the possibility of this outcome may be less important for most groups in differentiating between courses of action.

For all strategies, respondents preferring immediate withdrawal see a reunited, Communist Vietnam as the most likely outcome; they are the only one of our five groups to do so. Curiously, those favoring strategies two, three and four all see a partitioned South Vietnam as the most likely outcome. However, twos and three are closer to ones in reporting a reunited, Communist Vietnam as next most likely, while those favoring four see an anti-Communist South Vietnam as next most likely. The advocates of present policy see an anti-Communist South Vietnam as the most likely outcome of all.

Another question we can ask of this data is whether some of these outcomes were more salient than others to respondents when they first gave us their strategy preferences. For instance, a respondent whose ideal strategy is number four on our scale might have the preference order 4325167. If he preferred strategies to the extent that they were seen as leading to some particular outcome, that outcome (or outcomes) would have to be most probable given 4, next mostly likely for 3, then for 2, 5, 1, 6, and finally for 7. For each group, as it turns out, one and only one of the outcomes orders the strategies in the same way as the group members themselves did initially. For those favoring immediate withdrawal this outcome is a reunited, Communist Vietnam; if we assume that these respondents preferred strategies to the extent that they increased the chances for this outcome, we can predict their strategy preferences exactly, while we cannot predict them using any other outcome as our reference point. For those preferring phased withdrawal or general de-escalation, a reunited neutralized Vietnam orders the strategies precisely as they did, while no other outcome does. For those favoring the enclave holding strategy, perhaps surprisingly, the outcome of a partitioned South Vietnam is the only one that could, taken by itself, account for their preference structure (though this accounting places fours closer to number five than to one). Finally, for present policy advocates, the probability of an anti-Communist Vietnam seems to have been the most salient of the four, for it alone orders their strategy preferences. These relationships can be seen by inspecting the four columns for each strategy choice group, and comparing the resultant orderings of strategies with the ordering that each group prefers when placed appropriately along the scale presented in Table 3.

PERCEPTIONS OF U.S. CONTROL AND U.S. CHOICE IN VIETNAM

We asked people two questions designed to assess the amount of responsibility they felt the U.S. had in determining the outcome in Vietnam. If some people were advocating a strategy even with full knowledge that it would lead to undesirable outcomes, the explanation could be that these people felt it would not make much difference what the U.S. did or believed that the U.S. had relatively little choice. The results are presented in Table 6.

Once again, we encounter a striking monotonic relationship between answers to these questions and strategy preference. People favoring immediate or phased withdrawal are more likely to say that the outcome in Vietnam will be mainly a result of factors beyond our control—a position that is consistent with their tendency to deny that even further escalation would succeed in bringing about an anti-Communist South Vietnam. More militant groups see the U.S. as more powerful, or more in control, in Vietnam; and yet they also see the U.S. as having less choice

TABLE 6.   Perceptions of U.S. Control and Choice in Vietnam by
            Respondents with Different Strategy Choices

	Strategy Choice				
Statement	1	2	3	4	5
"The outcome in Vietnam will be mainly a result of factors beyond our control"	24.7%	19.4	13.9	11.1	5.2
"The U.S. has no real choice in Vietnam—we are pretty much trapped by the situation"	1.9	3.3	12.3	18.8	26.8

Each number in this table represents the percentage of respondents in the
column endorsing the statement at the left of the row.

in Vietnam, as being "trapped by the situation." In some sense, of
course, those favoring either the present policy or immediate withdrawal
are advocating policies they know to have undesirable or unpleasant aspects, and they do make use of this chance to justify their choices. But
they justify their commitments very differently—the former by seeing the
U.S. as having less control, the latter by seeing the U.S. as having less
choice.

IMPORTANCE OF OTHER GOALS

Vietnam is only one among many American concerns.   A person
may feel that the U.S. can bear certain costs in Vietnam because he sees
these costs as being offset by benefits in other areas.   We asked respondents to judge the importance of a dozen other political goals, categoriz-
ing each one as "extremely important," "important," "unimportant," or
"completely unimportant."   Again, assigning values of 400, 300, 200,
and 100 to these categories, respectively, means that any item with a
mean of more than 250 is seen as important, while items with means of
less than 250 are considered unimportant.

Once more we find that people who favor different strategies differ
significantly on every one of these values.   These values, and their perceived degree of importance, are presented in Table 7.   Again, on the
items on which differences are greatest, the differences are perfectly
monotonic.   All of the following, each clearly related to the "anti-Communism" dimension emerging repeatedly in the study, are considered
more important by the more militant respondents: limiting the spread of
Communism; maintaining the unity of the Western Alliance; safeguard-

ing our national military security; discouraging external aggression; and also, as the Administration argues, "honoring our moral commitments."

TABLE 7. Importance of Other Goals*

Goals	Strategy Choice				
	1	2	3	4	5
Preserving world peace and reducing the danger of nuclear war	448	439	435	429	418
Eliminating poverty and racial inequality in the U.S.	401	399	400	398	387
Protecting freedom of dissent in the U.S.	398	394	393	384	362
Aiding the social and economic progress of the developing nations	365	353	360	334	339
Protecting the independence of developing nations	326	319	319	326	351
Discouraging external aggression	274	303	304	327	340
Honoring our moral commitments	274	288	290	312	346
Maintaining economic prosperity in the U.S.	263	287	291	317	267
Safeguarding our national military security	236	275	283	308	315
Following of majority opinion by the U.S. government	234	249	298	255	248
Maintaining the unity of the Western Alliance	197	236	248	267	277
Limiting the spread of Communism	184	233	249	287	323

*Each number in the table represents the mean importance of the goal at the left to the group at the head of the column. Respondents were allowed to place a star by any item they felt was "so important it must be achieved no matter what happens to the other values." Starred items were given scores of 500, which accounts for the fact that some numbers in the table are larger than 400 (the score for "extremely important").

Not surprisingly, the "doves" rate the importance of preserving world peace and reducing the danger of nuclear war more highly, but this goal is seen by all groups as the most important single goal of all.

Group five sees protecting the independence of developing nations as more important than aiding their social and economic progress, while the other groups see the latter as more important. All groups agree that eliminating poverty and racial inequality in the U.S. is more important than aiding developing nations.

There is one point at which both ends of the spectrum agree: both groups one and five rate the importance of maintaining economic prosperity in the U.S. as less important than do the other groups.

Interestingly enough, all groups in the sample rate protecting freedom of dissent in the U.S. as considerably more important than the following of majority opinion by the U.S. government. However, fives rate freedom of dissent as less important than do others.

Despite the substantial and pervasive differences of opinion, there is still considerable agreement on which goals are most important. Besides the importance of preserving peace, all groups agree on the next most important goal: eliminating poverty and racial inequality. The implication of the analysis as a whole, however, is that the disagreement about what the U.S. should do in Vietnam is indicative of a fundamental dissensus about what American goals should be. And this seems to be true despite the fact that we are sampling a group of social scientists who have designated themselves not only by their training but by their organizational membership as people who are committed to liberal social values.

IMPACT OF STRATEGIES ON OTHER GOALS

As we did with the outcomes in Vietnam, we selected four of the goals that we felt might be relevant to strategy preferences in Vietnam —preserving world peace, safeguarding U.S. security, protecting the independence of developing nations, and eliminating poverty and racial inequality in the U.S.—and listed them at the heads of four columns, with the seven strategy options listed as rows. For each strategy respondents indicated how likely they thought each of the goals would be, again using the same four category scale. These results are presented in Table 8.

This matrix differs in several ways from the previous one. First, while we hypothesized that these goals would be seen as relevant to the choices in Vietnam, we did not assume so. Respondents could tell us that the choices in Vietnam were irrelevant to one or all of these goals by telling us that these goals would be equally likely no matter what choice was made in Vietnam. Thus, some of the relationships we observed between strategy preferences and perceived probability of outcomes in Vietnam (in Table 5) might be attenuated for these goals. On

the other hand, given these somewhat more general (perhaps more am-
biguous) goals, there is more room for respondents to distort their perceptions such that everyone sees his own strategy choice as optimal on
all counts.   (Or, in an alternative interpretation, these wider goals may
be more important in determining peoples' strategy choices than any
consideration of possible outcomes in Vietnam.)   Also, in this matrix,
unlike the previous one, there is no implication that the different goals
are mutually exclusive.

TABLE 8. Impact of Different Strategies on General Goals

Table 8a: Probability of Preserving World Peace

	Strategy Choice				
	1	2	3	4	5
1. Immediate withdrawal	363	283	241	220	151
2. Phased withdrawal	313	339	305	295	237
3. General de-escalation	309	324	334	298	195
4. Enclave holding	249	271	263	315	221
5. Present policy	163	167	190	214	295
6. General escalation	117	124	136	146	198
7. All-out escalation	104	111	113	107	123

Table 8b: Probability of Safeguarding U.S. Security

	1	2	3	4	5
1. Immediate withdrawal	321	263	227	209	163
2. Phased withdrawal	300	319	277	273	230
3. General de-escalation	300	306	297	281	198
4. Enclave holding	251	274	263	298	228
5. Present policy	192	201	217	237	305
6. General escalation	147	155	166	175	219
7. All-out escalation	119	120	127	127	161

Table 8c: Probability of Protecting the Independence of Developing Nations

	1	2	3	4	5
1. Immediate withdrawal	303	248	214	195	149
2. Phased withdrawal	280	301	276	263	219
3. General de-escalation	267	280	285	266	179
4. Enclave holding	220	241	246	280	209
5. Present policy	172	193	215	229	307
6. General escalation	133	152	171	181	242
7. All-out escalation	116	127	133	139	181

TABLE 8 (cont.)

Table 8d: Probability of Eliminating Poverty and Racial Inequality in the U.S.

	1	2	3	4	5
1. Immediate withdrawal	312	294	255	256	193
2. Phased withdrawal	260	287	252	258	212
3. General de-escalation	262	279	268	263	191
4. Enclave holding	201	226	219	246	186
5. Present policy	150	155	158	164	193
6. General escalation	120	125	131	139	167
7. All-out escalation	109	114	116	129	140

Again, in order to make multiple comparisons in a meaningful way, we performed an overall analysis of variance on the entire set of probability estimates. The overall effect for all groups and for all four of these goals is an extremely strong selective perception. In almost every instance, the diagonal entries of these matrices are not only the largest numbers in their row, but also the largest numbers in their column. Each group sees its own strategy as most likely to bring about the desired goals.

Looking first at the probability estimates for preserving world peace, all the diagonal entries are the largest in their rows and columns. Those favoring immediate withdrawal think this strategy is an excellent means of preserving world peace; those favoring present policy think immediate withdrawal would be disastrous for peace. Those favoring general de-escalation think this would be the best means of preserving world peace; next they favor phased withdrawal, enclave holding, immediate withdrawal, and then the present policy (i.e., closely following their initial scale positions). One might note, however, that while all groups consider their own preference optimal for preserving peace, the perceived chance for this value given the group's favorite strategy decreases as one moves from immediate withdrawal to present policy. This is indicated by the fact that the diagonal entries become successively smaller.

The same pattern is dominant in the next case as well, where respondents are considering the impact of strategies in Vietnam on U.S. security. For example, those favoring the holding strategy think this would be optimal for safeguarding the security of the U.S., preferring general de-escalation next, then phased withdrawal, then present policy, then immediate withdrawal.

In this table, as in the others, these estimates of the probability of obtaining desirable goals order the outcomes extremely well with respect to the scale values initially derived—with two exceptions.   The first is that those favoring present policy seem to find phased withdrawal a more desirable alternative than any other save their own choice.   Those favoring five do not suffer from this inconsistency when considering the probability of effecting their desired outcome in Vietnam.   One possible explanation for this is that their strategy choice was determined more by consideration of immediate outcomes than of wider goals, with the reverse being the case for the choices of other groups.   The other difference is that, as in considering outcomes within Vietnam, those favoring enclave holding seem closer to the militants than to other non-militants.

Ones do not see their strategy as having any detrimental effect on U.S. security.   The other groups are progressively more likely to reject the strategy of immediate withdrawal on these grounds.

The same pattern is repeated when we come to the prospects for protecting the independence of developing nations.   The interpreter is tempted to conclude that the different groups are using these words quite differently—that immediate withdrawers, for instance, also have in mind protecting their independence from American aggression.

The last of our goals, eliminating poverty and racial inequality in the U.S., is the only domestic (rather than international) issue considered. While there is some tendency for the different groups to generalize the virtues of their favorite strategies to extend to this goal as well, the overall pattern indicates that the various Vietnam strategies are not well ordered (according to our initial scale) at all by this consideration.   For none of the groups does this goal order the strategy preferences in the same way as derivable from our initial scaling.   Interestingly, there is an overall difference between groups, with those favoring Administration policy seeing the general chances for eliminating poverty and inequality as less than do other groups.

PERCEPTIONS OF COMMUNIST THREAT

In all of these calculations there are certainly important assumptions being made about the nature of the enemy and the enemy's motives and capacities.   White[7] has discussed how psychologically unsophisticated assumptions about the nature of the enemy may lead to dangerous miscalculations.   In our survey, we asked people to indicate which of sev-

---

[7] R. K. White, "Misperceptions and the Vietnam War," *Journal of Social Issues,* XII, 1966.

eral possible motives were the "most important" motives behind Communist revolutions in developing nations. These motives and the percentages in each group endorsing them or attributing them to Communist revolutions are presented in Table 9.

TABLE 9. "Most Important" Motives Behind Communist
Revolutions in Developing Nations

Motives	Groups				
	1	2	3	4	5
Desire for social and economic progress	83.2%	79.0	75.2	80.2	55.7
Nationalism and patriotism	60.9	50.8	52.0	56.8	49.1
Opposition to undemocratic governments in their own countries	60.9	50.5	48.8	54.3	26.2
Desire for world revolution and spread of Communism	11.8	18.1	26.4	23.5	54.1
Hatred of the West and of the U.S. in particular	11.8	14.6	10.4	14.8	29.5
Personal ambition and the desire for power for its own sake	12.4	19.3	22.4	32.1	32.8

Each number in this table represents the percentage of respondents in each column who rate the item on the left as one of the most important.

People favoring immediate withdrawal have a relatively favorable picture of Communism in underdeveloped countries. Desire for social and economic progress is seen as a most important motive by 83% of this group, with majorities also rating nationalism and patriotism and opposition to undemocratic governments in their own countries as very important. Other more threatening motives—desire for world revolution, hatred of the West, and desire for power—are attributed to Communist movements only by small minorities. The first two of these unfavorable motives become progressively more important for groups favoring more militant strategies, although only fives see desire for world revolution as more important than nationalism or opposition to undemocratic governments. Fives are also less likely to rate desire for social and economic progress as most important.

The ordering of the strategies by these general considerations is only roughly the same as the ordering of them by our initial scaling. This suggests that general views of Communist revolutions may be less important determinants of strategy preferences for Vietnam than specific perceptions of the nature of the conflict and of the enemy in Vietnam. This hypothesis is borne out by the striking effects obtained in answer to questions about the source of aggression in Vietnam; the results are presented in Table 10.

TABLE 10. Perceptions of Aggression in Vietnam

Statement	Strategy Choice				
	1	2	3	4	5
"North Vietnam has clearly committed aggression in Vietnam."	16.4%	34.6	40.5	55.0	76.7
"The U.S. has clearly committed aggression in Vietnam."	98.1	85.1	73.8	53.8	25.0
"The North Vietnamese leaders probably believe their main purpose in this war is to defend their homeland against U.S. aggression" (vs. "to spread Communism into South Vietnam").	93.5	81.5	70.6	52.8	25.9
"Among those South Vietnamese who have strong feelings about the outcome of the war, more than half favor the Vietcong."	78.3	49.1	49.5	34.4	11.8

Each number in this table represents the percentage of people favoring the strategy at the head of the column who endorsed the statement at the beginning of the row.

The statement "North Vietnam has clearly committed aggression in Vietnam" is endorsed by 16% of those favoring strategy one, and by 35%, 41%, 55%, and 77% of those favoring two through five. These percentages differentiate groups almost precisely as they were differentiated by our initial scaling. Endorsement of the statement "the U.S. has clearly committed aggression in Vietnam" is a mirror image of the previous question, since relatively few people in the various groups endorse both statements, or the idea of mutual aggression. The percentages of each group attributing self-defense as the main motivation of the North Vietnamese, and pro-Vietcong sentiment as predominant among "those South Vietnamese who have strong feelings about the outcome of the war," also distinguish all groups by amounts comparable to their distances on the strategy scale. Since self-defense is the psychological rationale for most wars, it is somewhat surprising that so few of those favoring Administration policy, or even the holding strategy, are willing to concede that it is the major motivation of the North Vietnamese in their own eyes.

DISCUSSION

We know that people try, when possible, to make choices that are both internally consistent and also consistent with their beliefs about the consequences of these choices for their important values. In this paper, we have seen the extent to which people are consistent in their views on Vietnam, and how they achieve this consistency.

First of all, we saw that people chose among strategies in an internally consistent manner. Having in mind some "ideal" or "optimal" degree of militancy, a respondent apparently ordered the strategies according to militancy and, when comparing two alternatives, regularly chose the one that was closer to his ideal point on this dimension. Not only can we characterize both militants and anti-militants as having made their choices in this way, but we can say that a sizable majority of our sample agreed on just how militant the different strategies were. Apart from further escalation, which almost no one in our sample favored, the present policy (as of December, 1967) involving increasing military pressure was clearly distinguished from various forms of graduated de-escalation, which were in turn separated from immediate withdrawal.

Secondly, we saw that people were consistent in choosing strategies that maximized the likelihood of a preferred outcome (with the exception of fours): a Communist Vietnam for ones, a reunited, neutralized Vietnam for two and threes, and an anti-Communist South Vietnam for fives. Fours, who advocated enclave holding, seemed to have in mind a "realistic" outcome rather than a highly valued one; for them, the outcome that best ordered their choices was a partitioned South Vietnam. If these outcomes were in fact salient in people's minds as they made their strategy choices, then discussion might be aided by making the differences in this regard explicit.

Thirdly, we saw that respondents were also consistent in preferring strategies that they saw as maximizing the important general values of preserving world peace, protecting developing nations, safeguarding U.S. security, and even eliminating poverty and racial inequality in the U.S. The belief conflict in this domain is striking. Militants believe their strategy is the best means for preserving peace, safeguarding U.S. security, and protecting developing nations; anti-militants believe the same things about their strategy, immediate withdrawal. In some sense, these contradictions are encouraging, for if one ignored all other differences between groups, these disagreements over means would be sufficient to explain the different strategy choices; it might therefore be possible to reduce disagreement between militants and anti-militants to a dispute over means to shared goals.

Finally, people are highly consistent in justifying their strategies by their conceptions of the enemy. Anti-militants see the U.S. as the aggressor, the North Vietnamese as defending their homeland, and the South Vietnamese as favoring the Vietcong; non-militants are divided; militants believe the opposite. There is little indication in our results that social scientists conceive of this conflict as involving mutual aggression or factors unknown to them, such as the opinion of the South Vietnamese.

Degree of anti-Communism seemed to be the best predictor of differences within our sample. The relationship between anti-Communism and militancy was strong and linear. If a person was not at all anti-Communist, he was not at all militant; if he was slightly anti-Communist, he was slightly militant; and so on. It should be recalled that our sample did not span the range from Robert Welch to Stokely Carmichael, but consisted entirely of relatively liberal people with academic backgrounds.[8] If anti-Communism is less salient for academicians than for the American public, as Robinson and Hefner report,[9] it is nevertheless quite salient indeed.

Besides preferring more militant strategies, the strong anti-Communists in our sample seemed to differ from all the others in the way they made their choices. First, in evaluating outcomes in Vietnam (ignoring for the moment the consensus choice of a "neutralized" Vietnam) the militants saw an anti-Communist South Vietnam as most desirable, a

---

[8] It is not clear from previous research whether positions on the war in Vietnam correspond to differences in social status. A study by Verba, *et al.* found no relationship in a national sample, while a study by Armor, *et al.* found that, among college professors, those affiliated with large public schools were more likely to oppose the war than those affiliated with small private schools. We cannot shed light on this issue since we did not collect demographic information on our sample. S. Verba, R. A. Brody, E. B. Parker, N. H. Nie, N. W. Polsby, P. Ekman, and G. S. Black, "Public Opinion and the War in Vietnam," *American Political Science Review,* Vol. 61 (1967), pp. 317-333; D. J. Armor, J. B. Giacquinta, R. G. McIntosh, and D. E. H. Russell, "Professors' Attitudes toward the Vietnam War," *Public Opinion Quarterly,* Vol. 31 (1967), pp. 159-175.

[9] J. P. Robinson and R. Hefner, "Multidimensional Differences in Public and Academic Perceptions of Nations," *Journal of Personality and Social Psychology,* Vol. 7 (1967), pp. 251-259.

Communist South Vietnam as least acceptable, and the other alternatives as intermediate; that is, they seemed to be using a dimension from Communist to anti-Communist. The others saw a neutral South Vietnam with a coalition government as most desirable and a military stalemate without a peace settlement as least acceptable, with the other possibilities in between; they used a different dimension, perhaps one reflecting how "stable" the solution in Vietnam would be. Secondly, militants seemed to restrict their thinking more than others to immediate outcomes in Vietnam, for general goals predicted their strategy preferences somewhat less well. One way of changing militant opinion—and a way in which opinion may actually be changing in the U.S.—would be to demonstrate that such wider goals are relevant, yet inconsistent with militant strategies in Vietnam.

At this point in our research we have characterized the consistency in several domains of respondents with different views on Vietnam.[10] From the data reported here we are ready to compute overall indices of the extent to which each respondent was rational in making choices that maximized his expected gain. In addition, we have information about respondents' reference groups, their factual knowledge of the war, the subjective certainty of their views, and their interest in receiving new information. We propose to explore the interrelationships among different kinds of cognitive consistency—e.g., to compare the extent to which a person makes rational choices and the extent to which he perceives agreement between his views and those of his reference groups.

---

[10] Some of this consistency is no doubt due to the fact that respondents were implicitly asked for a coherent statement of their views, but it is nonetheless interesting to see how well and in what ways they achieved this coherence.

PART III

THE BIG POWER CONFRONTATION: RELEVANCE FOR THE RESOLUTION OF THE CONFLICT

CHAPTER 8. VIETNAM: AN ARENA OF THE BIG POWERS

By Robert Strausz-Hupé*

The author sets the Vietnamese problem in the context of a world-wide bipolar Soviet-U.S. confrontation. His thesis is that there can be no effective solution to the Vietnam conflict without a "give-and-take" in the multi-dimensional U.S.-Soviet negotiations space. Ed.

I presume that it is the purpose of the United States to disengage itself from Vietnam and not to perpetuate its presence beyond the making of a political settlement. I can conceive of a number of possibilities for such a settlement as, for example, those which Goodman discusses in the following chapter. Certainly, a Vietnamese settlement must meet one requirement: it must prove viable *after* the withdrawal of the American military forces presently deployed in Vietnam. The question is not only how we are to disengage, but also what happens after we have disengaged? I can conceive of no other satisfactory answer to this question than an agreement between the Great Powers, the United States and the Soviet Union.

There are several precedents of regional conflicts settled by the anterior agreement, albeit implicit rather than explicit, of the superpowers, the most important ones being that of the Middle East conflict in 1948 and 1956, and that of the Cyprus conflict. In these cases, the outcome was determined not so much by the activities of the opposing factions

*The author is associated with the Foreign Policy Research Institute of the University of Pennsylvania.

within the area—in the one case, Arabs and Israelis, and, in the other case, Greeks and Turks—as by what the Great Powers did or did not do. Now it seems to me that the making of peace in Vietnam and in the rest of Indo-China—and no settlement for Vietnam that does not provide also for the security of Laos, Cambodia and Thailand can prove viable—requires the making of an agreement between the Soviet Union and the United States. No matter how intransigent and valorous are the local factions, they are largely the proxies of the Great Powers. The North Vietnamese could not fight the South Vietnamese and us without the aid which they receive from the Soviet Union and, the South Vietnamese could not fight the North without the support of the United States.

The Indo-Chinese conflict will remain incomprehensible as long as it is not placed in the proper historical context. The war in Vietnam did not erupt in a historical vacuum. The origin of our involvement in South Vietnam is the so-called Laotian (Geneva) agreement of 1962. This agreement was supposed to settle the civil war in Laos by dividing that country into three parts, namely the Communist-controlled Pathet Lao in the North; a neutral belt in the middle; and the Royalist-controlled Laos in the South. This arrangement was guaranteed by the United States, the Soviet Union, and Britain. Britain's guarantee was largely a diplomatic formality. Only the United States and the Soviet Union possessed the leverage necessary for compelling their respective proxies to keep within the territories assigned to them. President Kennedy said that the United States would be able to assess the advisability of further steps toward a détente by the measure of fidelity with which the Soviets would live up to their obligations under the Geneva agreement of 1962. The gist of this statement was repeated by Mr. Harriman testifying on Laos before the Senate Foreign Relations Committee.

Indeed, it would have been difficult, if not impossible, to take the "next step," namely, the conclusion of the Partial Nuclear Test Ban, if the sincerity of the Soviets' pledge to Laos had been in doubt. If the Soviets were not to carry out their side of this agreement, then what would be, one might ask, the worth of their signature on any other agreement? Immediately after the signing of the Geneva agreement, the Pathet Lao occupied the Plain of Jarres, the one and only feasible access route from North Vietnam to South Vietnam. It was only by virtue of the Pathet-Laos' occupation of this area of passage which parallels the Western frontier of Vietnam and abuts Cambodia, that it became possible for the North Vietnamese to infiltrate South Vietnam; to ship material to the Vietcong; and to reenforce the Vietcong with contingents raised and trained in North Vietnam. The solution of this logistical problem by the Pathet Lao, acting in concert with North Vietnam, marks the beginning of the stepped-up operations by organized insurgent forces and regular North Vietnamese troops in South Vietnam. It is at this point, too, that the question of stepped-up U. S. military support of Vietnam arose. Obviously, the South Vietnamese had now to deal with massive foreign intervention rather than domestic insurgency. President Kennedy now had to choose between leaving the South Vietnamese to their fate or to escalate the U.S. involvement from the dispatch of "advisors" to the unambiguous U.S. military presence. Now, it seems to me that, at this fork of the road, President Kennedy might well have addressed the following observations to the Soviets: "We presume that your desire for a détente matches ours in sincerity; that you deem a Partial Nuclear Test Ban as important to the welfare of mankind as do we; that you want cultural exchanges at least as ardently as we; and that you want trade with the West in order to approximate your average standard of living to that of the Western peoples. But does the fulfillment of these aspirations not hinge on the degree of the fulfillment of the obligations which you assumed under the 1962 agreement of Geneva on Laos?" I am sure that, if President Kennedy's advisors could have couched these questions in the proper diplomatic language, their gist could have been made quite clear to the Soviets. For one reason or the other, President Kennedy does not seem to have ventured upon such a confrontation with the Soviet Union. "Next steps" were taken; yet the Soviets did not restrain either the Pathet Lao or the North Vietnamese.

Globally, very little has changed since 1962. In Vietnam, the United States is still confronted by the proxies of the Soviet Union, i.e. the North Vietnamese and the Vietcong, while the Pathet Lao operate from staging areas just across the borders of Vietnam. All these elements depend critically on supplies originating in the Soviet Union and communist Eastern Europe.

It has been argued in the Western press that the Soviets in their relations to Hanoi are not free agents. According to this version, the Soviets see themselves compelled to assist the fraternal Communist party of North Vietnam, lest the Chinese communists accuse the Soviet Union of treason to Marxist-Leninism; gain ascendancy over Hanoi; and precipitate a world war. Significantly, no indication of this concern can be found in the Soviet press. More important still, the Chinese communists do not produce those sophisticated weapons systems—antiaircraft rockets, fighter bombers and sundry electronic gear—which now enable the North Vietnamese forces to inflict heavy losses on the U.S., or do not produce these items in quantities sufficient for export.

In fact, the United States is bogged down in an immensely costly Asian war which strains U.S. commitments in Europe and the Middle East, and erodes the U.S. defense budget for the development of strategic weaponry. It is immaterial as to whether the Soviets contrived deliberately this situation: the advantages, strategic and political, which have accrued to the Soviets have been considerable. There is no reason why the Soviets should halt the drain on U.S. power—except in return for solid gains to their global posture. This hypothesis is not subject to rigorous testing; it is inferentially more plausible than the hypothesis of Soviet concern with Chinese bellicosity and the good opinion of fraternal communist parties.

It is inconceivable that the war in Vietnam as well as the guerrilla wars in Laos and Northern Thailand could continue on the scale on which they are now being waged, without the supplies and the "advisors" that are now being shipped into the region by the Soviets. Certainly, the North Vietnamese and Vietcong enjoy the unstinting propagandistic and diplomatic support of the Soviets and, at innumerable occasions, have expressed their gratitude and loyalty to the Soviet Union. So, it seems to me that the very key to the situation has been and still is the United States-Soviet relationship.

How can we engage in a meaningful dialogue on peace in Vietnam with the Soviets? Clearly, such a dialogue cannot be confined to Vietnam, nor even to all of Indo-China. It will have to encompass the Middle East and Europe. A settlement in Vietnam, if it is to be equitable and enduring, must be a part of a much wider settlement—a settlement negotiated between the Soviets and ourselves, reconciling issues-in-conflict not only in Indo-China, but also in Europe and the Middle East. The war in Vietnam is inseparable from the U.S.-Soviet confrontation. This is why it is both so bitterly contested and so widely misunderstood. If such a settlement does not lie within reach—and, not being in the confidence of either President Johnson or Chairman Brezhnev, I do not know whether it lies within reach—I cannot see any issue to the fighting in Vietnam except the stabilization of the local military situation. Such a stabilization would require a greater effort than we are now making, and possibly involves the risk of a confrontation with the Soviets more direct than the present, proxy-buffered relationship.

The other alternative is the withdrawal of the United States from

Vietnam, leaving Indo-China in the sphere of influence of the Soviet Union—and, to reiterate my above stated opinion, *not* in the sphere of influence of China. Such a withdrawal would pose many problems. Not all of these will be of concern to the Vietnamese alone. The disengagement of the American forces under the guns of the North Vietnamese would be fraught with many difficulties familiar to the student of military history. Even if these difficulties could be successfully surmounted, the evacuation by the U. S. of Vietnam would not have contributed anything —except negatively—to the making of a global settlement between the U.S. and the Soviet Union.

PART IV

ANALYTIC MODELS: POSSIBLE SOLUTIONS, PROCEDURES FOR REACHING AGREEMENT, AND STATISTICAL PREDICTIONS

CHAPTER 9. DIPLOMATIC AND STRATEGIC OUTCOMES OF THE CONFLICT

By Allan E. Goodman*

In the first paper of this part dealing with the potentials for solutions, the author follows a rather traditional approach. In a perceptive manner he presents a set of key considerations which might be expected to guide discussions and negotiations for a Vietnam settlement, and in particular a withdrawl without defeat or weakness by a major power in a position of strength. He presents a diplomatic scenario for ending the Vietnam conflict which consists of three phases: a cease-fire declaration and establishment of regroupment zones; negotiations involving the parties to the conflict and the U.N.; and the establishment of a control and inspection commission, a plebiscite, and demilitarization of foreign assistance.

Vietnamese chess is similar to Vietnamese wars: the lesson of both is that it is possible for a combatant to sacrifice all his pieces but one and

*The author is associated with the Department of Government, Harvard University. This article was written in late May, 1968, and served as the basis for a discussion of the prospects and probabilities of various possible outcomes of the Vietnam war. The apparent stalemating of the Paris talks, the association of South Vietnamese Communists and neutralists into an "Alliance for National Democratic and Peace Forces", the functional "liberalization" of the Thieu government with the expected return to South Vietnam of former political actors such as Gens. Duong van Minh and Nguyen chanh Thi, and the apparent victory of Thieu over Vice President Ky in the struggle for control of the executive have undoubtedly altered the substance and probabilities of the scenarios presented here. These developments, however, are still unfolding in the effects they are likely to have on any resolution of the war. Analyses of these developments constitute a sequel to this article and the scenarios presented; such a sequel is now in preparation.

still win. Conversely, it is possible that the opponent with the most powerful force can win a large number of encounters and still lose. Clearly, the United States, as long as it has the will, cannot be decisively defeated in Vietnam, but this condition does not make victory any more possible. Rather, victory on the battlefield has been as elusive as it has been difficult to define in either domestic or international politics.

Somewhere between defeat and victory probably lies the solution to war in Vietnam, a solution not unlike others we have sought, with peace without victory as its basic tenet. United States involvement in other countries' internal wars may vindicate American goals without necessarily achieving military victory. Indeed, limited wars and internal conflicts, rather than world wars, may come to be characterized by resolutions which place peace without victory as the major objective. The British withdrew from Cyprus after an unequivocal "never;" France withdrew from Indo-China and Algeria despite an emotional and material investment equal to that of the United States' in present-day Vietnam; China gradually disengaged herself from the contest over the off-shore islands; and the U.S.S.R., similarly, withdrew from the Greek civil war, the Berlin Blockade, and the Cuban missile crisis. All of these cases, while different to be sure in many respects, have one common element: these powerful countries could have chosen to remain engaged but instead withdrew while in positions of relative strength rather than from actual weakness or after clear-cut military defeat. In all of these cases withdrawal was in some sense regulated by explicit agreements or conducted in accordance with the more informal rules of great-power diplomacy.

The question of American de-escalation, disengagement, and withdrawal from South Vietnam has provoked much debate. Critics of the present policy tend to view such withdrawal as an end in itself: if the United States withdraws, they argue, an "immoral" war will end and further world crisis will be averted. Proponents of the present strategy, on the other hand, are deeply committed to the belief that to withdraw would also be immoral, precipitate the fall of a free Vietnam, and result in the assassination of thousands of Vietnamese committed to a non-Communist, non-Vietcong government in Saigon. While both extremes are within the realm of possibility, neither represent realistic appraisals of the milieu in which the Vietnamese war is occurring. Writers on both sides of the issue generally agree on a large number of details[1] but gen-

---

[1]This conclusion is drawn from an analysis of a year's worth of pro- and anti-war literature, articles, and policy statements. See also Sidney Verba *et al.,*

erally remain at loggerheads on the question of withdrawal vs. victory. As a result, there has been much debate but little attempt at synthesis.

It is also conceivable that the issue of American withdrawal is less important than is the question of the form such disengagement would take, and in this sense proposals to "end the war" both within and outside the administration are rather "formless." A timely and regulated withdrawal to either coastal enclaves or from South Vietnam itself may not avert world war just as it might not precipitate the fall of government in the South to the Communists or result in mass assassinations within the society. Indeed, a regulated reduction of the American presence may well stimulate a counter force to both the increasing "Americanization" of the war and the heightened sense of Vietnamese political cynicism and military malaise. Disengagement may foster the peace that escalation has failed to provide.

A "withdrawal in strength" tactic for the United States might involve three phases and a like number of strategic outcomes.

FIGURE 1. The Diplomatic Scenario for Ending the Vietnam War

Cease-Fire Declaration		Establishment of Control
	Dual Negotiations	and Inspection Commission
Establishment of Zones for "re-groupment"		Plebiscite
		De-militarization of Foreign Assistance in South Vietnam

Concurrently with the declaration of a cease-fire, zones for political and military regroupment will be established. Such zones were set up in 1954 to facilitate the return of soldiers and the migration of civilians to the North and the South. Part of what is here called "dual negotiation" has already begun in Paris between Hanoi and the United States and may eventually set the terms for their mutual military withdrawal. The terms of the debate between the NLFSVN and the GVN over the form of political reconstruction that will take place have yet to be estab-

"Public Opinion and the War in Vietnam," *American Political Science Review*, *LXI* (June, 1967), 317-33, where the authors found that despite the obvious polemics of the public debate on Vietnam, ". . . few respondents took *consistent* 'dove' or 'hawk' positions. . . . There seemed to be more willingness to see a reduction of the war but, symmetrical with the opposition to major escalation, was an opposition to precipitous withdrawal." p. 321 (Emphasis added).

lished. While the war will probably not be ultimately resolved on the basis of any meaningful cease-fire line, Hanoi-U.S. negotiations will in part involve the question of respecting the DMZ as the 1954 accords provide,[2] as well as mutual agreement to cease the infiltration and military use of Laos as specified in the 1962 agreements. Saigon-Vietcong negotiations will involve the questions of coalition and reunification and will no doubt reflect the strengths and political skills of the various Vietnamese political forces and groups. In addition, the VC have suggested that

> "Pending the reunification of the country, the people in both zones will make joint efforts to oppose foreign invasion and defend the fatherland at the same time (sic) endeavor to expand economic and cultural exchanges. The people in both zones are free to exchange letters, to go from one zone to another and to choose their place of residence."[3]

From the negotiations will come, in the final phase, establishment of a permanent inspection commission to administer the agreements and, perhaps, to supervise arrangements for local and provincial plebiscites. At the same time, both Hanoi and the U. S. will have begun to de-militarize their assistance to the Republic.

The diplomatic scenario suggested above and the various strategic outcomes presented below have several underlying assumptions. First, there can be little doubt that the Vietcong is in South Vietnam to stay, that it is an indigenous force politically aligned with the DRV and supported diplomatically and militarily by the northern regime. VC political cadre in the South have increased from the few hundred who remained behind in 1954, to 45,000 in January 1967, to an estimated 75,000 to 120,000 in March 1968.[4] Indeed, the political mobilization of the population which the presence of increasing numbers of political

---

[2]The fate of the DMZ as a rational political boundary between North and South Vietnam will ultimately have to be determined within the context of reunification. At other times, this area has served as a temporary and expedient boundary between North and South and the current line is close to the Dong Hoi wall built in 1631 to defend the Nguyen domains from the "Lords of the North." See D. G. E. Hall, *A History of Southeast Asia* (London, 1964), pp. 830ff.

[3]"Text of a Policy Statement by the National Liberation Front of South Vietnam," *New York Times,* December 15, 1967, p. 6.

[4]Previous National Intelligence Estimates placed VC political cadre in the South at between 75,000 to 85,000 before Tet. Since then, a revised CIA estimate places the VC presence at between 110,000 to 120,000 political cadre in South Vietnam. See *New York Times,* March 19, 1968, p. 3.

cadre fosters is an integral part of the "people's war." Not without some irony, Mao Tse-tung has stated that "To wish for victory and yet neglect political mobilization is like wishing to 'go south by driving the chariot north,' and the result would be to forfeit victory."[5] As will be evident in the discussion which follows, the Vietcong have stressed, when possible, political mobilization and to some of South Vietnam's population a Viet Minh-Vietcong government and administration have been the only ones they have known. Second, any series of negotiations and agreements must protect those who have committed themselves to the GVN, the Allies, or to a free, non-communist, non-VC South Vietnam. Not only must the means be available to offer people a choice but their ability to choose without reprisal must be defended. Third, it must be fully understood that a coalition government would be as precarious as it would be wise depending upon the degree to which the various political, ethnic, and religious forces in South Vietnam are involved. Neutralist or Communist control of the machinery of the state would be meaningful only in proportion to the diversity such a government would represent. Control of a government composed largely of members of a political and military elite would be control of little more than a few buildings in Saigon. Control of a government reflecting the Vietnamese political spectrum might be as difficult for the communists as it was for Diem in 1954. Indeed, the first quarter of Vietnam's independence has been characterized by precisely this problem. As leaders sought control they eliminated opposition; the more they came to power by this method the less, in fact, they actually controlled. There is little reason to believe that the Communists would be any more successful than Diem in effectively and decisively eliminating the power and influence of the sects, the students, or the Buddhists. Fourth, there is by no means a dearth of appealing leaders who would prove capable of competing on relatively equal footing with their Vietcong counterparts. Souvanna Phouma of Laos came to power, in part, not despite the fact that a relatively strong right and left opposed each other, but because of that confrontation. South Vietnam's neutralists, similarly, may well only become an effective voice when both right and left oppose each other in the *political* arena.

Finally, the milieu of the conflict in Vietnam has changed markedly since both the signing of the Geneva Accords in 1954 and United States entry into the war in force. Red China has suffered both advances and set-backs in its domestic and foreign policies; it is a different kind of

---

[5] *On Protracted War* (Peking, 1966), p. 60.

Southeast Asian power than it was a decade ago. In 1954, the NLF did not exist in the form in which it is found today; it was less significant and less in evidence, too, a decade ago. Time and events have also eroded the efficacy of the ICC and little short of a transplant of vital organs could revive it from its moribund state. On balance, a "restorative" end to the war along the terms of the 1954 agreements may well not be in the interests of United States policy since that solution itself led to conflict and might today simply postpone or only move such conflict westward, into Laos, for example. Indeed, for the United States the war has proven costlier in men, money and international prestige than the planners of the original commitment envisioned, and any solution would have to be made in an effort to prevent other conflicts requiring similar involvements. However, the United States also confronts both a stronger Southeast Asia and South Vietnam than it did five or ten years ago. Any solution to the war in Vietnam should, therefore, involve a clear assessment of the strengths and weaknessess of the whole region as well as of South Vietnam itself. Negotiations, even more than a policy of military victory, make positions of strength essential to a solution of "the second Vietnam crisis" which would prevent another generation seeking such solutions to what might then be labeled the "first Southeast Asian crisis."

STRATEGIC OUTCOMES OF THE WAR

There is little doubt that some areas of South Vietnam have been under Viet Minh-Vietcong control since the end of World War II. In these areas, it can be assumed, the Vietcong have accomplished their most sophisticated political mobilization of the population and government to the Vietnamese living there means government by the Vietcong. Map 1 depicts the military situation in Vietnam in 1954 and indicates the zones of Viet Minh control. These zones roughly correspond to the Camau peninsula, the western border of Kien Phong and Kien Tuong provinces (the Plain of Reeds), the northwestern border of Tay Ninh province, portions of the coastal area of Phuoc Tuy province, the PMS highland area north of Kontum, and "the street without joy." Since 1960, these areas have also been characterized by the most intense fighting of the war and the least success in pacification. The tree lines of the delta bordering the Plain, the swamps, and Cambodia are infamous, as is the Black Widow mountain in Tay Ninh, Ap Bac, War Zones "C," "D," and the "Iron Triangle," and the Marine Corps chain of bases

MILITARY SITUATION IN INDOCHINA AS OF MAY 1954 AND REGROUPING AFTER PARTITION

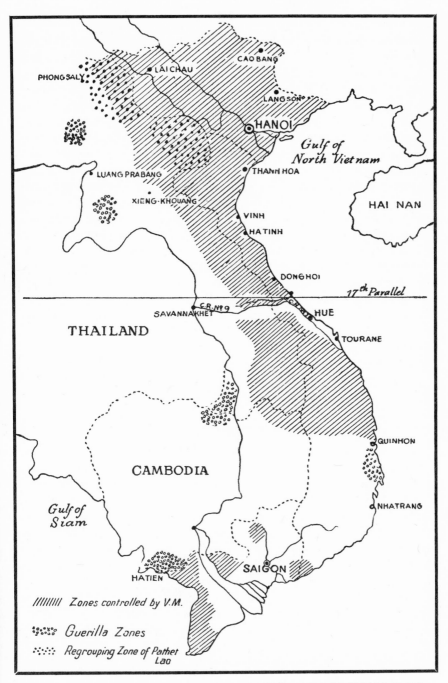

From: Nguyen phut Tan, A MODERN HISTORY OF VIET-NAM (1802-1954), Appendix. Saigon: Khai-Tri, 1964.

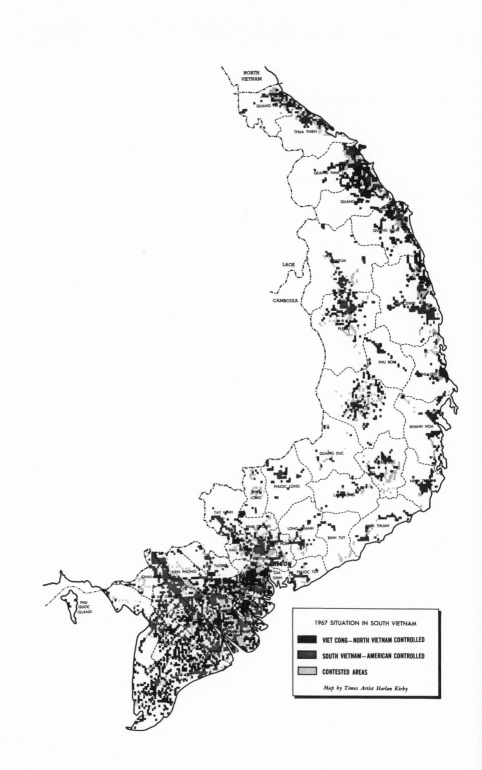

1967 SITUATION IN SOUTH VIETNAM

VIET CONG — NORTH VIETNAM CONTROLLED

SOUTH VIETNAM — AMERICAN CONTROLLED

CONTESTED AREAS

Map by Times Artist Harlan Kirby

from Khesanh to Rockpile to Con Thien, Pleiku, and the "street without joy." These areas have produced costly victories from Operation Starlight to Cedar Falls and Junction City, but they have not been the scene of any major pacification "success stories." Map 2 depicts the military situation at the end of 1967, and it does not differ very much from the situation 13 years earlier. The areas of strong Vietcong control and the largest number of "contested" areas still fall within the zones described above. Indeed, the Vietcong's summary of the military situation in 1961, for example, is strikingly similar to their predecessor's summary seven years earlier. The relative stability of the military fronts during the period from 1954-1961 reflects the fact that there was less warfare going on than there was political mobilization. This period was characterized by the reinfiltration of Vietcong agents to the South and Hanoi's general reluctance to expand the tempo of actual combat beyond what the strategy of political mobilization permitted. This was also a period when Diem made sorties against Vietcong-controlled areas but was never able to gain firm control over the zones. Vietcong who defected in 1961-1962, in part, gave as their reason for changing sides the reluctance of Hanoi to authorize anything beyond political action among the population. These areas, then, are probably the most stable in Vietnam today in terms of continuity of government and political organization. An offensive, furthermore, like the one at Tet could not have been carried out unless such "secure" areas still existed to base and supply VC-NVA forces.

Based upon the assumption that such zones of Vietcong control and influence do exist and are part of the permanent politico-military landscape in South Vietnam, three models of strategic outcomes of the war can be postulated.

1. Establishment of Re-Groupment Zones

This model postulates that the DMZ, as defined in the 1954 Geneva Accords, would be respected and the Vietcong and GVN forces would re-group to those areas where they are in clear control as was the case in 1954. This would mean essentially that past and current military fronts would be stabilized by a cease-fire agreement and that responsibility for the truce administration and eventual government administration would fall directly to the Vietcong and the GVN in those areas where they are strongest. Population would be allowed free access to each of these zones, presumably, for the purpose of returning to their homes if they so desired. Under this model by far the largest part of Vietnam's territory would be considered "contested" and it is in these areas that the population must be assured an opportunity to determine their loyalties. These contested areas, too, tend to also be the ones where indigenous, non-government, non-Vietcong forces are strong (e.g., the Tan Dai Viet in III Corps, FULRO in the highlands, and the Revolutionary Dai Viet and VNQDD in I Corps). Given the time and the incentive to do so, these political forces may well pose themselves as an alternative to either the Saigon government or the Vietcong as the Hoa Hao in the Delta did from 1940-1955, and from 1962 to the present. In any event, a joint national commission would have to administer such local and provincial plebiscites, while the established local communities would be able to use their elected village and hamlet councils to administer local affairs as was the case in Cyprus after the 1959 settlement there. Geographically, this outcome would look similar to the maps previously presented.

2. International Buffering

This outcome assumes that North Vietnam has failed in its original goal of reunification " . . . a failure the North Vietnamese have in fact repeatedly conceded since 1956—but the government emerging in Saigon from the war is not unfriendly to Hanoi. . . . ."[6] Thus, both parties might be willing to accept a peace-making machinery that would involve regulation of both foreign military withdrawal as well as the maintenance of a parallel strategic presence to assure peace. This might then involve two American bases at Da Nang and Cam Ranh, two North Vietnamese garrisons in the Camau peninsula and north of Kontum, as well as an international commission to administer the DMZ. In this scenario the United Nations might prove to be the most versatile institution through which the legitimation or rationalization of withdrawal could proceed.[7] It has not proved incapable in the past of supervising such withdrawals, registering population, and administering refugee programs of the sort that would be needed in postwar Vietnam. And use of the UN would not be without propaganda value or precedent for both sides. Future assistance, too, to both North and South Vietnam might also be best channeled through such an international organization. Indeed, the UN might be able to avoid negotiations of the variety that took place in Korea. There, US casualties were greater after negotiations began than before, and, if the casualty rate during the April bickering for a suitable site for Vietnam peace talks is any indication, the same phenomenon

[6]See "There Is Going to Be A Silence . . . ," in Bernard Fall, *Last Reflections on a War* (New York, 1967), pp. 281, and *passim*.
[7]See Connor Cruise O'Brien, "How the UN Could End the War," *New York Review of Books* (28 March 1968), 22-25.

may re-occur. The current negotiations in Paris are also likely to be conducted in the context of "talk and fight" diplomacy, with each side seeking to improve its position by military victories, as recent captured documents from Hanoi and pronouncements on American military operations suggest. Putting the matter before the UN might avoid the tensions, petty squabbles, and breakdowns inherent in bilateral negotiations.

3. Coup-to-Coalition

This model assumes that peace could not be achieved (other than total GVN victory over the Vietcong or vice versa) unless the present government leadership in Saigon changes. A military government, dedicated to the defeat of the Vietcong, could not pose as the vanguard of neutralism nor would the Vietcong negotiate and respect political concessions made by its foes who may not be altogether legitimate to non-Vietcong Vietnamese as well. Recent public statements by Thieu, Ky and Foreign Minister Tran van Do, in addition, indicate the strong GVN sentiments against coalition and recent GVN arrests of those political figures advocating such a development tend to bear this out. Thus, Thieu and Ky would have to be replaced (but not necessarily the elected assemblies or the April Constitution) by a neutralist figure who would then negotiate with the Vietcong. For example, former head of state, General Nguyen Khanh, called for "a national reconciliation of South Vietnam without foreign interference." He said that he would favor giving the National Liberation Front "a role measured by the support it might win in an election."[8] In this scenario the military front would be stabilized by a cease-fire agreement, but not by the maintenance of any foreign military presence. Indeed, part of neutralism's appeal in Vietnam may well be its anti-American and generally anti-foreign bent. Thus, coalition government would have to be the order of the day with local and provincial elections for representatives to councils and national assemblies. Such elections would invariably reflect the diversity of the political system in the South and provide incentives for villages and political groups alike to organize themselves. Indeed, the prospects of election and coalition provide a strong imperative: the future of government in South Vietnam will depend upon who organizes its politics.

---

[8]Cited in John L. Hess, "Vietnam Exiles Split on Tactics," *New York Times* (12 May 1968), p. 16.

CHAPTER 10. METAGAME ANALYSIS OF VIETNAM POLICY

By Nigel Howard*

Against the background of relatively little success achieved by traditional disciplines in identifying ways and means to resolve conflicts, the author probes a fresh approach. He develops "metagame" analysis. He is able to suggest how deadlocks (stalemates) can be avoided, and desirable cooperative solutions reached when emphasis is shifted onto policies rather than actions. He simulates the Vietnam conflict and applies his new concepts of rationality. Ed.

During the past two years the author, working on a project for the U. S. Arms Control and Disarmament Agency, has pursued two research objectives. The first has been to develop the theory of metagames, which is a new approach to n-person variable-sum games. The second objective has been to develop a method by which these theoretical results can be used *by laymen* to analyze *actual real-life political situations.*[1]

In this paper, the method for analyzing real-life political situations is

*The author is associated with the Management Science Center, University of Pennsylvania. His research was carried out under a project supported by the U. S. Arms Control and Disarmament Agency.

[1] Most of this research has not yet been published. In references (1) and (2) the theory of metagames was presented while it was at an early stage of development. It has since been discussed in references (3) and (4). The author plans to publish an up-dated account, in General Systems, Vol. XIV (1969), ed. L. von Bertalanffy and A. Rapoport, Society for General Systems Research, Box 228, Bedford, Mass. 01730. A second paper is being published in Volume 9, *Papers, Peace Research Society (International).*

applied to the Vietnam conflict. The method can be considered on its own, independently of the theoretical work from which it is derived. Nevertheless, we shall begin with a sketch of this theoretical background before proceeding to analyze the situation in Vietnam.

METAGAME THEORY

The Metagame Tree

The game of Prisoners' Dilemma (Figure 1) has only one (Nash) equilibrium (an outcome such that no player can gain by unilaterally moving away from it). It is the outcome (d,d).[2] Yet if we are interested in which outcomes of a game may be *stable,* we find experimentally that (c,c) may be stable as well as (d,d).

FIGURE 1. Prisoner's Dilemma and its 2-Metagame

Player 2

		c	d
Player 1	c	3,3	1,4
	d	4,1	(2,2)

	c/c	d/d	c/d	d/c
c	3,3	1,4	3,3	1,4
d	4,1	(2,2)	2,2	4,1

Note: The policy "x against c, y against d" is represented by "x/y".

Metagame theory explains this by taking into consideration the possible reactions of players to each other's strategy-choices (c or d). If player 2 (the column-player) can react to player 1's choice, he must make his own choice in knowledge of 1's choice. This gives rise to the 2-metagame (Figure 1). In this game we call 2's choices "policies." A policy is a function from 1's choices to 2's choices. It represents a possible pattern of reaction by 2 to player 1's choices.

In the 2-metagame we find that $(d, d/d)$ is the only equilibrium, giving rise to the outcome (d,d) as before. The next step, therefore, is to form the 1-2-metagame (Figure 2). Here, player 1 reacts to 2's reaction to his (1's) strategy-choice. He has 16 "policies" (functions from 2's *policies* to his own strategy-choice).

---

[2]Note that we use the word "outcome" to refer to a pair of *strategies,* not a pair of *payoffs,* as often used in game theory.

FIGURE 2. The 1-2-Metagame of Prisoner's Dilemma

	c/c	d/d	c/d	d/c
c/c/c/c	3,3	1,4	3,3	1,4
d/d/d/d	4,1	(2,2)	2,2	4,1
d/d/d/c	4,1	2,2	2,2	1,4
d/d/c/d	4,1	2,2	(3,3)	4,1
d/d/c/c	4,1	2,2	3,3	1,4
d/c/d/d	4,1	1,4	2,2	4,1
d/c/d/c	4,1	1,4	2,2	1,4
d/c/c/d	4,1	1,4	3,3	4,1
d/c/c/c	4,1	1,4	3,3	1,4
c/d/d/d	3,3	2,2	2,2	4,1
c/d/d/c	3,3	2,2	2,2	1,4
c/d/c/d	3,3	2,2	(3,3)	4,1
c/d/c/c	3,3	2,2	3,3	1,4
c/c/d/d	3,3	1,4	2,2	4,1
c/c/d/c	3,3	1,4	2,2	1,4
c/c/c/d	3,3	1,4	3,3	4,1

Note: "w/x/y/z" represents the policy "w against c/c, x against d/d, y against c/d, z against d/c."

In the 1-2-metagame we find three equilibria, two of which give rise to the outcome (*d,d*) as before, while the third gives rise to the (*c,c*) outcome which is also experimentally stable.

Now we could have started by forming the 1-metagame first, then the 2-1-metagame. By symmetry, this would not have made any difference in this case, but in general it may make a difference. Also, there is no reason to stop at the 1-2- or the 2-1-metagame. We should go on to consider, in general, the k_1-...-k_r-metagame, where each k_i is either "1" or "2", and *r* is any positive integer. The reason for this is that, though we can be sure that the process of players reacting to each other's reactions to reactions to . . . etc., will not be carried to infinity, we cannot set any predetermined limit to how far this process will be carried.

The process of constructing metagames can be generalized to the case of an n-person game as follows. Given a game *G,* with players 1,...,*n,* we construct n *first-stage* metagames *kG* (for *k=1...,n*). In the game *kG* (called the "*k*-metagame") player *k* chooses a "policy", a *function* from the strategy-choices of the other players to his own strategy-choice, while the other players choose strategies as in the game

G. Next, n² *second-stage* metagames *jkG* (for *j,k=1,...,n*) are constructed, the metagame *jkG* being constructed from *kG* just as *kG* was constructed from *G.* And so on.

Hence, the mathematical object studied in metagame theory is the infinite tree of metagames shown in Figure 3. By using this tree as a model of the situation originally modelled by the game *G,* we take account of players' reactions to each other's moves.

FIGURE 3. The Tree of Metagames

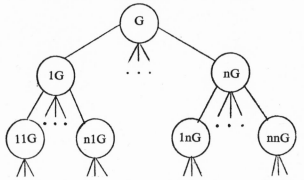

Note. In our example we have considered a so-called "pure-strategy" game of Prisoner's Dilemma. Had we wished, we could have considered a "mixed-strategy" game instead. We simply replace the pure-strategy game *G* with a mixed-strategy game. In the metagame *kG* where *G* is a mixed-strategy game, player *k* chooses a "policy" which is now any function from the others' *mixed* strategies to his own *mixed* strategy. And so on.

QUESTIONS AND ANSWERS CONCERNING THE METAGAME TREE

In order to discuss the tree of Figure 3, let us first state some definitions.

Rational outcomes. An outcome of the game *G* is said to be *rational for player k* if it is such that, given the others' strategy-choices, he cannot reach an outcome he prefers to the given outcome. For example, we see from Figure 1 that *(d,c)* and *(d,d)* are the rational outcomes for player 1 of the game of Prisoner's Dilemma.

(Nash) equilibria. A Nash equilibrium may now be defined simply as an outcome which is *rational for all players.*

Metarational Outcomes. An outcome of the game *G* is said to be *metarational for player k from the metagame $k_1...k_rG$* if it is derived from an outcome of $k_1...k_rG$ which is *rational for player k*. For example, we see from Figure 1 that $(d,c/c)$, $(d,d/d)$, $(c,c/d)$ *and* $(d,d/c)$ are the outcomes of $2G$ which are rational for player 1. Hence (d,c), (d,d) and (c,c) are player 1's metarational outcomes from $2G$.

Metaequilibria. An outcome of the game G is said to be a *metaequilibrium from $k_1...k_rG$* if it derives from an equilibrium of $k_1...k_rG$. For example, (c,c) is a metaequilibrium from $12G$ in our example because it is derived from $(d/d/c/d, c/d)$, which from Figure 2 is an equilibrium of $12G$.

We focus attention particularly on metarational outcomes, since these are the outcomes which may be made the "best attainable" for a player by a certain type of policies pursued by the other players—this "type" being defined as the set of policies available in a particular metagame.

We now ask and answer certain questions.

Q. 1. Are the *rational* outcomes for a given player *metarational* for him from every metagame?

Ans. Yes. In fact, a metarational outcome for a player from a metagame H is metarational for him from every metagame *based on H* (i.e., from every descendant of H in the metagame tree).

Q. 2. Do metaequilibria have the same "descendance" property?

Ans. Yes.

Q. 3. Do metarational outcomes "converge"? That is, is there a point in the metagame tree after which no additional metarational outcomes for a player can be found by going further?

Ans. Yes. When a metagame $k_1...k_rG$ is *complete* (i.e., every player's name occurs in the title) all its descendants have the same set of metarational outcomes for every player as it itself does.

Q. 4. Are metarational outcomes ever affected by a player's name appearing *more than once* in the title of a metagame?

Ans. No. The metarational outcomes for each player from $k_1...k_rG$ are the same as from the *prime representative* of $k_1...k_rG$—which is the metagame obtained by striking out all but the *last occurrence* of each player's name from the title of $k_1...k_rG$.

Q. 5. It follows that the *complete prime* metagames (in which every player's name occurs in the title just once, and of which there must be $n!$, corresponding to the $n!$ ways of ordering the names of the players) together yield all the metarational outcomes for any player. Can we characterize the outcomes which are metarational for a given player from *every one* of these complete prime metagames?

Ans. Yes. Such outcomes are called *symmetric metarational* for the player. The following are alternative necessary and sufficient conditions for an outcome *s* to be symmetric metarational for player *k*.

(a) *s* is metarational for *k* from every branch of the tree (i.e., from *some* metagame based on *any* metagame in the tree).

(b) s is metarational *for* k from *some* metagame based on the game *kG*.

(c) *s* is metarational for *k* from every complete metagame.

(d) There exists a joint strategy of the other players such that, if they choose that joint strategy, player *k* cannot obtain an outcome which is preferred by him to *s*. This joint strategy of the other players is called an *inescapable sanction against k for s*. For example, in Prisoner's Dilemma we see that (*c,c*) is symmetric metarational for player 1 because 2's strategy *d* is an inescapable sanction against 1 for (*c,c*): if 2 chooses *d*, 1 cannot obtain an outcome he prefers to (*c,c*).

When we come to applying the theory, we shall be particularly interested in *symmetric* metarationality, which is the "strongest" kind of metarationality.

Q. 6. A Nash equilibrium is by definition an outcome which is *rational for all players*. Is it true that an outcome which is *metarational for all players* from a given metagame is a metaequilibrium from that metagame?

Ans. In general, this is true only in the case of a *two-person game*. However, it is always true that an outcome which is metarational for every player from a given metagame is a metaequilibrium from *another* metagame, a descendant of the first.

ALTERNATIVE METHOD OF ANALYZING PRISONER'S DILEMMA

Consider the game of Prisoner's Dilemma shown in Figure 1. Suppose we wish to know whether (*c,c*) is *rational* for player 1; if it is not, whether it is *symmetric metarational* for him, and if it is symmetric metarational, what kind of policy by player 2 would make it the "best attainable" outcome for him (player 1).

In order to answer these questions, all we need is the information in Figure 4. Here the outcomes of the game are represented by columns. The outcomes other than (*c,c*) have been bi-partitioned into two sets according to whether they are "preferred" or "not preferred" by player 1 to (*c,c*). The outcomes are represented by columns. From the arrow

FIGURE 4.   Inescapable Sanction in Prisoner's Dilemma

	Preferred Outcomes		Not Preferred Outcomes	
Player 1's strategy	d	c	d	c
Player 2's strategy	c	c	d	d

leading left, we see that player 1 can unilaterally improve his position starting from (c,c), so that (c,c) is not *rational* for him. From the arrow leading right to a set of outcomes from which 1 cannot escape (i.e., to an *inescapable sanction* against 1 for (c,c)), we see that (c,c) is *symmetric metarational* for 1; and the inescapable sanction which makes it so gives us a description of the kind of policy which would make it the "best attainable" outcome for him. For this, 2's policy must be that if 1 will accept the "offer" of (c,c), this will be the outcome; but if 1 will not accept this, 2 will apply the sanction by choosing his strategy d.

The procedure followed here is essentially the method by which we shall analyze the Vietnam conflict. We shall take particular outcomes which are of interest, and ask concerning each player in turn whether the others can influence him to accept that outcome—and if so, how they can do this. That is, we shall look to see whether the outcome is rational for the player, and if it is not, we shall look for inescapable sanctions which might lead him to accept it. In doing this, we shall in fact (though this is not proved rigorously here) be investigating whether the outcome is symmetric metarational for him in the metagame tree.

Before going on to this, however, we must stress two points which arise from the paucity of assumptions used in Figure 4.

(1) In order to apply our theory and method, we do *not* need to assume numerical "payoffs" obtained by the players from the outcomes of the game. We only need to assume a general "preference relation" for each player over the set of outcomes. In fact, we can replace "payoff functions" with general reflexive preference relations "not preferred." That is, for each player associate with each outcome a set of "not preferred" outcomes. This set must include the given outcome (an outcome is always "not preferred" to itself) but otherwise the set can be chosen arbitrarily. It is thus allowable that, of three outcomes *a,b,c, a* may be preferred to *b, b* to *c,* and *c* to *a.* Thus, preferences need not be transitive. Indeed, we may allow *a* to be preferred to *b* while simul-

taneously *b* is preferred to *a*! An interpretation of this would be that a players' preferences *depend on the current outcome*.

(2) In Figure 4 nothing is assumed about player 2's preferences. Thus our theory and method are independent of all assumptions about players' knowledge of or beliefs about *each others' payoffs*. We are analyzing the effect on one's behavior of knowing *one's own* payoffs. This, however, means that while we can find the sanctions which, if they were credible, would make a given outcome acceptable by a given player, we can say nothing inside the theory about whether these sanctions *will* be credible. This important question is left to the judgment of the person using the method.

THE VIETNAM CONFLICT

In applying our technique to the Vietnam conflict, we begin by making a list of the main issues involved.

List of Issues

1. U.S. bombing in North Vietnam
2. North Vietnamese (N.V.N.) infiltration into the South.
3. South Vietnamese (S.V.N.) and Vietcong (N.L.F.) acceptance of some peaceful governmental arrangement in the South (e.g., a coalition, an election).
4. U.S. military withdrawal from S. Vietnam.
5. N.V.N. military withdrawal from S. Vietnam.
6. Continuation of warfare in the South by the U.S.A., S.V.N., N.L.F. and N.V.N.

From this list we extract the names of all decision-making parties. These will be the players. We extract the names US, SVN, NLF and NVN. Next, we extract from the list enough "yes/no options" to represent the decisions which in the list of issues are controlled by the players —the decisions by virtue of which the players appear in that list as "decision-making parties." We extract the following "yes/no" options for each player.

US: (1) BOMB (in North)
(2) FIGHT (continue war in South)
(3) WITHDRAW
SVN: (4) FIGHT (continue war in South)
(5) SETTLE (be willing to accept peaceful settlement in South)

NLF: (6) FIGHT
      (7) SETTLE
NVN: (8) INFILTRATE
      (9) FIGHT
     (10) WITHDRAW

When the list of options is drawn up it may happen that a value of
one option *implies* a value of another—in that we would assume that if a
player chooses one, he necessarily must (or must not) choose the
other. We make a note of such cases. Here we shall assume the following *implications* between options.

$$3 \;\rightarrow\; \text{not } 2 \;\rightarrow\; \text{not } 1;$$
$$9 \;\rightarrow\; 8;$$
$$10 \;\rightarrow\; \text{not } 9;$$
$$10 \;\rightarrow\; \text{not } 8.$$

A *strategy* for a particular player is now represented by a column of
1's and 0's, where "1" stands for "yes" (the option is taken). Thus
the first three entries in the column of Figure 5 represent the U.S. strategy of ceasing to bomb the North and withdrawing militarily from the
South. The whole column represents an *outcome* of the game. We interpret it as the outcome which a "negotiated settlement" of the conflict
would require. An asterisk is placed next to the value (0 or 1) of an
option if that value is implied by the value of some other option in the
outcome.

FIGURE 5. The "Negotiated Settlement" Outcome
US:

BOMB	0*
FIGHT	0*
WITHDRAW	1

SVN:

FIGHT	0
SETTLE	1

NLF:

FIGHT	0
SETTLE	1

NVN:

INFILTRATE	0*
FIGHT	0*
WITHDRAW	1

At this point we have defined a four-person game which rather crudely represents the Vietnam conflict. But we have not yet made any assumptions about the preferences of the players between outcomes of the game. Now the game has 320 outcomes. To state all preferences between these would be a lengthy process. Instead, we proceed by stating a specific *question* which we wish the analysis to answer, then making the minimum assumptions necessary to answer that question. This method has the added advantage that we can see exactly which assumptions lead to each answer.

Figure 6 shows how in this way we answer the question: how can South Vietnam be influenced to accept the "negotiated settlement" shown in Figure 5?

FIGURE 6. Sanctions Against SVN for a Settlement

US:	Preferred by SVN				Not Preferred by SVN
Bomb	–	–	–	0*	0*
Fight	1	–	–	0*	0
Withdraw	0*	–	–	1	–
SVN:					
Fight	1	1	1	0	–
Settle	0	0	0	1	–
NLF:					
Fight	–	0	–	0	1
Settle	–	–	–	1	–
NVN:					
Infiltrate	–	–	–	0*	1*
Fight	–	–	0	0*	1
Withdraw	–	–	–	1	0*

(Ω denotes the bracketed group of columns)

Note: The symbol "–" stands for "either/or"—the option may or may not be taken.

A column in Figure 6 represents a *class* of outcomes obtained by filling in the *blanks* in the column (represented by "–") with 0's and 1's in every possible way. Each column is assigned to "preferred" or "not preferred" by South Vietnam *to* the settlement. Thus the following assumptions have been made.[3]

---

[3]In these assumptions we are really interpreting the "settlement" as one which would be seen by the SVN as so counter to their interests that any fighting which held out some hope for them would be preferred.

First Column: If the US continues to fight, the SVN, by fighting and refusing a settlement, are sure to obtain a preferred outcome. *Second and Third Columns:* The same strategy will guarantee them a preferred outcome *whatever the US does* if either the NLF or the NVN *do not* "fight". *Fifth Column:* If the US does not fight, but both the NLF and the NVN do fight, the outcome is bound to be "not preferred" by the SVN.

In Figure 6 the "not preferred" columns (in this example there is only one) have *all blanks* outside the set Ω—which is the set of options open to the players other than South Vietnam. Thus the outcomes assigned to the "not preferred" side are *inescapable sanctions* against South Vietnam; that is, if the other players choose in accordance with one of these outcomes, South Vietnam can only obtain outcomes which are not preferred by her to the settlement. The "preferred" columns have *no blanks* outside the set Ω. Thus if the other players choose in accordance with one of the "preferred" outcomes, this will *not* be an inescapable sanction against South Vietnam, since there exists a strategy for South Vietnam by which, in this eventuality, she can reach a preferred outcome.

The "preferred" and "not preferred" outcomes together "complete" the set Ω; that is, every combination of the options in the set Ω occurs either on the "not preferred" side (so that it is a sanction) or on the "preferred" side (so that it is not a sanction). The analysis is thus complete because the set Ω is "complete"; that is, we know that we have formed *all* the sanctions against South Vietnam.

The assumptions made thus suffice to answer two questions: Is the settlement *rational* for South Vietnam so that she cannot by unilateral action improve her position? If it is not rational for her, is it *symmetric metarational,* so that the others have an inescapable sanction by which she may be induced to comply?

To answer the first question, we look to see whether the "Ω-part" of the settlement (i.e., the combination of Ω-options which occurs in the settlement outcome) appears on the "preferred" or "not preferred" side. *Since it appears on the preferred side* (in both the 2nd and 3rd columns) *the settlement is not rational for the SVN.* They can improve their position by fighting and refusing to settle.

We look, therefore, for inescapable sanctions, the fear of which might nevertheless induce the SVN to accept the settlement. We find that for an effective sanction the SVN must fear that if they defect from the settlement, the NLF and NVN will resume fighting, but the US will not.

> *Note:* The analysis finds all the sanctions which *exist*. However, it tells us nothing about whether a sanction is *credible*—as it must be to be effective. In this case, it seems the sanction might be credible. But we must expect at times to find sanctions which are obviously not credible. At the moment, this is an extra-theoretical matter which must be judged intuitively.

This stage of the analysis is now concluded. We have answered one question, making the minimum assumptions necessary to answer it. We could, of course, go on to further stages in which we ask further questions. By defining the "given outcome" (in this case the "settlement" outcome) differently, and choosing different Ω-sets, we can investigate how various players or "coalitions" of players can be induced to accept various outcomes.

At each stage it is perfectly clear that *we get out of the analysis no more than we put in*. We have stripped away the air of "magic" which often invests the deductions made from a model. Finally, these deductions reduce to a simple matter of stating an assumption which—since it assumes *no more* than the conclusion drawn from it, and, of course, cannot assume less—is actually *equivalent* to that conclusion. The theoretical contribution lies entirely in "phrasing the questionnaire"— i.e., in the standard form of the questions which we ask.

So far, however, only a tiny part of the model has been explored. Our method is analogous to the exploration of a large, dark warehouse using a tiny flashlight. When we ask a question and answer it, we direct our light to a small area which we have pre-selected. But in this way, using our present model, it would take rather long for us to see much of the warehouse! Had we set up a model with more detailed options—for example, had we split up the military options into various types and levels of military activity—our answer would be more detailed but would take still more time to obtain.

In the next section, therefore, we drastically simplify our model so as to try to see the "shape" of the Vietnam problem as a whole. The method by which we shall simplify our present model will indicate precisely how the present model may be regarded as itself a "simplification" of the more detailed models we could construct.

THE SIMPLIFIED MODEL

We select from the set of strategies available to each player in our previous model, a proper subset of those strategies. Then we construct a model in which each player has a single option—whether or not to choose a strategy which falls within that selected proper subset of his strategies.

A good choice of subsets in our case would seem to be as follows. The "fight" option appears to be the most important for each player. We, therefore, select, for each player, that subset of his strategies in which the "fight" option is taken.

We now define for each player a *new* option called FIGHT. For this option to be taken means simply that *some* strategy involving "continuation of warfare in the South" is chosen. For our new option not to be taken means that *no* such strategy is chosen.

We now proceed to analyze this simplified model.

(i) In Figure 7 we look at how each player might be influenced to accept a "settlement"—which now corresponds to no player choosing the FIGHT option. We see that the settlement is *rational* for the US, but not for any other player. The sanctions which must, therefore, be feared by the players if the settlement is to be stable are: the SVN must fear that if they re-start the fighting the NLF and NVN will fight but the US will not; while the NLF and NVN must each believe that if *they* restart the fighting, the SVN and *also* the US will fight. This points to the danger that, even if these sanctions were credible, the SVN might start fighting and blame the NLF and/or NVN; or that one of the Communist forces would start fighting and blame the SVN. In addition, if the "settlement" involved US *withdrawal,* the problem would have to be met of making credible to the Communist forces that US forces, having withdrawn, would be likely to return and fight after all.

(ii) Next, consider the outcome in which all parties choose to continue FIGHTing. One conclusion concerning this outcome is so simple that we do not show it in a figure. We assume the outcome is *rational for all players*—i.e., a Nash equilibrium—since we assume that for each player, unilaterally ceasing to fight would be "not preferred." On this assumption, to "escape" from this outcome will require some kind of joint, cooperative action by the players.

In Figure 8 we analyze the outcome from the viewpoint of two coalitions—the US/SVN coalition and the NVN/NLF coalition. In dealing with coalitions, our method is to regard a coalition as if it were a single

FIGURE 7. Sanctions Against Each Player for a Settlement

US Preferences

US:	Fight	0	—
SVN:	Fight	0	0
NLF:	Fight	0	0
NVN:	Fight	0	0

SVN Preferences

US:	Fight	1	—	—	0	0
SVN:	Fight	1	1	1	0	—
NLF:	Fight	—	0	—	0	1
NVN:	Fight	—	—	0	0	1

NLF Preferences

US:	Fight	0	—	0	1
SVN:	Fight	—	0	0	1
NLF:	Fight	1	1	0	—
NVN:	Fight	—	—	0	—

NVN Preferences

US:	Fight	0	—	0	1
SVN:	Fight	—	0	0	1
NLF:	Fight	—	—	0	—
NVN:	Fight	1	1	0	—

Note: These difficulties in ensuring the *stability* of a settlement may also be interpreted as difficulties involved in *reaching* it.

player. However, an outcome "preferred" by the coalition has to be *preferred by all its members;* all other outcomes are "not preferred" by the coalition—even though they may be preferred by *some* of its members.

The result is again a simple one. From Figure 8 we see that the outcome is *rational for both coalitions;* we may say it is a *Nash equilibrium for these coalitions.* Thus forming *these* coalitions will not enable the players to "escape" from continuation of the war. Joint "cooperative" action of some other kind is required.

FIGURE 8. The Nash Equilibrium at Continuation of the War

US + SVN Preferences

US:	Fight	1	–
SVN:	Fight	1	–
NLF:	Fight	1	1
NVN:	Fight	1	1

NLF + NVN Preferences

US:	Fight	1	1
SVN:	Fight	1	1
NLF:	Fight	1	–
NVN:	Fight	1	–

(iii) In Figure 9, we look at the same outcome from the viewpoint of a US/NVN "coalition". The question being asked here is—can these two players move to an outcome which they jointly prefer, and if so, are there any sanctions by which the others can dissuade them?

FIGURE 9. Sanctions Against a US/NVN "Coalition"

US + NVN Preferences

US:	Fight	0	0	1	–	–	
SVN:	Fight	0	1	1	1	0	$\Big\}\Omega$
NLF:	Fight	0	1	1	0	1	
NVN:	Fight	0	0	1	–	–	

The assumption in Figure 9 is that the coalition can unilaterally move to a preferred outcome by both members ceasing to fight. The sanctions which they might fear are that either the SVN or NLF, but not both, would cease to fight. The assumption used in writing these sanctions is, of course, that if such a sanction were applied, then whatever the US and NVN jointly chose to do, *one* of them (not necessarily both) would be in a "not preferred" position.

Intuitively, however, these sanctions are not very credible, since they would involve one of the South Vietnamese forces failing to respond to an attack by the other. We may, therefore, conclude that the outcome is *not* likely to be stable against a US/NVN "coalition". However, of course, since we have previously assumed that the outcome *is* a Nash equilibrium, the joint action required for the US/NVN "coalition" to move away from the outcome would necessitate mutual trust and/or firm and enforceable agreements between the US and NVN. We investigate this next.

(iv) In Figure 10 we look at the outcome in which only the SVN and NLF are fighting. We ask whether each player could be induced to accept this, and if so, how they could be induced. We see that on our assumptions the outcome is *rational* for the SVN and NLF, so that there is no problem as regards these players. Both the US and the NVN, however, would be tempted to re-start the fighting.

Looking at the sanctions which might dissuade them, we may suppose that for the US the sanctions in which the SVN cease fighting are certainly not credible; but the sanction in which the NLF continue fighting and the NVN also re-start fighting is quite credible. Similarly there is a credible sanction to dissuade NVN from breaking this "cease-fire".

FIGURE 10. Sanctions for a Cease-Fire Between US and NVN

US Preferences

US: Fight	0	1	1	0	–	–	–	
SVN: Fight	0	1	1	1	–	0	0	}Ω
NLF: Fight	0	0	–	1	1	1	–	
NVN: Fight	0	–	0	0	1	–	1	

SVN Preferences

US: Fight	0	0
SVN: Fight	1	–
NLF: Fight	1	1
NVN: Fight	0	0

NLF Preferences

US: Fight	0	0
SVN: Fight	1	1
NLF: Fight	1	–
NVN: Fight	0	0

NVN Preferences

US: Fight	0	–		0	1	
SVN: Fight	–	0		1	1	}Ω
NLF: Fight	–	–		1	–	
NVN: Fight	1	1		0	–	

This outcome—involving a reduction in military activity by both the NVN and the US—thus seems quite likely. If levels of reduction could be agreed to by these players, the credible threat of a "non-preferred" situation if the agreement were violated might be sufficient to keep it stable.

In conclusion, we emphasize—what is really apparent from the nature of the method—that all the "conclusions" depend on the assumptions made concerning preferences. The method does not give any guidance concerning which assumptions to make—i.e., we have no theory as to how preferences arise. Preferences are data, arising from outside the model. The method is thus really one by which the user can set down and analyze *his own* assumptions concerning the situation. Furthermore, of course, there is no reason to suppose that preferences are static; we might, for instance, try assuming that once the *US ceases fighting,* her preferences will change in the direction of giving less preference to oucomes which would involve her starting to fight again. This would alter the assumptions in Figures 7 and 10—though not in 8 or 9.[4] Such assumptions could also be made for other parties, of course.

REFERENCES

(1) Howard, N., "The Theory of Metagames," *General Systems,* Vol. 11, pp. 167-168; 1966.

(2) ——————, "The Mathematics of Metagames," *General Systems,* Vol. 11, pp. 187-200; 1966.

(3) Rapoport, A., "Escape From Paradox," *Scientific American,* July, 1967, pp. 50-56.

(4) Ackoff, R. L. and M.W. Sasieni, *Fundamentals of Operations Research,* John Wiley and Sons, New York, 1968.

---

[4]Recall that we make no assumption that preferences are *ordinal;* hence we are free to assume, as suggested here, that preferences *depend on the current outcome.*

CHAPTER 11. NOTES ON POLICIES, GAMES, META-GAMES, AND VIETNAM

By Thomas C. Schelling*

In this paper, the author critically evaluates Howard's new concepts. He makes an important contribution in demonstrating how by assuming successive rather than simultaneous credulity, the four-party Vietnam conflict simulated by Howard can be reduced to a two-party coalition conflict. With one coalition headed by the U.S., and the other by North Vietnam, the application of Howard's new concepts can be extended— should these concepts be found relevant and valid. Ed.

Mr. Howard's paper implies, and his oral presentation emphasized, that to achieve a four-party cease-fire is difficult in the game he has described, because it requires the United States to persuade South Vietnam (SVN) that the United States will not fight, even if South Vietnam faces two opponents, while "simultaneously" persuading North Vietnam (NVN) that the US will. Making these contradictory commitments simultaneously credible to these two participants may indeed require special assumptions about deceit or credulity. But the difficulty seems to disappear if we demand only successive, not simultaneous, credulity. Take it in two stages. The US threatens to withdraw unconditionally unless South Vietnam (SVN) commits itself to cease conditionally, the condition being that both parties on the other side cease. (This step can be construed as the formation of a US-SVN coa-

---

*The author is associated with the Center for International Affairs, Harvard University.

lition, the rules of the coalition requiring conditional acceptance of a cease-fire, SVN's decision to join the coalition having been coerced by a US threat.) Step Two: Having already used the credible threat of unconditional withdrawal, and the threat, having succeeded, being no longer necessary, the US now threatens North Vietnam (NVN) that it will fight unless North Vietnam (NVN) and the National Liberation Front (NLF) accept a cease-fire. The credibility of this threat is no longer jeopardized by an outstanding contradictory threat to South Vietnam (SVN), because that one is no longer outstanding. Even if NVN begs off, claiming it has no control over NLF, US can explain to NVN the tactic it just used on SVN and propose that NVN similarly coerce NLF into a coalition that is committed conditionally to a cease-fire. In effect, the number of participants has been reduced from four independent parties to two coalitions, and the conditional cease-fire may now be negotiated unembarrassed by that original credibility problem.

Within the game as defined, even within the war that the game attempts to model, one can go even further. The United States threatens to join the NVN-NLF coalition and fight against SVN unless the latter agrees to a US-SVN coalition committed to a conditional cease-fire. (NVN might make a similar threat to NLF.) This choice is actually not available to the US, or to NVN, in the summary version of the game that Mr. Howard presents, but he acknowledges that to make analysis practical he has somewhat reduced the list of available "options." The point I want to emphasize is that, until one has identified those various conditional strategies that Mr. Howard calls "policies," one cannot be sure just which strategies can safely be eliminated in simplifying the game. In particular, a strategy that is "dominated" in the original matrix of strategies, the one that precedes "metagame" considerations, need not be dominated once conditional strategies are allowed, that is, once the adoption of "policies" regarding the ultimate choice of strategies and the communication of these policies to an adversary has been allowed in the larger game.

Various suicidal or purely destructive options may initially appear sufficiently preposterous to be left out of the game; later on, when a "metagame" has been generated by the addition of policy options, it may be too late to recall some options that, originally irrelevant because dominated, should now be reinstated as relevant. For a factory labor force, disgruntled about wages, to stop working yet refuse to go work elsewhere might seem preposterous until one recognizes that a credible declaration of intent to strike may be an effective policy in the metagame. The danger, then, of attempting to define the original game with a manageable set of "reasonable" options prior to the introduction of "metagame" possibilities is that one will have missed some relevant strategies at the time he rejected them as "unreasonable." This consideration suggests to me that, when one has in mind an actual situation for which a game is to serve as a model, the "policy options" might best be considered as basic parts of the game itself rather than something superimposed in pursuit of a metagame.

Furthermore, they typically are indeed basic parts of the game itself. That is to say, the "policy options" are not analytical constructs but typically an integral part of the description of the situation. Whether agreements are binding, whether forfeits can be pledged, whether information can be credibly released as evidence, whether secrets can be kept, whether irrevocable steps can be taken, whether negotiations with different partners and adversaries can be taken in sequence and in what order they can be taken, are usually part of the given situation.

Analytically, I like the idea of distinguishing between those ultimate moves that determine the "outcome" and all of those "policies" whose contents are functions relating the ultimate moves to other players' moves and policies. One can discover a lot about "policies" by making the distinction. But there are two important qualifications. One, which I've mentioned, is that in any real situation—even in any real game—the policy options are there to be discovered, not invented by the analyst and not arbitrary with the analyst.

Second, there never is a unique metagame. There are as many metagames to be constructed as there are ways to specify the policy options and the sequences in which they can be adopted and made known. Not only is there no limit to this number, but the specification of a very few policy options to be taken in a specified short sequence of steps can generate an astronomical number of strategies.

Let me illustrate that this is true even in a game, a real "game", and not just a model of some more complex "real" situation. One might define bridge as a game in which cards, having been dealt, are laid down in a certain order, tricks taken, and score computed when the hands have been depleted. One can then introduce a variety of rules about bidding, doubling and signaling. But each set of rules defines a different game, and each set of rules is integral to the game that results. It determines what is trump, how tricks are scored, what information partners can share, and even the duration of the game. There is some correspondence between the bidding in bridge and the metagame superstructure in

Mr. Howard's concept; the correspondence is enough to convince me that the distinction between game and metagame is of limited usefulness. I will even propose that the terminology go in another direction. The game that includes all the policy options should be identified as "the game." We then distinguish, within the game, between those moves that ultimately determine the "outcome"—the moves that the policies are about, not the policy moves—and give this one a new name. This way we identify something that is central to the game, a matrix that specifies all the ultimate states of the world (on the assumption that "policies" themselves have no lasting significance beyond the choices that they are about), and we have all the cells out of which the full game matrix is constructed. Even with this we have to be careful, because a way that is often useful to express policy choices is to change the payoffs themselves, and if we do choose to represent certain policy choices (e.g., incurring a penalty on nonfulfillment of a bargain or commitment) as changes in the "original" payoffs, this central schedule of outcomes will not contain all the payoff combinations that go into the matrix of the game itself.

A final point about "policies" needs to be emphasized. As I have said, the policy options are part of the game itself; but to be part of the game they must be more than permutations of possible responses, more than silent intentions, more than hypothetical specifications of behavior. There must be a procedure within the game by which a policy is actually adopted, and to be significant within the game and to constitute a rational policy it must constrain a choice in a way that somebody can appreciate or change the information available within the game, or change the payoffs. If a "policy" is merely a silent resolution regarding how to behave, it can influence no one's choice and is therefore either a profitless reduction of a player's own freedom or cognizance, or else merely a "final" decision taken in advance. In Mr. Howard's model the US can neither respond to the private plans of North Vietnam (NVN) nor make its own action conditional on the private intentions of North Vietnam (NVN). If indeed NVN can reach a binding decision that either can be communicated to the US or is bound to leak to the US, as, for example, the way a Congressional resolution may structure a President's future choice, then the policy is part of the game, and, furthermore, the US may try to adopt a prior policy that includes as a variable the policy that NVN will adopt. Failing this, the US can have policies only relating to observed behavior or observed states of the world.

To illustrate, if the only two ultimate "actions" are "escalate" and "do not escalate," NVN may choose, as Mr. Howard indicated in his oral presentation, among four strategies for reacting to a US action. NVN can escalate no matter what, it can decline to escalate no matter what, it can escalate if US does but not otherwise, and it can escalate if US does not but not if US does. If these are binding policies taken by a politburo and known to the US, the game matrix is 2 x 4; if the US has a prior option to make its own choice of escalation dependent on which of the four policies NVN adopts, the US can choose among sixteen different policies in which the subsequent NVN policy choice is a variable capable of four different values, and the matrix of the game is 16 x 4. But if binding policies cannot credibly be communicated, the US (if it moves first in the action game) has only two choices. The metagame requires that these policy choices have status within the game and that they be part of its legal structure and information structure. And this legal structure must indicate who moves first in the choice of actions or whether moves are simultaneous. If nobody has to move first, a time dimension of the game has to be acknowledged. In that case, as a bare minimum there are at any given moment three strategies: escalate, do not escalate, and wait. (If a binding decision not to escalate cannot be taken, we are back to two, escalate and wait.) The crucial question now is whether there's a penalty on waiting. If the "first strike" is important in escalation, the inability of the participants to incur binding policies or to make bargains may condemn them to a jointly dispreferred outcome in which both escalate. If the value of the first strike is modest or negative, "wait" strategies will appeal and will be as effective as conditional policies would have been.

Finally, if bargains are feasible within the game structure but the payoffs are such that the bargain is unattractive to one party, another one of those discarded strategies may be reinstated, a strategy of double escalation, i.e., of escalating more than the situation calls for, a strategy that may be relevant in a conditional policy if the threat of it can induce the adversary to accept second best, namely, non-escalation, to avoid the worse outcome of double escalation. Mr. Howard's metagame will not discover this policy if its component strategy was eliminated in advance as "unreasonable." In Vietnam it may be unreasonable, but Mr. Howard's game will not discover it so.

CHAPTER 12. THE VETO-INCREMAX PROCEDURE: POTENTIAL FOR VIETNAM CONFLICT RESOLUTION

By Walter Isard*

In this paper the author proceeds to supplement the Howard-Schelling analysis. He develops a "veto-incremax" procedure which has a number of properties which might be found appealing by the parties to a conflict. He demonstrates how this procedure might induce parties, such as the U.S. and North Vietnam, to move gradually by a series of steps from a position of zero percent joint disengagement to a position of 100 percent joint disengagement. Ed.

This paper is an attempt to develop further the general rationale for cooperative solutions to game situations, particularly of the Prisoners' Dilemma type. It therefore is in keeping with the work of Howard and Schelling. Specifically, it is aimed at supplementing the Howard analysis at a place where the Howard analysis is weakest. While some analysts will admit that participants should be able to appreciate and perceive clearly the logic (metarationality) of a cooperative (c,c) solution to a Prisoner's Dilemma or similar game, these analysts may well contend that such logic does not provide the basis, or a procedure, by which participants can get there. It is in this connection that we present the "veto-incremax" procedure. This procedure may be able to induce

*The author is associated with the Department of Regional Science, University of Pennsylvania

the participants, through a series of moves of a single play, to reach the cooperative (c,c) solution. In this sense, this procedure provides another type of rationale to supplement the Howard-Schelling rationale, and perhaps even to be synthesized with the latter to yield a still stronger "logical" basis for the cooperative solution.[1]

There are several possible veto-incremax procedures. (Incremax is an abbreviation for incremental maximization, and involves a maximization process taken over each of a series of small steps.) Each has the following appealing features:

(1) each can be presented in a relatively simple form for a given situation, and can be rigorously defined mathematically;

(2) each gives each participant a full veto power which he may exercise at any time, and assures each participant that he will end no worse off than at the start if any participant does exercise his veto power;

(3) each clearly points up the inefficiency of the existing position (deadlock, threat point, current-stand point or prominent reference point) and identifies a common goal (the achievement of a mutually preferred outcome which is efficient);

(4) each requires that each participant be able to state consistently his preferences among outcomes. Thus, each depends on no intercomparisons of utility, and only requires the assumption of ordinal utility;

(5) each assures that no participant will ever be made worse off on any move, except by the exercise of the veto power;

(6) each allows each participant to be as conservative and cautious as he desires with respect to the amount of change in proposed actions on any move; that is, within extreme limits, each participant is allowed to make as small a commitment on change as he desires;

(7) provided the veto power is not exercised, each insures that an efficient outcome will be reached, but that no participant is able be-

---

[1] A fuller and more precise discussion of a number of aspects of this paper is contained in Walter Isard, Tony E. Smith, Tze H. Tung, Peter Isard and Michael Dacey, *General Theory: Social, Political, Economic and Regional*, M.I.T. Press, Cambridge, Mass., forthcoming Spring 1969, chapter 7. This paper also draws upon: Walter Isard and Tony E. Smith, "A Practical Application of Game Theoretical Approaches to Arms Reduction (and to Goal Determination Among Regional Planning Authorities)" *Papers*, Peace Research Society (International), Vol. 4, pp. 85-98.

The ideas in this paper are further developed in a manuscript by the senior author presented at the November 1968 conference of the Peace Research Society (International) to be published in Vol. 12 *Papers*, Peace Research Society, (International) 1969.

fore hand to identify the specific set of changes in the joint proposals, or steps, required to achieve that outcome;

(8) each suggests a "fair compromise" or "equitable" procedure by which all participants may share in the gains from the gradual advancement to a mutually more efficient state of affairs;

(9) each allows the participants considerable flexibility in combining its appealing features with the appealing features of several other veto-incremax procedures into a single synthesized procedure.

More formally, we may proceed to state the general properties of veto-incremax procedures as follows:

Property (1) (Veto Power). On any move the procedure allows each participant to exercise the veto power, which exercise commits the participants only to the joint action in effect before the first move.

Further, *except when the veto power is exercised*:

Property (2) (Objective Achievement). The procedure insures that the participants' objective will be achieved[2] after a finite number of steps;

Property (3) (Pre-indeterminacy). The procedure allows each participant to insure that for any number of initial steps, the joint proposals which may be reached cannot be determined uniquely by the other participant prior to these steps;

Property (4) (Guaranteed Improvement). The procedure insures that on any move the joint proposal reached will not be less preferred by any participant to the joint proposal reached on the previous move, and will be preferred by at least one participant;

Property (5) (Limited Commitment). On any move the procedure allows each participant to limit the extent of change in the joint proposal (action) reached on the previous move[3] to which he is willing to agree (commit himself).

We now wish to illustrate the use of this procedure. In doing so we shall make a number of concrete modifications of its general properties in order to make the procedure more directly applicable to the Vietnam-type of conflict situation being examined.[4]

---

[2] By "achieved" we mean reaching a position imperceptibly close to the objective frontier. See W. Isard and T. E. Smith, "On the Resolution of Conflicts Among Regions of a System," *Papers,* Regional Science Association, Vol. 17, 1966.

[3] On the first move, the relevant position from which change is measured is the initial position (joint action) of the two participants.

[4] Strictly speaking, we should restate the properties so that they are consistent with the application of rules 4 and 5 to be stated below. However, because of space limitations, we do not do so.

We begin by examining the following Prisoners' Dilemma game.

TABLE 1. A Payoff Matrix

		Player 2	
		c	d
Player	c	5,5	-10,12
1	d	12,-10	-2,-2

There are two participants: Players 1 and 2. Each player may choose one of the two actions, c and d. Player 1's actions correspond to the rows c and d. Player 2's actions correspond to the columns c and d. The numbers in the cells of the matrix (Table 1) represent the payoffs of each player, when Player 1 chooses the action corresponding to the row of that cell, and when Player 2 chooses the action corresponding to the column of that cell. The first number in each cell is the payoff to Player 1; and the second number is the payoff to Player 2.

We assume that each player is strictly self-interested and is motivated to maximize his payoff (or achieve his most preferred outcome). Thus it is clear that given the action of the other player, it is always best for a given player to choose d. For example, suppose Player 1 has chosen action c. Then Player 2 finds it better to choose d than c, for if he chooses d he gets a payoff of 12; if the choice had been c, he would get a payoff of only 5. Or suppose Player 1 has chosen action d. Then Player 2 still finds it better to choose d than c, for if he chooses c his payoff is -10, whereas if he chooses d his payoff is -2.

Since this payoff matrix is symmetrical, it also always pays Player 1 to choose d for any given action that Player 2 may take. Hence, in this game, each chooses d, and the equilibrium payoff[5] to each is -2. It does not pay for either to change his action unilaterally.

It also may be argued that if by chance each of the two players had erroneously chosen action c at the start, so that their payoffs would be 5, 5, this outcome would not be an equilibrium outcome. For where actions are independent, unrestricted and retractable, and where this game is played only once, each player would then, out of pure self-interest, find it profitable to switch to action d.

It is with respect to breaking away from the deadlock equilibrium

---

[5] An equilibrium joint action is defined to be one in which neither player is motivated to change his action unilaterally. Equilibrium payoffs and outcomes are payoffs and outcomes associated with such action.

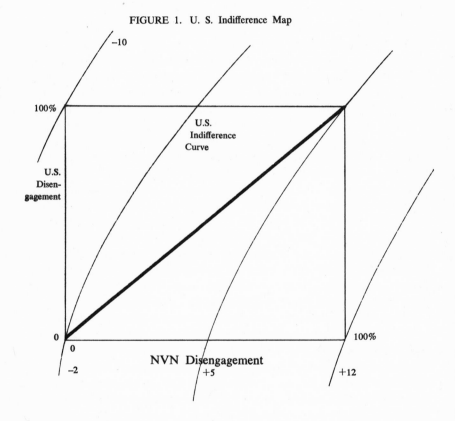

FIGURE 1. U. S. Indifference Map

position *d,d,* which yields the payoff -2,-2, that we propose the use of the veto-incremax procedure. The application of this procedure is best demonstrated with a series of figures. In Figure 1, we measure along the horizontal axis the percentage of disengagement (cease-fire and withdrawal by the North Vietnamese).

This axis from the 0% point to the 100% point then constitutes the (continuous) set of actions which the North Vietnamese can choose from in the particular game we are considering. Along the vertical axis we measure the percentage of U.S. disengagement (cease-fire and withdrawal). The axis from the 0% point to the 100% point then represents the (continuous) set of actions which the U.S. can choose from. Next we construct the box of Figure 1 by constructing perpendiculars at the 100% points. This box then constitutes all possible combinations of actions, that is the set of possible joint actions. We assume that the U.S. can state its preferences over all joint actions in the box drawn in Figure 1.

For this game of disengagement we make one basic assumption about the preferences of both participants. We assume that each participant always prefers more disengagement than less when both participants are committed to the same percent of disengagement. Hence, if we draw a straight line from the 0%-0% point to the 100%-100% point, each participant prefers the joint action represented by a given point on that line to any joint action represented by any point lower and to the left on that line. Thus, as we go from the lower left-hand corner to the upper right-hand corner, we proceed onto joint actions which are more and more preferred by both participants.

Next we indicate on Figure 1 the preferences of the United States. Consider the current position—joint action—represented by the 0%-0% point. The payoff to U.S., who may be taken to be Player 1, is -2 according to Table 1. Let us then use this number to designate the curve that we will construct through the 0%-0% point. Now, as already indicated, if both the U.S. and NVN were to disengage by some equal percentage—say 10%—U.S. would prefer this joint action to the current position. If U.S. were to disengage by 10%, and the NVN by 9.9%, the U.S. might still prefer such a joint action to the current position. If U.S. were to disengage by 10% and NVN by 9.5%, or by 9.0%, or by 8.8%, U.S. still may prefer each of such joint actions to the current position. But it is clear that at some low enough percent of disengagement by NVN (with U.S. at 10%), U.S. will no longer prefer the resulting joint action to the current position. At that percent of disengagement by NVN, U.S. might be *indifferent* between the joint action so defined and the joint action defined by the 0%-0% point. Both these two points may then be said to lie on the same *indifference curve* for the U.S. In similar fashion, for 11%, 12%, 13% . . . disengagement by U.S., we determine the corresponding disengagement by NVN which defines a joint action which U.S. neither prefers *more* nor *less* than the joint action defined by the 0%-0% point. The locus of all these points then forms the indifference curve designated by the number -2.

In similar manner, we can derive the set of all joint actions which U.S. neither prefers more nor less than the joint action defined by the 100%-100% point. We connect these by a curve, and associate with it the number +5, since this is the payoff in Table 1 for the (*c,c*) joint action (the 100%-100% point). Likewise, we can determine other indifference curves of the set which orders U.S. preferences among all possible joint actions. Some of the indifference curves in Figure 1 involve hypothetical joint actions outside the box. For our purposes we do not need to interpret those segments of the indifference curves not in the box. We are concerned only with preferences for the joint actions contained by the box and its boundary lines. However, note that the least preferred action by U.S. lies on the -10 indifference curve, and the most preferred on the +12 indifference curve.

It should be stressed at this point that the numbers associated with these indifferences curves are not basic to the analysis which follows. Any other set of numbers which orders the indifference curves of the U.S. in the same way is just as relevant. We use the numbers of Figure 1 simply because they have been already used in Table 1.[6]

In a similar manner we construct in Figure 2 the indifference curves for North Vietnam, who may be taken to be Player 2. These curves are dashed in order to distinguish them from those for the U.S. In Figure 3 we superimpose those indifference curves of the two sets which are relevant for the analysis to ensue. Now, to repeat, the problem is how to go from the lower left-hand corner of Figure 3, which corresponds to 0% disengagement by each of the parties, and which lies on each one's indifference curve of -2, to the point at the upper right-hand corner of the box, which corresponds to 100% disengagement by each party and the indifference curves of +5.

---

[6]Because of lack of space, we can not indicate here the various other assumptions re: the indifference curves, which are either required or desirable in terms of the use of a veto-incremax procedure. Some relevant discussion is contained in the references cited in footnote 1. Additionally, further thought on the question is required in terms of the specific game situation being considered in this paper.

FIGURE 2. NVN Indifference Map

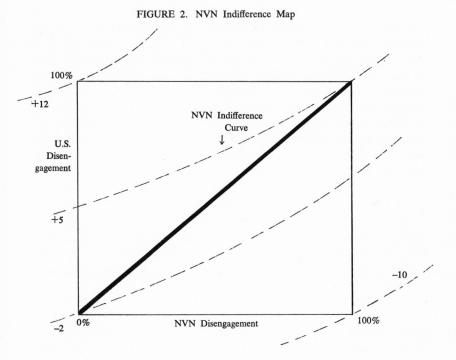

We now envisage a series of moves in a step-by-step improvement process for each party. On each move, each party is to make a proposal for a joint action. These proposals are, however, to be subject to the following rules:

RULE 1: *In making any proposal for a joint action, each player shall not consider a joint action which would yield any participant an outcome less preferred than the joint proposal reached in the preceding move.* On move 1 this rule means that each participant's proposal for a joint action must lie within or on the boundary of that shaded area defined within the larger box by the pair of indifference curves which course through the initial position of 0%-0% disengagement.

RULE 2: *On each move no player can propose a joint action which lies outside the commitment set.* In Figure 1 the commitment set for the first move is the small, heavily shaded box which centers around the 0%-0% point. This commitment set is obtained by first identifying the maximum change along both the vertical and horizontal which each participant is willing to allow on that move, and then by taking the least of these maximums first along the vertical and then along the horizontal. Recall that change along the vertical represents percentage change in U.S. disengagement and that change along the horizontal represents percentage change in NVN disengagement.[7]

Assuming that all possible joint actions within the commitment set in the first move are less preferred by both participants to the 100%-100% joint action, as is the case in Figure 3, we may imagine that the U.S. will then propose the joint action designated by U_1—since that joint action of all joint actions in both the commitment set and improvement set lies on the highest U.S. indifference curve, that is, is the most preferred of these points by U.S. Also, we may imagine that NVN will propose N_1 for the same reason. Since these two proposed joint actions are not identical, we now invoke a third rule, which may be as follows:

RULE 3. *If on any move the proposed joint actions of the participants are not identical, the participants shall adopt as a compromise proposal that joint action defined by the mid-point of the straight line connecting the proposed joint actions of the two participants.* In Figure 3, the point P_1 is the midpoint of the straight line connecting N_1 and U_1, the proposed joint actions of NVN and U.S., respectively. Thus, P_1 represents a compromise or joint proposal reached at the end of the first

---

[7]For this paper, it is not necessary to examine changes which take the participants to points outside the large box of possible joint actions.

FIGURE 3. The Determination of the Joint Proposal of the
First Move

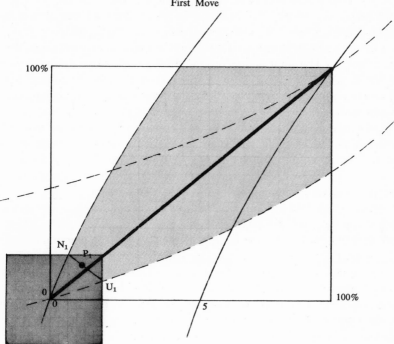

move. The principle by which the compromise itself is reached may be designated a split-the-difference principle.

Assuming a split-the-difference principle is acceptable to the participants we may proceed to the second move. The second move is illustrated with the use of Figure 4. On Figure 4, we plot the joint action P_1, the compromise proposal reached at the end of the first move. This joint action serves as the reference point for improvement during the second move. We next identify the two indifference curves which course through P_1, one for the U.S. and one for NVN. These two indifference curves then define for the second move the improvement set within the large box. This improvement set is the shaded area extending upward and to the right from point P_1, between these two indifference curves. The joint action proposed by any participant on the second move must lie within or on the boundary of this shaded area, none of whose points correspond to a joint action less preferred by any participant to P_1.

Next we construct around P_1 the commitment set for move two which is the small, heavily-shaded box. This set is determined by the maximum commitments which the participants state at the beginning of the second move. These commitments will generally be different than the corresponding commitments made at the start of the first move. By Rule 2, the joint action proposed by any participant on the second move must also lie within this commitment set.

Accordingly, if all possible joint actions within the commitment set on the second move are less preferred by both participants to the 100%-100% joint action, we may imagine that U.S. will then propose the joint action designated by U_2—since that joint action of all joint actions which lie in both the commitment set and improvement set is most preferred by U.S. Also, we may imagine that NVN will propose N_2 for the same reason. Since these two proposed joint actions are not identical, we invoke the third rule again and split the difference. This then yields P_2 (the midpoint of the straight line N_2U_2) as the joint proposal (compromise joint action) reached at the end of the second move.

In like manner, we may imagine that the joint proposals P_3, P_4 . . . in Figure 4 are obtained at the end of the third round, fourth round, etc. . . . On each round the objective, namely, the 100%-100% point, is more closely approached.

However, before the attainment of the objective, another constraint on one or both of the participants becomes operative. We may well imagine that in the particular type of conflict situation envisaged, each

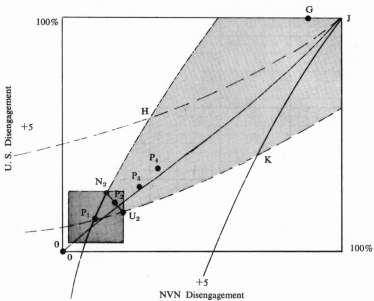

FIGURE 4. A Sequence of Joint Proposals

participant recognizes that he may become 100% disengaged before the other; for example, point G might be attained after a series of moves.[8] For obvious reasons, he is concerned and has perhaps grave misgivings about this outcome which leaves the other player partially engaged. And he knows that no further moves in the game are possible since, for example, a shift from such a point forces the other party to a less preferred joint action and this violates Rule 1.   (For example, a shift from G toward the 100%-100% disengagement point would involve the acceptance to joint actions less preferred by NVN). Therefore, to preclude such an outcome, and to insure that the 100%-100% disengagement point is attained, we add the following:

RULE 4.   *On any move, no player can propose a joint action which is more preferred by him to the 100% joint disengagement action.* By this rule we define a restricted improvement set.   This set on any move is bounded by the indifference curves of the two participants which pass through the 100%-100% disengagement point and those which pass through the joint proposal reached on the previous move.[9] In Figure 4, the restricted improvement set on the second move is thus P_1HJKP_1.[10]

It is now evident that the sequence of joint proposals which yield participants more and more preferred outcomes can never lie outside the area defined by the pair of indifferences curves in Figure 4 which course through the 100% joint disengagement point. Hence, the joint proposals over a sequence of moves must approach and attain the 100% joint disengagement point, the objective.[11].

Additionally, to avoid a series of small steps, the participants may agree beforehand that once the improvement process has progressed to the point where a joint action is contained within the commitment set which some participant prefers at least as much as the 100%-100% point, then the other participant may set the final joint action, without being limited to the commitment set, provided that that joint action (1) lies in the restricted improvement set, and (2) is not less preferred

---

[8] In the sense of Property 2.

[9] Or the initial position (joint action) if the first move is being considered. Note that this rule only insures that the 100%-100% point is reached because it has been assumed that each participant always prefers more disengagement than less when both participants are committed to the same percent of disengagement.

[10] This set includes all its boundary points except its reference point, which is the initial position (joint action) on the first move or the joint proposal reached on the previous move for all other moves.

[11] When the players come imperceptibly close to the objective, for practical purposes we say that the objective has been attained.

by the first participant to the 100%-100% disengagement point. That is:

RULE 5. *Once a move is reached where one player can propose a joint action whose outcome is not less preferred by him to the 100% joint disengagement point, the other player may choose as a final joint action any joint action which is not less preferred by the first to the 100% joint disengagement point.*

It is evident that whenever Rule 5 is applicable, the objective can be immediately attained through a proposal of a joint action by the second player.

We have now illustrated a possible use of one type of veto-incremax procedure. There are at least several other types that can be constructed and examined for applicability. One would substitute for the split-the-difference principle in Rule 3 an alternating leader-follower principle. Another might substitute a weighted compromise principle where different rather than equal weights are assigned to joint actions proposed by the participants on any move. The commitment sets might be defined differently. And so forth. The reader is referred elsewhere[12] for further discussion. The important point is that one of the variants of this procedure can permit the gradual advancement from a position of 0% joint disengagement to one of 100% joint disengagement. The procedure is rational in the sense that participants may find appealing the properties of *unqualified veto power, objective achievement, guaranteed improvement* over each of many steps, *limited commitment to change* (e.g., in percent of disengagement on any move), and the use of some equitable principle, such as the *split-the-difference* to resolve differences in proposals on any move. Since in the Vietnam conflict situation simulated by Howard, the veto-incremax procedure yields the same outcome as the Howard metagame supplemented by the Schelling successive credulity hypothesis,[13] it may then be said that the rationale of the veto-incremax procedure complements the rationale of the Howard-Schelling approach.

Recall the appeal of the Howard analysis. If one participant adopts a certain policy strategy it guarantees that if the other participant acts rationally from a strategy standpoint, both will end up at the desired

---

[12] See literature cited in footnote 1.
[13] Recall that the successive credulity hypothesis can reduce Howard's 4-participant game down to a 2-participant game, where one participant is a coalition dominated by NVN and the other is a coalition dominated by U.S.

goal, namely, a cooperative-type outcome. Moreover, and equally important, no matter how irrational the second participant may turn out to be, the first can never be made worse off than he would be by the noncooperative (d,d) outcome. Therefore, he has nothing to lose at all by playing in accord with the Howard metagame when the outcome he otherwise confronts is 0% joint disengagement. Moreover, it is to be noted that when any participant in the Howard game chooses a policy which would lead to a (c,c) outcome if the other participant were rational, this choice also serves as an *inescapable sanction* to the other party—that is, the other party cannot do anything that would give him (the other party) a more preferred outcome than what would be achieved if he followed that policy consistent with a (c,c) outcome, (the desired goal).

The complementarity of the Howard-Schelling approach and the veto-incremax procedure may even be of a more subtle nature in a real situation. Suppose in a conflict one party is primarily strategy-oriented and not phased by the thought of large shifts in policy (as is often the case for small nations who have not much to lose if a serious error is made in a shift). Suppose the other party is primarily conservative and cautious, partly because it has much to lose from a major error and therefore wishes to consider at any time only small changes (as is often the case for major powers). Then the ability of a mediator to point out the logic of the 100% joint disengagement point from both a strategy standpoint and a limited commitment standpoint (as in the veto-incremax procedure) may provide that arbitrator with more forceful means to achieve his goal—namely to convince both parties of not only the rationality of the 100% joint disengagement but also the existence of a workable negotiation procedure to reach that joint action.

*   *   *

We conclude with the hope that we have now laid bare several procedures which can be examined and investigated in terms of their potential applicability to major conflict situations. It is not expected that these procedures may have direct application to all conflict situations, or even to a large fraction of such situations—or even to existing situations such as the Paris talks, the Middle East, or the urban confrontations in the United States. If however they do provide some assistance in mediating some important conflict, the effort that has gone into the development of game theory and these procedures will have been justified.

CHAPTER 13. DYNAMICS OF THE VIETNAM CONFLICT: A QUANTITATIVE ANALYSIS AND PREDICTIVE COMPUTER SIMULATION

By Jeffrey S. Milstein and William Charles Mitchell*

In the final paper of this book, the authors present new methods of statistical prediction. They thereby provide to decision-makers a means of evaluating the reliability and validity of the models used in developing ongoing policy. These methods also provide a means of observing probable outcomes of alternative policies. The authors study the dynamics of the Vietnam conflict with these methods. Ed.

INTRODUCTION

We have all observed the major events of the Vietnam War since 1964. These events include what is commonly called the escalation of

*The authors are associated with the Political Science Department, Michigan State University and the Institute of Political Studies, Stanford University, respectively. A second paper is to appear in Volume 12, *Papers,* Peace Research Society (International), 1969.

The authors would like to express their thanks to the following: Jane Milstein, Diane Sorben, and Alain Robert for invaluable assistance, suggestions, and criticisms; Hayward R. Alker, Jr., Raymond C. Tanter, Robert C. North, Richard A. Brody, William Vickery, Jerome Feldman, and George Woodworth for helpful comments; Representative Charles S. Gubser and Martin B. Reilly and Gerry M. Argraves of the Office of the Assistant Secretary of Defense for Public Affairs for help in gathering military data; and to Mike A. Etemad for data on black market piastre values.

the war as represented by increases in armed hostilities and casualties on both sides, the introduction of large numbers of American combat troops and their assumption of the major burden of the ground war, the increased use of North Vietnamese Army combat troops in South Vietnam, and the massive bombing of North Vietnam. We have also witnessed each side's attempt to bring the war to a satisfactory conclusion through both military and diplomatic means.

An important question concerning the war is what the relationships are among the belligerents' behaviors, their expectations as to the effect of their behaviors, and actual outcomes. This question is both of academic and of policy interest. Roger Hilsman, former Assistant Secretary of State for Far Eastern Affairs, has recently written about policymakers' need for knowledge concerning these *relationships*.

> Effective foreign policy depends on the capacity to predict events in the social affairs of men, and a better capacity to predict would mean better and more effective policy. But more is required than simple factual information. Predicting the outcome of alternative policies requires knowledge in the sense of an ability to identify and weigh the different factors bearing on the particular situation and an understanding of the dynamism by which those different factors interact.[1]

That policy-makers do relate events can be inferred from the fact that they do express preferences for goals and exhibit behavior which presumably they believe to be means towards their ends. In addition, policy-makers make explicit statements regarding their perception of the relationship between their behavior and their goals. These statements suggest that policy-makers have a set of such relationships which we can consider to be their models of the conflict.

It is our purpose in this paper to explicate the models held by each of the belligerents in the war from their public statements. We justify accepting public statements as authentic reports of the policy-makers' models on the grounds that people generally believe what they say for psychological reasons, and say what they believe for reasons of long-range credibility. It is also our purpose to test these models with quantitative data. The use of quantitative data requires that we operationalize the concepts used in policymakers' models.

We know that the decision-makers' models have failed to predict accurately, since we have all observed such major unintended conse-

---

[1]Roger Hilsman, *To Move a Nation,* New York; Doubleday, 1967, p. 565.

quences as the general failure of the policy-makers on each side to achieve their military and political goals in the conflict or to anticipate the major patterns of behavior that have occurred in the war so far: escalation to overcome a disadvantage or gain a new advantage, matched by the other side's counter-escalation, leading to a new stalemate at higher levels of violence, greater costs to both sides, and the prolongation of the war.

Noting the incongruity between policy-makers' goals and the consequences of their policies, we have attempted to construct a model which would better predict behavior and outcomes in the war. We desire to build a *systematic* model so that we can use it to predict the consequences of assumed alternative behavior. This predictive ability not only has practical importance, but also represents one of the major purposes of scientific inquiry.

> The purpose of science is to describe the world in an orderly scheme or language which will help us to look ahead. We want to forecast what we can of the future behavior of the world; particularly we want to forecast how it would behave under several alternative actions of our own between which we are usually trying to choose.[2]

DATA

The data used in this study are all publicly available. The complete set of data one would like to have to test completely the models of the policy-makers and to develop a complete theoretical model were not available to us. To a certain degree, the incompleteness of the data available to us is due to the circumstances under which researchers in international relations normally operate. For example, direct measures of policy-makers preferences and perceptions were not available to us. Additional incompleteness of data occurred because data on some theoretically interesting variables have never been collected, some available data were incomplete, and some data were classified.

The data were of four general kinds: military, economic, public opinion, and communications. For each variable used in this study, complete data were collected for the three years 1965, 1966, and 1967, and aggregated by month. Although representing only a subset of all possible data on the war, the data available do allow us to test hypoth-

---

[2] J. Bronowski, *The Common Sense of Science*, New York, Alfred A. Knopf, Inc., and Random House, p. 70.

eses relating to some of the most significant behavior in the war such as the escalation of commitment by both American and North Vietnamese forces and the bombing of North Vietnam. The data cover the time period during which much of the significant escalation of the conflict has occurred.

We have constructed quantitative indices as operational definitions and measures of the conceptual variables in the policy-makers' models and our own theoretical models. Some of these indices are single variables, others are weighted sums of two or more variables. We constructed indices to obtain more *valid* indicators of theoretical concepts, to obtain more *reliable* measures of conceptual variables, to transform some kinds of data into a form appropriate for quantitative analysis, and to make our models and analysis more *parsimonious*.

Valid indicators of theoretical concepts are of importance to policy-makers as well as to social scientists. People in the Department of Defense were reported to have constructed an "index of victory" consisting of the composite variables of the number of enemy killed, the number of hamlets pacified, the number of enemy infiltrated and recruited, and the number of miles of roads cleared in South Vietnam.[3]

A composite index of two or more variables is more reliable than a single variable since it is less subject to random fluctuations and less likely to be subject to non-random error due to biases.

We also considered differences or proportional differences of all military, economic, and public opinion variables. The justification for this is that many decisions are made on an incremental basis rather than in absolute terms. Policy-makers make decisions regarding how many troops will be committed this month. If no decision is made, the number of troops will remain at last month's level. For this reason, we considered the change in troop commitments from month to month to be a more reliable indicator of the decision process than the absolute level of troops committed. The use of proportional differences, a form of logarithmic transformation of the data, is indicative of the concept that larger changes in some variable, like bombing of the North, are possible with the same effort after a high level of activity has been obtained. The addition of 100 bombing sorties over North Vietnam was a major decision in 1964 but a bureaucratic one in 1967. It is more relevant to speak of an increase of 10% in bombing missions than of the actual increase.

---

[3] *Wall Street Journal,* October 27, 1967, p. 1.

The variables and indices we used in this study are as follows: As an indicator of North Vietnamese and Vietcong behavior: the change from one month to the next in the reported number of *Vietcong and North Vietnamese troops* in South Vietnam, including main force divisions, regiments, and battalions, Vietcong guerrilla platoons, Vietcong administrative and logistical personnel, but *not* political cadres or irregular self-defense militia.

As an indicator of United States military effort: the change from one month to the next in the level of *U.S. commitment,* a weighted sum equal to .025 times the number of *U.S. troops* in South Vietnam, plus 50 times the number of *U.S. ground operations* of battalion-size or larger, plus .67 times the number of U.S. *bombing sorties over South Vietnam,* plus 1.0 times the number of hundreds of short tons of *cargo sealifted* by the U.S. Military Sea Transport Service.[4]

As another indicator of U.S. military behavior, we use the number of U.S. *bombing sorties over North Vietnam.* For 1965, this is the number of sorties; for 1966 and 1967, this is the reported number of missions times 3. We also use the *proportional change* from one month to the next in U.S. bombing of North Vietnam as an additional variable.

As indicators of military outcomes or consequences of the military behavior of both sides in the war, we use the following indices and variables:

As *military initiative,* we take the ratio of the number of U.S. ground operations of battalion-size or larger to the number of U.S. troops killed in action. As a separate index, we take the *change in* this ratio from one month to the next.

To index *U.S. casualties,* we took the sum of 10 times U.S. killed in action, the number of U.S. wounded in action requiring hospitalization, and half the number of U.S. wounded in action not requiring hospitalization.

To indicate *North Vietnamese and Vietcong attrition,* we took the sum of 2.5 times the number of reported Communist troops killed, 3 times the total number of reported weapons captured from the Communists, and 1 times the number of reported Communists captured. We also used as an additional index the *percentage change* in this index from one month to the next.

---

[4]Since the impact of each component of an index is proportional to the variance due to that component and not due to the mean, we chose weightings so that the product of weighting and standard deviation would be of the desired relative magnitude. This accounts for some of the unusual coefficients.

To index *South Vietnamese casualties,* we took the sum of 4 times the number of the Army of the Republic of Vietnam troops reported killed in action plus the number of the Army of the Republic of Vietnam troops reported as seriously wounded. We used the percentage increase in this index from one month to the next as an additional index.

One indicator we used, the "kill ratio" of the number of Vietcong and North Vietnamese troops killed in action divided by the number of U.S. plus the Army of the Republic of Vietnam troops killed in action, is an index which Department of Defense officials have been reported to use as an indicator of relative progress in the war. We have also used the *change* in this ratio from one month to the next as an additional index. We did not include the number of "third nation" (e.g., South Korean) casualties in this index because these data were not completely reported over the entire time period we were studying.

As indicators of political support we have chosen the following variables and indices: To measure *U.S. domestic support* for the Johnson administration, we have taken the *change* from month to month of the difference between the percent who approve and the percent who disapprove of the way President Johnson handles his job as President. These data come from the Gallup Poll taken each month during the period studied. We unfortunately were unable to use the Gallup Poll data on the question of approval or disapproval of the way President Johnson is handling the situation in Vietnam. This question was not asked in the poll on a monthly basis until July, 1965. However, the correlation between popular disapproval of President Johnson's handling of his job as President and his handling of the situation in Vietnam since July, 1965, is very high, .89. Similarly, the popular approval of the President on these two items correlates .80.

We have chosen the number of Vietcong and North Vietnamese *defectors* as an indicator of Communist morale and support. Data on defectors (called "Chieu Hoi" or "ralliers") are collected by the Defense Department, and are used by them as an indicator of morale. We assume that the greater the number of defectors, the lower the Communist troop morale. As an additional index we also use the *change* in this number from one month to the next.

Confidence in the government of South Vietnam by the people in that country has often been called one of the key criterion of how well or badly the war is going. In this war of "national liberation" the achievement of *political* objectives is the real payoff, and military successes are only a means to the end of controlling the population of the country and winning their allegiance. (These objectives are pursued in the program jocularly referred to as "WHAMing"—"Winning Hearts and Minds.")

The Department of Defense tries to measure population control with its survey questionnnaires called Hamlet Evaluation System. To use an unobtrusive measure[5] of popular confidence in the government, we have used the *black market dollar value of the piastre,* hand-payment *in Saigon.* This value is the average exchange ratio of cents to piastres for the buy and sell values. We assume that people's confidence in the government is reflected in their confidence in the currency printed and circulated by that government, as demonstrated in a free market. Therefore, we assume that the higher the dollar value of the piastre, the greater the popular confidence of the government. These data are quoted at least twice a month by financial firms in Hong Kong who have agents in the Saigon money market. They were made available to us by a money dealer in San Francisco. As another index, we use the *change* in this value from one month to the next.

Another similar indicator which we used as a measure of external *international confidence* in the government of South Vietnam was the *dollar value of the South Vietnamese piastre, in the Hong Kong* free money market. We use the average cents to piastre ratio of the buy and sell values. We assume that this indicates confidence in the currency of the government on the part of foreign financial and business concerns. It is of interest that the Saigon and Hong Kong piastre rates are correlated .93, thus indicating that domestic and foreign perceptions of the stability of the government are similar. However, we do note that the *difference* between the two rates is a significant predictor of some dependent variables in our regression analysis. Again, we used the *change* in this value from one month to the next as an additional indicator.

The communications data are composed of *public statements* made by major political and military *policy-makers* in the United States, South Vietnam, North Vietnam, and the National Liberation Front. All statements made by these men relevant to the Vietnam War during the years 1965, 1966, and 1967 which were reported in *The New York Times* and indexed in the *New York Times Index* were content analyzed from the *Index* according to a coding scheme which recorded separately speakers' preferences and perceptions of forty-one separate items of actual or possible behavior or events in the war. These forty-one items

---

[5]Eugene J. Webb et al., *Unobtrusive Measures,* Chicago; Rand McNally, Co., 1966.

form as complete a list as possible of the general statements leaders on both sides made about the war. Using the coding scheme and the Communications Appendix, we measured the speakers' *preferences* for increasing, continuing unchanged, or decreasing the particular behaviors or events referred to in the statements on an ordinal scale, and the speakers' *perceptions* of the behaviors or events as certainly decreasing, possibly decreasing, remaining unchanged, possibly increasing, or certainly increasing, also on an ordinal scale. These data were collected on a daily basis from the *Index,* and aggregated by month. In all, for the three years 1965-1967, 1857 separate statements were coded. These included 3941 specific perceptions and preferences.

The forty-one topics were combined into the following eight communication indices: 1) North Vietnamese and Vietcong preferences for their own military and political activities; 2) North Vietnamese and Vietcong perceptions of United States and South Vietnamese military and political activities; 3) North Vietnamese and Vietcong preferences for negotiating; 4) North Vietnamese and Vietcong preferences for outcomes and goals; 5) United States and South Vietnamese perceptions of North Vietnamese and Vietcong military and political activities; (6) United States and South Vietnamese preferences for U.S. and South Vietnamese military and political activities; 7) United States and South Vietnamese preferences for negotiations; and 8) United States and South Vietnamese perceptions and preferences for outcomes and goals. The components of these communications indices are fully described in the Communications Appendix. See pages 196-202.

These indices are composed of sums of scores of measures of those topics we considered relevant. Depending upon the nature of the statements about some topic, we chose either the frequency of statement, or the frequency times the typical comment, or the frequency times the differences between preferences and perception for some topic. For instance, the United States never expresses a preference for either continuing unchanged or increasing North Vietnamese troop strength in South Vietnam. However, the *frequency* of statement of preference for decreasing North Vietnamese troop strength should be indicative of the saliance of that factor to the decision-maker. Many topics were discussed too infrequently to permit sophisticated measures of intent.

Since our measures of preference and perception are ordinal, and our frequency counts are interval, something should be said about the use of the product-moment correlation. The coder of the communications was instructed to evaluate strength of feeling in a linear manner, and the fact that we had only three and five ordinal classifications makes the ordinal to interval transition reasonable. The justification for multiplying interval data and then considering it to be continuous data after summing several measures lies in aspects of the central-limit theorem.

The effects of converting ordinal to interval data are less when several measures are combined into a single index because errors should not be systematic and should thus be expected to cancel somewhat. This conversion enables us to compare the communications, as interval data, with the military variables such as casualties, which are also interval data.

METHODS

Mathematical analysis involved four phases. The first phase of analysis was to prepare graphs of all variables against time. We found these to be an important aid in comprehending the data as they facilitated pattern recognition. For instance, from these graphs we noticed that there have been three phases of the war during the period of our study, 1965-1967. During each phase of the war the maximum monthly casualty figures fall below the minimum of the next phase, and the minimum monthly casualty figures are higher than the maximum casualties of the previous period.

The second phase of analysis was to calculate correlations among the various variables, including time lags and leads. For instance, not only did we examine the relationship between this month's bombing level and this month's rate of Communist troop commitment, but we also compared this month's commitment rate with previous bombing levels to see if heavy bombing means fewer troops begin the infiltration process resulting in lower troop commitments appearing in South Vietnam in later months. For troops going from North Vietnam to Saigon or the Mekong Delta area we would expect lags of up to 5 months to be significant. Similarly, it required 4 months for the United States to get 100,000 troops into the field in Vietnam after the decision was made to commit them in Washington in 1965.

Correlation results are of interest in testing the hypotheses of the decision-makers, but they are of primary interest as a preliminary to regression analysis. We also used some preliminary correlation analysis in the choice of variables to be used and in index construction.

The third phase of the analysis was the calculation of predictive models for each of the 20 indices through multiple regression. We also allowed lagged variables and differences to be used as explanatory variables. We used lags of 1 and 3 months for most variables plus lags of 5 months for bombing of the North and changes in the rate of U.S. commitment to South Vietnam. We also included four exogenous season variables to account for the effect of weather and the Christmas-Tet period. The type of regression we used (BMD 02R)[6] has been called stepwise regression, but is really repeated multiple regression with a decision rule for the selection of the next variable to be included in the regression. The first variable used as an independent variable is that variable which has the highest correlation with the dependent variable. The second variable brought in is that which has the highest partial correlation with the dependent variable after allowing for predictive ability of the first independent variable. The coefficient of the first independent variable may change when the second independent variable is brought in. We repeated this process until we had 6 independent variables for each dependent variable. We had some additional control over the selection process since we designated some variables not to be considered for inclusion in the analysis to avoid reciprocal predictive loops. For instance, it makes little sense to explain U.S. casualties from Communist casualties and to explain Vietcong casualties in terms of American casualties as these variables are both indicators of the same phenomenon, level of hostilities. The results of the regression analysis with different possible explanatory variables appear in the Regression Appendix. See pp. 203-213.

In order to attach causal significance to such regression the explanatory variables must be independent. As our variables are not independent we have not attempted causal modeling in this study.

The fourth phase of the mathematical analysis was simulation and prediction. Regression analysis is one form of prediction in which each variable is predicted in terms of the known values of other variables. While such techniques permit extrapolation to other wars they do not allow extrapolation into the future since we have no known values upon which to base our predictions. Other studies have attempted to extrapolate a single curve into the future. We desired to extrapolate the entire system into the future much as Richardson[7] studied the arms race system.

Techniques were required that permitted predictions based on pre-

---

[6]W. J. Dixon (ed.), Biomedical Computer Programs, Los Angeles Health Science Computer Facility, Department of Preventive Medicine and Public Health, School of Medicine, University of California at Los Angeles, 1964.

[7]Lewis F. Richardson, *Arms and Insecurity,* Chicago, Quadrangle, 1960.

vious values in order to provide a time continuity not present in concurrent-time regression. If present values are sufficiently dependent upon past values then one can confidently predict into the future. This process is similar to methods used in numerical analysis for the numerical solution of differential equations. For instance, the same equations could be derived from Richardson's model of the arms race process using either numerical techniques for the solution of his differential equations or using lagged regression analysis as we have done in this research.

To simulate such a system, we put in five real months' data values (since we have lags up to five months) and made the first month's prediction just as is done in regular regression prediction. However, we made the second month's prediction from four real data points and the first predicted values. We continued this bootstrapping process until, after the 10th month we were basing predictions only upon previously predicted values.

Regular regression analysis leads to a system of simultaneous equations whose solution is the prediction. However, a general system presents possible problems of stability, and consultation with an econometrician led us to attempt to develop a recursive system.

Simultaneous systems also require much difficult parameter calculation in order to prevent biased estimation of parameters. We did encounter problems of this sort when using a simultaneous system. A recursive system provides simple calculation of predictions. A recursive system demands a hierarchy of variables for concurrent interaction. For instance, if the current value of U.S. casualties is used to predict this month's Communist casualties, then this month's Communist casualties cannot be used in the prediction of this month's allied casualties. However, previous values of Communist casualties can be used to predict current U.S. casualties. All such causal loops must be avoided. However, we have found that establishment of a hierarchy, which may seem artificial, is actually an aid to understanding the system.

We considered three different forms of hierarchy. The first, which we refer to as empirical, was designed to give us the highest amount of variance accounted for in the regression and to provide the best predictive simulation, though the process significance of the model would be less. We put troop commitments at the top of the hierarchy, followed by military joint outcomes and then changes in levels of will among the participants. Communication variables were at the bottom of the hierarchy. Thus, within a single month, an increase in Communist commitments can lead to an increase in U.S. commitments (airborne troops can go into action in South Vietnam one week after the decision is made to commit them from the United States). These developments lead to increased bombing, increased casualties, and then to changes in Communist defectors, piastre rates, and U.S. popular approval of the President. Finally, the decision-makers react verbally with statements of perception and preference. We did not allow this month's communications to influence this month's military variables, since we believed that communications have a quicker reaction time than military matters.

Since the influence of statements upon action variables is of more interest to policymakers than the opposite relationship, we also developed control models for both sides of the conflict. For this model we divided the variables into those which the decision-makers could explicitly control (statements, troop commitments, and bombing), and those which they hoped to influence. Each control model had two parts. First a model of the war attempted to predict the effect of the decision-maker's actions upon all aspects of the war not under his direct control. How well do Johnson's statements and bombing predict Communist defectors? The second part of the control model was a model of the decision-maker. Upon what do Johnson and Ho Chi Minh base their decisions? This model completed the system, as is required for system simulation. After studying both the regression results for each of these models and the simulation resulting, we developed a fourth model composed of the best parts of each of these within the constraints of hierarchy. The process described above is a simple attempt to develop a system model from empirical results.

We believe that simulation offers several advantages over regression analysis. First, it allows interactive effects to become apparent even though we have considered only additive regression models. Interaction must take place over time, but it is a factor just as it was in Richardson's studies of arms races. We feel that this is a more realistic method of studying interaction in international reactions than multiplicative models since the assumptions necessary for such multiplicative terms are difficult to support.

TESTS OF POLICY-MAKERS' MODELS

The model of the Vietnam War held by American policymakers can be best observed when we focus on a few key policy-relevant dependent variables. When talking about the level of *North Vietnamese and Vietcong troops in South Vietnam* and the military commitment they represent, the political and military leaders in the Executive branch of the United States government often voice their ideas as to what effects *changes in the level* of the numbers of these troops, especially in regard to what they can do to affect *changes in these levels.* One way that the United States policy-makers believe that the *rate of Communist military effort* can be decreased is by *increasing the rate of United States commitments* of troops, supplies, and its own military effort. General Westmoreland stated this hypothesis in his answers to questions on *Meet the Press* on November 19, 1967. Asked about his request for additional troops, he expressed the belief that this increase in American forces would reduce Communist forces. "I believe that a force of the strength of 525,000 will put us in an excellent military posture. Based on the situation as I see it now, and as I project, we should continue to grind down the enemy so that he will be progressively weakened."[8]

Similarly, American policy-makers have repeatedly stated that the rate of Communist troop commitments can be decreased *by U.S. bombing of North Vietnam.* For example, President Johnson stated in his Johns Hopkins University speech in Baltimore on April 7, 1965: "In recent months attacks on South Vietnam were stepped up. Thus, it became necessary for us to increase our response and to make attacks by air. . . . We do this in order to slow down aggression."[9]

An alternative hypothesis about the relationship between North Vietnamese infiltration and U.S. bombing of the North was held within the administration. However, Secretary of Defense McNamara has stated an important qualification to the administration's belief that U.S. bombing of North Vietnam will reduce the rate of communist troop commitments. Speaking about bombing policy before the Preparedness Investigating Subcommittee of the Senate Armed Services Committee he stated on August 25, 1967 that: "Our primary objective was to reduce the flow and/or to increase the cost of the continued infiltration of men and supplies from North to South Vietnam." But he further stated: "It must, however, be recognized that no improvement and refinements can be expected to accomplish much more than to continue to put a high price tag on N.V.N.'s continued aggression."[10] It is interesting to observe that some policy-makers do seem to modify their models of the conflict on the basis of their experience.

---

[8]General William Westmoreland, Interview on *Meet The Press,* Washington, D. C., Merkle Press, Inc., November 19, 1967, XI, No. 47, p. 17.
[9]Marcus G. Raskin and Bernard B. Fall (eds.), *The Vietnam Reader,* New York, Vintage Books, 1965, pp. 344-345.
[10]*The New York Times,* August 26, 1967, p. 4.

We present empirical evidence testing these hypotheses in the following tables. In these tables, the numbers represent correlation coefficients:

$\triangle$ = change in value from month to month

$\triangle^*$ = proportional change in value from month to month

Hyp stands for Hypothesized relationship in the policy-makers' models

+ stands for positive hypothesized relationship

− stands for negative hypothesized relationship

lag 0, lag 1, lag 2, lag 3 indicate the lag in months between the dependent variable listed at the top of the table and each of the independent variables listed at the left-hand tab.

Significant correlations are underlined. Correlations not significant because of outlying values are not underlined.

In testing these hypotheses, we find no empirical evidence that the change in U.S. commitment predicts the change in Communist troop commitments. The greater the level of U.S. bombing of North Vietnam in current and past months, the lower the rate of Communist troop commitments during the current month. The face validity of time lags of up to five months is indicated by the report that it takes five months to infiltrate troops from North Vietnam to Saigon and Mekong Delta areas of South Vietnam.

Those periods of the war with high proportional increases of bombing (or escalation) have corresponded to increased Communist troop commitments two months later. Thus, it appears that U.S. bombing of North Vietnam may physically decrease infiltration, but *escalation* of the bombing is matched by North Vietnamese escalation of troop commitments. Thus, the North Vietnamese appear to be reacting to proportional changes in U.S. bombing rather than the actual levels.

This finding confirms McNamara's hypothesis that bombing will increase the cost of infiltration, but denies President Johnson's hypothesis that escalation of the bombing will reduce Communist commitments of troops. In fact, escalation of the bombing produces subsequent North Vietnamese counter-escalation, as predicted by the Richardson hypothesis. Once a high level of bombing is obtained, however, Communist troop commitments are subsequently at a lower level.

Inherent in the concept of the Vietnamese conflict as a war of attrition is the notion that increased Communist casualties should result in decreased Communist troop commitment. General Westmoreland, referring to the North Vietnamese, stated: "He could send more troops to the South: he will send more troops to the South. He has to, in order to make up for the guerrillas that he cannot recruit and to fill his depleted ranks, and we will continue to deplete these ranks through the casualties that we will inflict upon him.

"If he sends more units down—and he may—I think he will be hard pressed to support these units with a constant flow of manpower."[11]

We confirm the administration hypothesis that higher Communist attrition reduces the rate of Communist troop commitment. Note, however, that our definition of troop commitment is a composite variable which includes infiltration plus recruitment in South Vietnam minus attrition and defectors. Thus some negative correlation would be expected between attrition and troop commitments as a mathematical artifact.

An often-referred to index of the war is the *kill ratio*. As an indicator of the progress of the war, policy-makers would be interested in the relationship between this variable and the rate of Communist troop commitment. Does allied progress, as indicated by a high kill ratio or positive increase in the kill ratio from previous values, deter the Communists from further commitments, or does it force them to greater efforts in the face of adversity?

The empirical evidence on this point is that the higher the kill ratio

△ NV + VC TROOPS[12]

	Hyp	lag 0	lag 1	lag 2	lag 3
△ US Commitment	−	.08	.21	.14	.05
US Bomb NV	−	−.39	−.40	−.48	−.49
△* US Bomb NV	−	.09	.14	.43	.05
NV + VC Attrition	−	−.39	−.43	−.38	−.38
△ NV + VC Attrition	−		.27		
Kill Ratio	−	−.26	−.52		
△ Kill Ratio	−	.37	.10		
△ NV + VC Troops	+	1.00	.35	−.19	.22
NV Preferences for Outcomes	+	−.05	−.25		
△ US Domestic Support	−	−.11	.07	.12	.06

[11] General William Westmoreland, *Meet The Press*, November 19, 1967, p. 17.
[12] The following values of *r* are reported by Hays (William L. Hays, *Statistics for Psychologists*, Holt, Rinehart and Winston, 1963, p. 531) as necessary for rejection of the null hypothesis that $r = 0$ with 33 observations:

Significance level	Two-tailed	One-tailed
.05	.343	.292
.01	.439	.402
.001	.545	.512

in the previous month, the *lower* the rate of Communist troop commitments in the current month. However, the higher the *increase* in the kill ratio from the previous month to the current month, the *greater* will be the rate of Communist troop commitments in the current month. This finding indicates again that the North Vietnamese are reacting to *changes* in the status of the war.

Another part of the model of the Vietnam conflict held by policymakers in the United States is that the war is a war of attrition of *will*, and, therefore, U.S. bombing of North Vietnam demonstrates our determination to continue the war. In their words, we bomb the North "to convince the leaders of North Vietnam—and all who seek to share their conquest—of a simple fact: We will not be defeated. We will not grow tired. We will not withdraw, either openly or under the cloak of a meaningless agreement."[13] (Johnson, April 17, 1965.) These leaders believe that heavy bombing will decrease the Communist preference for military victory and increase their desire for negotiations.

Contrary to the notion that the United States can coerce or compel the North Vietnamese to prefer to negotiate ("bomb them to the conference table"), we find empirically that the more the U.S. bombs North Vietnam and escalates the bombing the *less* the North Vietnamese desire to negotiate. This finding confirms the earnestness of North Vietnam's primary demand for decreased bombing before meaningful negotiation begins.

We find no empirical relationship between rates of U.S. military commitments and stated North Vietnamese and Vietcong preferences for either negotiating or changing their military and political activities.

NV PREFERENCE FOR NEGOTIATION

	Hyp	lag 0	lag 1	lag 2	lag 3
US Bomb NV	+	−.29	−.15	−.27	−.10
△* US Bomb NV	+	−.31		−.14	
△ US Commitment	+	−.01	−.04	−.01	.17

NV PREFERENCES FOR NV ACTIVITIES

	Hyp	lag 0	lag 1	lag 2	lag 3
US Bomb NV	−	−.14	.01	−.10	.11
△* US Bomb NV	−	−.08	−.29	−.14	
△ US Commitment	−	−.08	.16	.06	−.24

[13] Marcus G. Raskin and B. B. Fall, *The Vietnam Reader*, Vintage Books, New York, 1965, pp. 344-345.

American military commitment to South Vietnam has as its objective the maintenance of the integrity of the South Vietnamese government. The American policy-makers' model thus implies that confidence in the South Vietnamese government will be raised by increased U.S. commitment to South Vietnam and increased bombing of the North. "It was also anticipated that these air operations would raise the morale of the South Vietnamese people who, at the time the bombing started, were under severe military pressure."[14] From this model we would also infer that increased Communist commitments and increased Army of the Republic of Vietnam (ARVN) casualties would decrease confidence in the South Vietnamese government.

We find empirically that neither the level of the bombing nor the proportional change in the bombing have any systematic effect on the value of the piastre.

We also find a slight positive relation between the previous two months' levels of Army of the Republic of Vietnam (ARVN) casualties and the piastre value in Saigon. This might be interpreted that increased ARVN activity increases confidence in the Vietnamese government.

We find that increases in the rate of Communist troop commitments precede decreases in confidence in the government.

We also find no significant correlation between *changes* in the rate of U.S. commitment and changes in the piastre value. This lack of correlation is contrary to the Johnson administration's belief and also to the assumption that confidence in the South Vietnamese government is based largely on U.S. commitment. This lack of systematic relationship suggests that while the piastre rate is a good predictor in the political sphere it cannot itself be explained upon the basis of political variables alone. This explanation must be sought in the realm of econometrics rather than politicometrics.

PIASTRE—SAIGON

	Hyp	lag 0	lag 1	lag 2	lag 3
△ US Commitments	+	−.04	.14	.05	−.07
US Bomb NV	+	−.13	−.11	−.16	−.14
△* US Bomb NV	+	.12	−.02		
ARVN Casualties	−	.12	.25	.31	.15
△ NV + VC Troops	−	−.36	−.42	.08	.17
Kill Ratio	+	−.21	−.30		
△ Kill Ratio	+	.11	.12		

[14]*New York Times,* August 26, 1967, p. 4.

△ PIASTRE—SAIGON

	Hyp	lag 0	lag 1	lag 2
△ US Commitment	+	.12		−.06
US Bomb NV	+	.21		.08
△* US Bomb NV	+	.05		−.07
ARVN Casualties	−	.01		.03
△ NV + VC Troops	−	−.07		−.37
Kill Ratio	+	.15		
△ Kill Ratio	+	.26		

Included in the U.S. policy-makers' model of the Vietnam War is the belief that the morale of North Vietnam and the Vietcong will decline with increases in U.S. military commitment. "In the past two and one-half years I have seen the progressive commitment of United States troops in support of the Vietnamese. I am absolutely certain that

NV + VC DEFECTORS

	Hyp	lag 0	lag 1	lag 2	lag 3
△ US Commitment	+	.04	.10	.09	−.12
US Bomb NV	+	.24	.16	.35	.31
△* US Bomb NV	+	.01	−.22	−.29	−.26
Military Initiative	+	.03	.23	.39	.35
△ Military Initiative	+	−.20	−.13		
Kill Ratio	+	.44	.42		
△ Kill Ratio	+	−.04	.02		
NV + VC Attrition	+	.63	.38	.38	.24
△* NV + VC Attrition	+	.14	.07		
△ US Domestic Support	+	−.07	.11	.12	.11

△ NV + VC DEFECTORS

	Hyp	lag 0	lag 2
△ US Commitment	+	.16	−.08
US Bomb NV	+	−.20	−.01
△* US Bomb NV	+	.16	−.06
Military Initiative	+	−.02	.04
Kill Ratio	+	.17	
△ Kill Ratio	+	−.25	
NV + VC Attrition	+	.03	−.25
△* NV + VC Attrition	+	.48	
△ US Domestic Support	+	−.24	−.02

whereas in 1965 the enemy was winning today he is certainly losing. There are indications that the Vietcong and even Hanoi know this."[15]

We find, in agreement with the administration's model, that the higher bombing levels over North Vietnam predict more defectors, an indicator of lower Communist morale, in future months. Also increased military initiative on the part of the U.S. and higher Communist-to-allied kill ratios predict higher defection levels. Correspondingly, decreases in the kill ratio predict fewer defectors. Vietcong and North Vietnamese attrition also correlates positively with the number of Communist defectors. We find no relationship between changes in U.S. commitment and Communist defectors or between changes in U.S. domestic support for President Johnson and Communists defectors, contrary to the administration's belief.

The North Vietnamese and Vietcong have their own model of how variables are related in the conflict. For example, public statements made recently by Xuan Thuy, chief negotiator of the North Vietnamese at the Paris meetings with the Americans, reveal his belief that *increases in the rate of U.S. commitments to South Vietnam* occur when there is declining confidence in the government of South Vietnam, when U.S. spokesmen state that they want to negotiate, when U.S. spokesmen perceive increasing Communist military and political activity, and when U.S. spokesmen say they prefer less U.S. activity.[16]

We find no systematic significant empirical evidence for any of these stated relationships. Thus Xuan Thuys' stated model of the dynamics of the war is also inadequate for purposes of prediction.

△ US COMMITMENT

	Hyp	lag 0	lag 1	lag 2	lag 3
Piastre—Saigon	−	−.04	.14	.04	−.07
△ Piastre—Saigon	−	−.34	.24		
US Preferences for Negotiations	+	.08	−.02		
US Perceptions of NV	+	.02	.01		
US Preferences for US	−	−.07	.31		

Similarly, from our communications data we observed that the North Vietnamese associate increases in *U.S. bombing* with declining confidence in the government of South Vietnam, with more U.S. spokesmen's

---

[15] *The New York Times,* November 22, 1967, p. 2.
[16] See statements in the *New York Times,* May 14, 1968, p. 18, and May 16, 1968, p. 16.

statements of preference to negotiate, with U.S. spokesmen's perceptions of more North Vietnamese military and political activity, and with higher U.S. casualties absolutely and in relation to Communist casualties.

Stating the relationship betwen U.S. peace proposals and U.S. escalation, Xuan Thuy stated: "But it is common knowledge that every time the U.S. Government speaks of 'peace negotiations' it perpetrates still more dangerous acts of war."[17]

We find empirically that low confidence in the South Vietnamese government is followed by high bombing levels two to three months later. We also find that U.S. casualties in past and current months are highly correlated with U.S. bombing. However, since both of these variables are increasing over time, this is in part a spurious correlation, since there is no significant relationship when the time component is removed by using differences from month to month.

BOMB NV	Hyp	lag 0	lag 1	lag 2	lag 3
Piastre—Saigon	−	−.15	−.23	−.40	−.45
△ Piastre—Saigon	−	.21	.26		
US Preference for Negotiations	+	.21	.15		
US Perceptions of NV	+	.07	.04		
US Casualties	+	.73	.80	.84	.86
△ US Casualties	+	−.19	−.17		
Kill Ratio	−	.66	.71		
△ Kill Ratio	−	−.10	.01		
Military Initiative	−	.35	.25	.34	.30
△ Military Initiative	−	.01	−.06		

△* **BOMB NV**	Hyp	lag 0	lag 1	lag 2	lag 3
Piastre—Saigon	−	.12		−.02	
△ Piastre—Saigon	−	.04			
US Preferences for Negotiations	+	−.26			
US Perceptions of NV	+	−.09			
US Casualties	+	−.06	−.18	−.14	
△ US Casualties	+	.22			
Kill Ratio	−	−.01			
△ Kill Ratio	−	.21			
Military Initiative	−	−.25		−.13	
△ Military Initiative	−	.10			

[17] *The New York Times,* May 13, 1968.

Contrary to North Vietnamese statements, we find that the U.S. bombs North Vietnam *more* when it is winning and has been winning in the previous month as measured by the kill ratio.

With regard to U.S. communications, we find no significant relationship between U.S. preference for negotiations or U.S. perception of North Vietnamese activity and the level or change in the level of U.S. bombing.

At the second Paris session, Xuan Thuy stated: "Not only the American bombings against North Vietnam did not succeed in preventing the U.S. defeat in South Vietnam but they resulted in still more serious U.S. setbacks in both zones of Vietnam."[18] We verified this aspect of the North Vietnamese model. However, this positive relationship between U.S. bombing and U.S. casualties may also be spurious due to time trends because the differences from month to month in these variables are uncorrelated.

US CASUALTIES

	Hyp	lag 0	lag 1	lag 2	lag 3
△ US Commitment	+	−.12	−.21	.05	−.21
US Bomb NV	+	.72	.79	.84	.86
△* US Bomb NV	+	−.06		.14	

△ US CASUALTIES

	Hyp	lag 0	lag 1	lag 2	lag 3
△ US Commitment	+	.37		.09	
US Bomb NV	+	−.19		−.11	
△* US Bomb NV	+	.22		.19	

The North Vietnamese predict that the less domestic public support the Johnson administration has, the more U.S. leaders will want to negotiate. "An unprecedented, widespread movement, embracing various strata of the American people, ranging from professors, students, scientists, jurists, religious people, writers and artists to laboring people, has risen in the U.S.A., urging the U.S. Government to stop the bombings on North Vietnam and withdraw U.S. troops from South Vietnam. . . . In face of its ever-more-serious isolation in the world and at home, the U.S. Government, while continuing to step up the war, has had to resort to the 'peace offensive' maneuver to sooth public opinion."[19] Empiri-

---

[18] *The New York Times,* May 15, 1968.
[19] *The New York Times,* May 13, 1968.

cally, we find no relationship between U.S. public opinion support for President Johnson and U.S. preference for negotiations.

The North Vietnamese have stated that their determination in the North along with Communist tenacity in the South will force the U.S. to seek negotiations as a way out of the stalemate. Xuan Thuy has said: "Confronted with U.S. heavy defeats in both zones of Vietnam. . . . U.S. President Johnson had to announce on March 31, 1968, the 'limited bombings' of North Vietnam." This bombing limit was a prelude to the Paris negotiations.

We find that no empirical indicator of battle outcomes advantageous to the Communists correlates significantly with U.S. preference for negotiations. Indeed, we find that increased *U.S.* military initiative is a good predictor of U.S. preference for negotiations three months later. This suggests that U.S. peace offensives follow three months after U.S. military offensives.

US PREFERENCE FOR NEGOTIATIONS

	Hyp	lag 0	lag 1	lag 2	lag 3
△ US Domestic Support	−	.11	−.04	−.08	−.19
△ VC Troops	+	−.17	−.24	−.09	−.20
Kill Ratio	−	.18	.19		
△ Kill Ratio	−	−.05	−.11		
Military Initiative	−	.11	.24	.23	.50
US Perception of NV	+	.42	−.03		

METHODOLOGICAL FINDINGS

We calculated 110 separate regression equations in order to predict each of our 20 indices under the constraints of our different hierarchies and to predict differences, which were not used in simulation. The results of the most important of these are reported in the Regression Appendix. The average amounts of variance accounted for depend upon the freedom to select explanatory variables. The predictive ability of each simulation model is summarized below:

	Empirical Model	North Vietnam Control Model	United States Control Model
Minimum r^2	.53	.18	.31
Maximum r^2	.95	.76	.80
Average r^2	.74	.51	.61

The table of regression equations in the Regression Appendix presents the variance accounted for in each equation as well as the additional variance accounted for by each variable in the predictive equation.

We attempted simulations based on each of the four models. Three of them exhibited stable behavior. The North Vietnamese control model diverged rapidly, exhibiting oscillatory behavior, as is common for unstable differential systems. The second predicted value of U.S. casualties was negative. Investigation revealed that the regression equation for U.S. casualties for this model showed non-random effects. The first 7 predictions are too small whereas the last 10 values are too large. Such systematic, non-random effects are not accounted for.

The other three simulations were quite stable. The amount of unexplained variance in the simulation was from 30 to 60 percent greater than the unexplained variance of the regression equations. Thus we can explain about 50% of the variance even though we are forecasting up to 3 years from the initial exact data values. We believe that this systematic behavior is evidence that we have tapped some systematic aspects of the Vietnam conflict with at least three of our four models. We believe that this type of result is methodologically similar to the post-diction results of the Pool, Abelson, Popkin[20] election simulations, since our regression equations are based on the three years' data. Our forecasts into 1968 are true prediction. The best way of presenting the results of the simulation is to show the graphs of some variables. See pages 188-195 below. In these graphs, the lighter line connecting pluses through 1967 represents the actual values taken on by each variable, month by month. The heavy line connecting stars through 1968 represents the values predicted by the simulation of the empirical model. It is evident that we failed to predict the magnitude of the increase in casualties accompanying the recent Tet offensive, though we do predict some increase. The best indicator we have that a new process was underway is that our predictions of Communist defectors are increasing during the last months of 1967, whereas the actual defection levels were decreasing to all-time lows. This suggests that some systematic effect present which we have not tapped. On the other hand, the predictions of the bombing of the North are fairly accurate since bombing has continued at a high level in spite of the restriction of targets.

It should be noted that our predictions have a very regular yearly phase component. This is partially due to the fact that there are yearly

[20]Ithiel de Sola Pool, R. P. Abelson, Samuel L. Popkin, *Candidates, Issues, and Strategies,* M.I.T. Press, Cambridge, Mass., 1965.

components in the phenomena and partially because of mathematical artifact. To understand to what extent the war can be modeled as a linear trend and a yearly phase, we attempted to predict each variable from the linear time trend and the month. This regression accounted for an average of only 35% of the variance. This suggests that our phase component is more a time series analysis than mere yearly phase. As a mathematical exploration of the simulation, forecasts were attempted through 1972. After 1968 the predictions settled down to a yearly phase with no escalatory or de-escalatory trends. This stability leads us to believe that time series analysis would be relevant.

Comparison of the simulations reveals that the predictions are closer to each other than to the real values. This suggests that each model is tapping similar systematic aspects of the conflict, though the degrees of success vary slightly. All models exhibit the same behavior regarding the prediction of Communist defectors during the last months of 1967. The difference between prediction and actual data is of the same sign for all three stable simulations about 80% of the time.

CONCLUSION

Although policy-makers on either side of the war may not conceive of their military decisions as based upon models, it is clear from their public statements that they do hold and act on hypotheses about the dynamics of the Vietnamese conflict. It is also clear from our analysis that many of their hypotheses can be disproved by an empirical study of the interactions in the war. Policy-makers are apparently willing to modify their models when they become aware that those models do not adequately explain the course of the conflict. To the extent that they consciously formulate hypotheses and test them against their experience, they enhance their ability to predict and are in a position to develop more effective policies. We believe, however, that policy-makers are, at the present time, handicapped by an inadequate understanding of the dynamics of the war; that their predictions are too often inaccurate and they are, thus, too often unable to achieve their policy goals thereby imposing heavy costs on others and themselves.

We feel these handicaps are greater than necessary given the analytic tools available for predicting the dynamics of the war. In our research we have attempted systematically to test the current hypotheses of the policy-makers; we have corroborated parts of their existing models and revealed errors in other parts, and explored new techniques for predicting the course of the war, thereby developing new, more comprehensive models. We suggest that to the extent that our work has been accurate it represents an advance in predictive techniques and could provide the basis for more effective policies if employed by decision-makers.

On the basis of our work, simulation appears to us to be a particularly useful tool for social science research. Causal simulations are necessary to explore the consequences of alternative behavior. We regard our efforts in developing predictive simulation techniques as a first step in this direction.

GRAPHS

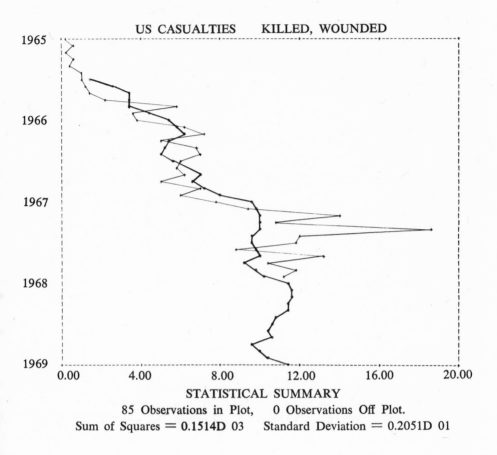

US CASUALTIES   KILLED, WOUNDED

STATISTICAL SUMMARY
85 Observations in Plot,   0 Observations Off Plot.
Sum of Squares = **0.1514D 03**   Standard Deviation = 0.2051D 01

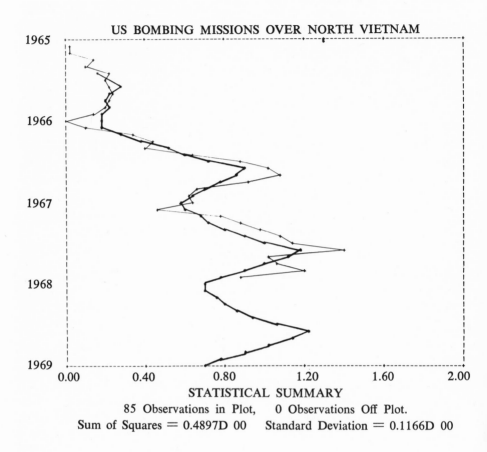

US BOMBING MISSIONS OVER NORTH VIETNAM

STATISTICAL SUMMARY
85 Observations in Plot,   0 Observations Off Plot.
Sum of Squares = 0.4897D 00   Standard Deviation = 0.1166D 00

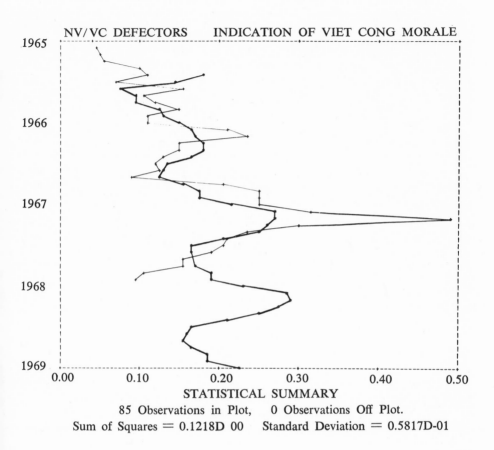

NV/VC DEFECTORS   INDICATION OF VIET CONG MORALE

STATISTICAL SUMMARY
85 Observations in Plot,   0 Observations Off Plot.
Sum of Squares = 0.1218D 00   Standard Deviation = 0.5817D-01

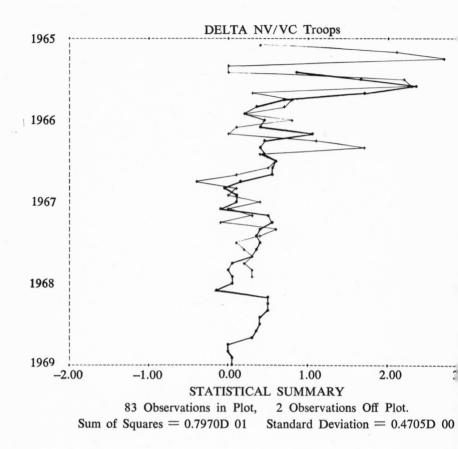

DELTA NV/VC Troops

1965

1966

1967

1968

1969

-2.00   -1.00   0.00   1.00   2.00

STATISTICAL SUMMARY

83 Observations in Plot,   2 Observations Off Plot.

Sum of Squares = 0.7970D 01   Standard Deviation = 0.4705D 00

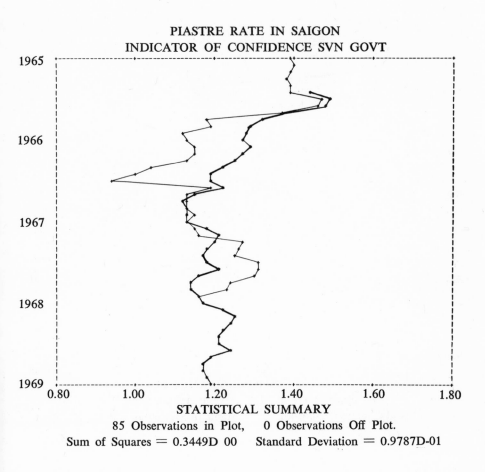

PIASTRE RATE IN SAIGON
INDICATOR OF CONFIDENCE SVN GOVT

STATISTICAL SUMMARY
85 Observations in Plot,   0 Observations Off Plot.
Sum of Squares = 0.3449D 00   Standard Deviation = 0.9787D-01

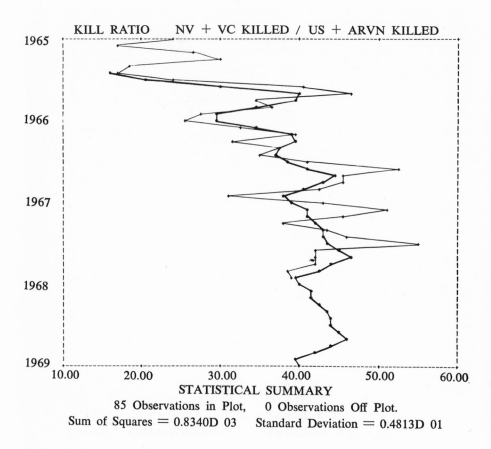

KILL RATIO   NV + VC KILLED / US + ARVN KILLED

STATISTICAL SUMMARY

85 Observations in Plot,   0 Observations Off Plot.
Sum of Squares = 0.8340D 03   Standard Deviation = 0.4813D 01

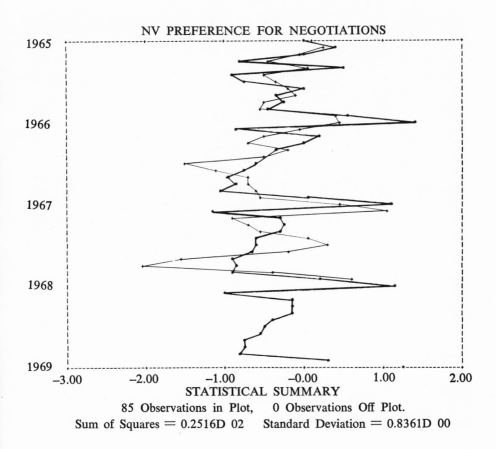

NV PREFERENCE FOR NEGOTIATIONS

STATISTICAL SUMMARY

85 Observations in Plot,   0 Observations Off Plot.

Sum of Squares = 0.2516D 02   Standard Deviation = 0.8361D 00

COMMUNICATIONS APPENDIX

For purposes of this study, the communication data were aggregated into the indices described below. Messages about the specific referents included within each index were coded to pick up two characteristics: one, how frequently the referent was mentioned, and two, whether the referent was perceived or preferred to be increasing or decreasing. The following code was used:

Blank = referent not in statement.

Perceptions:

0 certainly decreasing
1 possibly decreasing
2 unchanging
3 possibly increasing
4 certainly increasing

Preferences:

5 for decreasing
7 for continuing unchanged
9 for increasing

Thus, we reduced all policy-makers' communications about any of the specific referents to a single digit on one of two ordinal scales. A statement by President Johnson stating that domestic dissension weakened the U.S. posture of firmness in Vietnam would be coded "9" in column 36 (specific referent: U.S. domestic support of Johnson administration's Vietnam policy; popularity of L.B.J. and his Vietnam policy; determination, will, patience, of U.S. public for continuing war). We hypothesize that the sums of the numerical values of each specific referent comprising an index are related to the behavior of those who communicate.

The speakers or the sources of these communications reported in *The New York Times* and indexed in *The New York Times Index,* include the following:

In the *United States:* President L. B. Johnson; Secretary of Defense McNamara; Secretary of State Rusk; U. S. Ambassadors in Saigon H. C. Lodge, M. Taylor, U. A. Johnson, W. Porter, E. Bunker, E. Locke; Field

Commander Gen. Westmoreland; Gen. E. Wheeler and others on the Joint Chiefs of Staff; other U.S. military officials; Vice-President Humphrey; Presidential Assistants and Advisors McG. Bundy, B. D. Moyers, W. W. Rostow, R. W. Komer, G. Christian, T. Johnson, J. Califano, R. Kinter, Bryant, C. Clifford, A. Fortas, D. Acheson, J. Gardner; CIA Directors W. F. Raborn, R. Helms; Undersecretaries of State G. W. Ball, N. Katzenbach, E. V. Rostow; Assistant Secretary of State for East Asia W. P. Bundy; Deputy Assistant Secretary of State for East Asia L. Unger; Deputy Secretaries of Defense C. Vance, and P. Nitze; Assistant Secretary of Defense for International Security Affairs J. T. McNaughton; Deputy Director of AID W. S. Gaud; USIA Director L. Marks; Ambassador-at-Large A. Harriman; U.N. Ambassadors A. Stevenson and A. Goldberg; other "unidentified spokesmen" from the Executive Branch of the U.S. government; and other special U.S. envoys and ambassadors.

In *North Vietnam:* President Ho Chi Minh; Premier Pham Van Dong; Defense Minister Vo Nguyen Giap; Truong Chinh; other inner elite, including Foreign Minister Nguyen Duy Trinh, Communist Party Head Le Duan, President of the Vietnam Fatherland Front Ton Duc Thang; Le Duc Tho; official media including *Quan Doi Nhan Dan, Hoc Tap, Tien Phong,* and Hanoi Radio.

In the *National Liberation Front (Vietcong)*: Official spokesmen of the NLF including Nguyen Huu Tho, President of the Presidium of the NFLSV Central Committee; and Nguyen Van Tien, permanent representative of the NLF in Hanoi; official NLF media, including the clandestine Liberation Radio.

In *South Vietnam*: Presidents Thieu and Khan; Vice-President (former Premier) Ky; other South Vietnamese government spokesmen; and official South Vietnamese media.

1) *North Vietnamese and Vietcong preferences for their own military and political activities.* This index is a sum composed of a) the product of the *preference value* of North Vietnamese and Vietcong statements concerning their troop infiltration, troop strength, supplies, munitions, recruitment, and other military capabilities in South Vietnam and in the Demilitarized Zone, *times* the *frequency* of these statements; plus b) the product of the *preference value* of North Vietnamese and Vietcong statements concerning their armed hostilities (terrorism, conventional and guerrilla operations) and effectiveness (military control) in South Vietnam, *times* the *frequency* of these statements; plus c) the sum of the *frequency* of their *preference* statements plus the *frequency* of their *perception* statements referring to North Vietnamese

and Vietcong morale, determination, motivation, confidence, optimism, lack of defections, and will to continue the war; plus d) the *frequency* of their preference statements referring to Vietcong political activities, effectiveness, strength, structure, influence, popular support, political and administrative control, and implementation of the NLF program in South Vietnam. This index of *statements* is so constructed that high values should correspond to high military and political *activity* on the part of the Communists.

2) *North Vietnamese and Vietcong perceptions of United States and South Vietnamese military and political activities.* This index is composed of the sum of the *frequencies* of North Vietnamese and Vietcong statements concerning a) their perceptions of U.S. bombing, shelling, mining, invading, blockading, and other armed hostilities against North Vietnam, including the effects and effectiveness of these hostilities, destruction in North Vietnam, and military, economic, industrial, and agricultural costs to North Vietnam; b) their preferences concerning U.S. troop strength, bases, weapons, firepower, mobility, and other military capabilities in South Vietnam; c) their perception of U.S. domestic public support of the Johnson administration's Vietnam policy, the popularity of President Johnson and his Vietnam policy, and the determination, patience, and will of the U.S. public for continuing the war; d) their perceptions of ARVN military activity and effectiveness; e) their perceptions of civilian casualties in North Vietnam; plus f) the *value* of their perceptions of the South Vietnamese government's stability and its control of and support from the people of South Vietnam. This index of statements is so constructed that high values should correspond to high U.S. and South Vietnamese military and political activity.

3) *North Vietnamese and Vietcong preferences for negotiations.* This index of North Vietnamese and Vietcong statements is composed of the sum of a) the product of their *preference value* for third party (e.g. UN, non-belligerents) mediation in achieving peace negotiations and settlement, and in supervision of a settlement, *times* the *frequency* of these statements; *minus* b) the frequency of their preference statements concerning reciprocity in military de-escalation; plus c) the sum of the *preference value* of their statements concerning talks or negotiations between the U.S. and/or the South Vietnamese on the one hand and the North Vietnamese on the other, including a new international conference at Geneva or elsewhere, *times* the frequency of these statements, *plus* the *frequency* of their statements *perceiving* such talks; plus d) the product of their *preference value* of their statements concerning talks

between the U.S. and the Vietcong, including a recognized role for the Vietcong in negotiations, *times* the *frequency* of these statements; *minus* e) the frequency of the'r perception statements concerning the sincerity, trustworthiness, honesty, and seriousness of U.S. peace proposals and moves; plus f) the value of their perceptions of the sincerity, trustworthiness, honesty, and seriousness of their peace proposals and moves, times the frequency of such statements; plus g) the preference value of their statements for a cease fire, truce, armistice, or temporary cessation of the war, times the frequency of these statements; plus h) the frequency of North Vietnamese and Vietcong diplomatic contacts and communications the content of which are unreported. This index was constructed so that higher values of it should correspond to lower values of North Vietnamese and Vietcong military activity.

4) *North Vietnamese and Vietcong preferences for outcomes and goals.* This index of North Vietnamese and Vietcong statements is composed of the sum of a) the preference value of their statements concerning their victory, winning the war militarily, defeating or destroying their enemy, and having their enemy capitulate, withdraw, retreat, or fade out, times the frequency of these preference statements, plus the frequency of their statements perceiving such victory; *minus* b) the sum of their perception values times the frequency of such perceptions concerning a permanent cessation of warfare, peace, settlement, negotiated compromise, an end to aggression and hostilities, and international order and security, *plus* the frequency of their preference statements for such a peaceful settlement; plus c) the frequency of their preferences for the reunification of Vietnam, independence, sovereignty, territorial integrity, democratic freedom, and the implementation of the 1954 Geneva accords; plus d) the frequency of their preferences for neutralization and non-alignment of South Vietnam, and a coalition government which would include Vietcong and non-Vietcong. This index was constructed to have higher values as Communist activity was higher.

5) *U.S. and South Vietnamese perceptions of North Vietnamese and Vietcong military and political activities.* This index of communications is composed of the sum of the products of the perception value times the frequency of perception statements by the U.S. and South Vietnamese leaders of the following items: a) North Vietnamese and Vietcong infiltration, troop strength, supplies, munitions, recruitment and other military capabilities in South Vietnam and in the Demilitarized Zone; b) North Vietnamese and Vietcong armed hostilities (terrorism, conventional, and guerrilla operations) and effectiveness and military

control in South Vietnam; c) North Vietnamese and Vietcong morale, determination, motivation, confidence, will to continue war, optimism, and lack of defections; d) Vietcong political activities, effectiveness, strength, structure, influence, popular support, political and administrative control, and implementation of the NLF program in South Vietnam; e) Communist Chinese participation in the war and aid to North Vietnam and the Vietcong, including "volunteers," threats to U.S. security and interests, likelihood of U.S. war with China, possibility of U.S. (nuclear) bombing of China, and North Vietnamese dependence on China; f) Soviet participation in the war and aid to the North Vietnamese and Vietcong, including "volunteers," Soviet protection of North Vietnam, likelihood of U.S. war with the U.S.S.R., tensions between the U.S. and U.S.S.R. over Vietnam, and North Vietnamese dependence on the U.S.S.R. This index was constructed to have higher values when Communist activity was high.

6) *U.S. and South Vietnamese preferences for U.S. and South Vietnamese military and political activities.* This index of U.S. and South Vietnamese communications is composed of the sum of a) the preference value minus the perception value, times the frequency of preference statements concerning U.S. bombing, shelling, mining, invading, blockading, and other armed hostilities against North Vietnam, the effects and effectiveness of these hostilities, including destruction in North Vietnam, and military, economic, industrial, and agricultural costs to North Vietnam; plus b) the preference value minus the perception value, times the frequency of preference statements concerning U.S. troop strength, bases, weapons, firepower, mobility, and other military capabilities in South Vietnam; plus c) the preference value times the frequency of preference statements concerning U.S. bombing, armed hostilities, and effectiveness in South Vietnam; plus d) the preference value times the frequency of preference statements concerning U.S. aid to, alliance with, commitments to, shield for, interest in, influence on, support for, and strengthening of South Vietnam and South Vietnam's dependence on the U.S.; *minus* e) the frequency of preference statements concerning U.S. domestic public support of the Johnson administration's Vietnam policy, the popularity of President Johnson and his Vietnam policy, and the determination, patience, and will of the U.S. public for continuing the war; plus f) the frequency of preference statements concerning ARVN military activity and effectiveness; plus g) the frequency of perception statements concerning ARVN morale, determination, confidence, optimism, lack of defections, motivation, and will to

continue the war; plus h) the perception value times the frequency of perception statements concerning the government of South Vietnam's stability and control of and support from the South Vietnamese people. This index of communication was constructed so as to have high values when U.S. and South Vietnamese military and political activity were high.

7) *U.S. and South Vietnamese preferences for negotiations.* This index of U.S. and South Vietnamese statements is composed of the sum of a) the frequency of preference statements plus the frequency of perception statements concerning world opinion, prestige, and support of U.S. policy in Vietnam; plus b) the frequency of preference statements concerning reciprocity in military de-escalation; plus c) the frequency of diplomatic contacts and communications the content of which were unreported (e.g. special visits by envoys or ambassadors); plus d) the frequency of preference statements plus the perception values concerning third party mediation in achieving peace negotiations and supervision of a settlement; plus e) the frequency of preference statements plus the perception values concerning talks or negotiations between the U.S. and/or the South Vietnamese on the one hand, and the North Vietnamese on the other, including a new international conference at Geneva or elsewhere; plus f) the preference value times the frequency of preferences concerning talks of negotiations between the U.S. and the Vietcong, including a recognized role for the Vietcong in negotiations; plus g) the perception value times the frequency of U.S. statements concerning the sincerity, trustworthiness, honesty, and seriousness of U.S. peace proposals and moves; plus h) the perception value times the frequency of U.S. statements concerning the sincerity, trustworthiness, honesty, seriousness of North Vietnamese and Vietcong peace proposals and moves; plus i) the preference value times the frequency of U.S. and South Vietnamese statements concerning a cease-fire, truce, armistice, or temporary cessation of the war. This index was constructed to have a high value the *lower* the level of U.S. and South Vietnamese military and political activity.

8) *U.S. and South Vietnamese perceptions and preferences for outcomes and goals.* This index of U.S. and South Vietnamese statements is composed of the sum of a) the perception value times the frequency of perceptions concerning extension or spillover of the war to neighboring countries, *e.g.,* Laos, Cambodia, Thailand; plus b) the perception value times the sum of the frequency of perceptions plus the frequency of preferences of United States speakers concerning the extension of

Communism into Southeast Asian countries, the extension or lack of containment of Communist China and its influence in Southeast Asia, and the spread of other wars of national liberation; *minus* c) the perception value times the frequency of *United States* speakers' perceptions concerning military or political stalemate in the war, including reference to each side controlling only part of South Vietnam, enclaves, or *de facto* territorial division of South Vietnam; plus d) the preference value times the frequency of preferences, plus the frequency of perceptions concerning military victory in the war, defeat or destruction of the enemy, enemy capitulation, withdrawal, retreat, or fade-out; *minus* e) the perception value times the frequency of perceptions, plus the frequency of preferences concerning peace, permanent cessation of the war, settlement, negotiated compromise, end of aggression and hostilities, and international order and security; plus f) the frequency of preferences by the *South Vietnamese* concerning neutralization or non-alignment of South Vietnam, or a coalition government which would include Vietcong and non-Vietcong; plus g) the frequency of preferences concerning the independence, sovereignty, political self-determination, territorial integrity, absence of foreign interference, and security of South Vietnam; plus h) the frequency of preferences for material and economic reconstruction, development, and modernization in South Vietnam, including land and economic reform, price stability, and sharing of wealth.

REGRESSION APPENDIX

In the printouts which follow, the first definition of dependent variable is empirical model. The second definition is U.S. control model. The third definition is North Vietnamese and Vietcong control model.

The constant is the regression intercept. The lag is the time lag in months between the independent variables and the dependent variable. In the first column of coefficients are the b coefficients. In the second column of coefficients are normalized beta coefficients. The variance column is the amount of additional variance accounted for by each independent variable having taken out the effect of the independent variables preceding it in the stepwise regression.

The terms:

Del = Change in value from month to month.

Del* = Proportional change in value from month to month.

```
DEFINITION OF DEL NV+VC TROOPS
                     CONSTANT =    2.70245       NORMALIZED   VARIANCE
     KILL RATIO NV/US  LAG =  1    -0.05346      -0.68458       27 %
     NV PERCEIVE US    LAG =  1    -0.57759      -0.47145       10 %
     DELTA KILL RATIO  LAG =  1     0.50460       0.55131       15 %
     DEL MIL INITIATE  LAG =  1     0.29010       0.29897        8 %
     DEL VC DEFECTORS  LAG =  1    -0.22641      -0.20151        4 %
     NV PREFER NEGOT   LAG =  1    -0.16451      -0.19321        3 %
     TOTAL VARIANCE ACCOUNTED FOR 67 %

DEFINITION OF DEL NV+VC TROOPS
                     CONSTANT =    1.02326       NORMALIZED   VARIANCE
     US BOMBING OF NV  LAG =  3    -0.30604      -0.17382       24 %
     DEL US COMMITMNT  LAG =  5    -0.15240      -0.28583        6 %
     AUGUST WEATHER    LAG =  0     0.27337       0.34378        6 %
     US PREFER US ACT  LAG =  1     0.07074       0.15403        3 %
     US PERCEIVE NV    LAG =  1    -0.16282      -0.20958        3 %
     US BOMBING OF NV  LAG =  0    -0.54728      -0.30605        3 %
     TOTAL VARIANCE ACCOUNTED FOR 45 %

DEFINITION OF DEL NV+VC TROOPS
                     CONSTANT =    2.82514       NORMALIZED   VARIANCE
     KILL RATIO NV/US  LAG =  1    -0.05608      -0.71813       27 %
     NV PERCEIVE US    LAG =  1    -0.56593      -0.46193       10 %
     DELTA KILL RATIO  LAG =  1     0.49729       0.54332       15 %
     DEL* US CASULTY   LAG =  1    -0.08602      -0.23785        9 %
     NV PREFER NEGOT   LAG =  1    -0.18363      -0.21567        4 %
     DEL MIL INITIATE  LAG =  1     0.21637       0.22298        4 %
     TOTAL VARIANCE ACCOUNTED FOR 69 %

DEFINITION OF NV+VC ATTRITION
                     CONSTANT =    0.53724       NORMALIZED   VARIANCE
     US CASUALTIES     LAG =  0     0.18804       0.90854       85 %
     DELTA US SUPPORT  LAG =  1     0.37802       0.23516        2 %
     US BOMBING OF NV  LAG =  0     0.28915       0.12703        2 %
     DEL* NV ATTRITON  LAG =  1     0.08443       0.13863        1 %
     SPRING - FALL     LAG =  0    -0.01959      -0.15560        1 %
     DEL NV+VC TROOPS  LAG =  1     0.15242       0.12794        1 %
     TOTAL VARIANCE ACCOUNTED FOR 92 %

DEFINITION OF NV+VC ATTRITION
                     CONSTANT =    0.50377       NORMALIZED   VARIANCE
     US BOMBING OF NV  LAG =  0     1.20634       0.52997       55 %
     US BOMBING OF NV  LAG =  5     1.14579       0.47851       10 %
     SPRING - FALL     LAG =  0     0.02751       0.21851        3 %
     US PREFER OUTCM   LAG =  0     0.10259       0.13646        2 %
     DEL US COMMITMNT  LAG =  5     0.11805       0.17394        1 %
     DEL US COMMITMNT  LAG =  0     0.10486       0.15825        2 %
     TOTAL VARIANCE ACCOUNTED FOR 73 %

DEFINITION OF NV+VC ATTRITION
                     CONSTANT =    3.12119       NORMALIZED   VARIANCE
     DEL NV+VC TROOPS  LAG =  3    -0.61714      -0.51585       18 %
     DEL NV+VC TROOPS  LAG =  1    -0.43968      -0.36906       23 %
     CHRISTMAS - TET   LAG =  0    -0.55738      -0.33196        9 %
     NV PERCEIVE US    LAG =  1    -0.37445      -0.24011        1 %
     DEL NV+VC TROOPS  LAG =  0    -0.29133      -0.22881        3 %
     NV PREFER NV ACT  LAG =  0     0.11939       0.11108        1 %
     TOTAL VARIANCE ACCOUNTED FOR 55 %
```

```
DEFINITION OF NV+VC DEFECTORS
                     CONSTANT =    0.07446     NORMALIZED  VARIANCE
   NV+VC DEFECTORS   LAG =  1      0.41195     0.41965      55 %
   US PREFER OUTCM   LAG =  1     -0.02740    -0.35423      14 %
   NV PREFER NEGOT   LAG =  1      0.03328     0.32056       9 %
   NV+VC ATTRITION   LAG =  0      0.02759     0.28804       5 %
   NV PREFER OUTCM   LAG =  1      0.03477     0.20090       3 %
   WINTER - SUMMER   LAG =  0      0.00191     0.15309       2 %
   TOTAL VARIANCE ACCOUNTED FOR 88 %

DEFINITION OF NV+VC DEFECTORS
                     CONSTANT =    0.10131     NORMALIZED  VARIANCE
   US BOMBING OF NV  LAG =  5      0.15453     0.67375      26 %
   US PREFER OUTCM   LAG =  1     -0.03289    -0.42521      20 %
   SPRING - FALL     LAG =  0      0.00457     0.37896      12 %
   US PREFER US ACT  LAG =  0      0.01428     0.25622       9 %
   DEL US COMMITMNT  LAG =  5      0.01858     0.28580       5 %
   DEL US COMMITMNT  LAG =  0      0.01191     0.18764       3 %
   TOTAL VARIANCE ACCOUNTED FOR 75 %

DEFINITION OF NV+VC DEFECTORS
                     CONSTANT =    0.22131     NORMALIZED  VARIANCE
   NV PREFER OUTCM   LAG =  0      0.02514     0.14263      17 %
   NV PERCEIVE US    LAG =  0     -0.03449    -0.23329      17 %
   DEL NV+VC TROOPS  LAG =  3     -0.04574    -0.39915      12 %
   DEL NV+VC TROOPS  LAG =  1     -0.03672    -0.32178       6 %
   NV PREFER NEGOT   LAG =  1      0.03720     0.35832       6 %
   NV PREFER OUTCM   LAG =  1      0.04814     0.27815       6 %
   TOTAL VARIANCE ACCOUNTED FOR 64 %

DEFINITION OF KILL RATIO NV/US
                     CONSTANT =   31.52878     NORMALIZED  VARIANCE
   NV+VC ATTRITION   LAG =  0      6.61340     0.67411      44 %
   DELTA KILL RATIO  LAG =  1      2.89353     0.25315      26 %
   ARVN CASUALTIES   LAG =  0    -12.41088    -0.32446       9 %
   MILITARY INITIAT  LAG =  1      4.58797     0.39411       5 %
   TOTAL VARIANCE ACCOUNTED FOR 84 %

DEFINITION OF KILL RATIO NV/US
                     CONSTANT =   35.12360     NORMALIZED  VARIANCE
   US BOMBING OF NV  LAG =  0     13.14792     0.58876      43 %
   US PREFER US ACT  LAG =  1     -1.70227    -0.29680       7 %
   US PREFER OUTCM   LAG =  0     -1.79913    -0.24393       4 %
   DEL* BOMBING NV   LAG =  3     -0.44628    -0.17503       2 %
   US PERCEIVE NV    LAG =  1     -2.20396    -0.22717       2 %
   DEL* BOMBING NV   LAG =  1     -0.62885    -0.21845       4 %
   TOTAL VARIANCE ACCOUNTED FOR 62 %

DEFINITION OF KILL RATIO NV/US
                     CONSTANT =   42.37250     NORMALIZED  VARIANCE
   DEL NV+VC TROOPS  LAG =  3     -6.83697    -0.58252      16 %
   AUGUST WEATHER    LAG =  0      3.16388     0.31860      14 %
   DEL NV+VC TROOPS  LAG =  1     -3.94971    -0.33793      11 %
   CHRISTMAS - TET   LAG =  0     -4.88684    -0.29667       9 %
   SPRING - FALL     LAG =  0     -0.38143    -0.30881       5 %
   NV PREFER OUTCM   LAG =  1      3.49502     0.19716       3 %
   TOTAL VARIANCE ACCOUNTED FOR 58 %
```

```
DEFINITION OF ARVN CASUALTIES
                     CONSTANT =    0.27062     NORMALIZED   VARIANCE
    DEL* US CASULTY   LAG =  1     0.04998       0.42328     14 %
    DELTA KILL RATIO  LAG =  1    -0.09101      -0.30456     15 %
    DEL US COMMITMNT  LAG =  3    -0.02794      -0.16287      9 %
    DEL US COMMITMNT  LAG =  0     0.06408       0.37704      7 %
    US BOMBING OF NV  LAG =  5     0.27853       0.45353      7 %
    PIASTRE.HONGKONG  LAG =  3     0.56372       0.37172     11 %
    TOTAL VARIANCE ACCOUNTED FOR 63 %

DEFINITION OF ARVN CASUALTIES
                     CONSTANT =    0.94196     NORMALIZED   VARIANCE
    US PREFER OUTCM   LAG =  0     0.08641       0.44813     14 %
    AUGUST WEATHER    LAG =  0    -0.06577      -0.25334      9 %
    DEL US COMMITMNT  LAG =  3    -0.02820      -0.16439      7 %
    DEL US COMMITMNT  LAG =  1     0.06288       0.36495      6 %
    DEL US COMMITMNT  LAG =  0     0.05973       0.35145      5 %
    US BOMBING OF NV  LAG =  5     0.20737       0.33766      9 %
    TOTAL VARIANCE ACCOUNTED FOR 50 %

DEFINITION OF ARVN CASUALTIES
                     CONSTANT =    1.26577     NORMALIZED   VARIANCE
    WINTER - SUMMER   LAG =  0     0.00932       0.27898      7 %
    DEL NV+VC TROOPS  LAG =  3     0.10407       0.33916      6 %
    DEL NV+VC TROOPS  LAG =  0    -0.12471      -0.38198      6 %
    NV PERCEIVE US    LAG =  1    -0.05253      -0.13133      2 %
    SPRING - FALL     LAG =  0     0.00616       0.19077      1 %
    NV PREFER OUTCM   LAG =  1    -0.08824      -0.19041      3 %
    TOTAL VARIANCE ACCOUNTED FOR 25 %


DEFINITION OF PIASTRE SAIGON
                     CONSTANT =    0.17942     NORMALIZED   VARIANCE
    PIASTRE SAIGON    LAG =  1     0.77980       0.80072     72 %
    DELTA US SUPPORT  LAG =  1     0.03433       0.15751      4 %
    DEL VC DEFECTORS  LAG =  1     0.02440       0.12582      3 %
    DELTA US SUPPORT  LAG =  0    -0.05243      -0.26386     -3 %
    ARVN CASUALTIES   LAG =  1     0.10466       0.18369      3 %
    MILITARY INITIAT  LAG =  1    -0.02520      -0.15663      2 %
    TOTAL VARIANCE ACCOUNTED FOR 87 %

DEFINITICN OF PIASTRE SAIGON
                     CONSTANT =    1.19994     NORMALIZED   VARIANCE
    WINTER - SUMMER   LAG =  0    -0.00501      -0.28368     13 %
    US PREFER NEGOT   LAG =  0    -0.05062      -0.50124      7 %
    DEL US COMMITMNT  LAG =  5    -0.04153      -0.45130      8 %
    US PERCEIVE NV    LAG =  0     0.07157       0.53416      6 %
    DEL US COMMITMNT  LAG =  1     0.03648       0.40052      6 %
    DEL* BOMBING NV   LAG =  3     0.00945       0.26817      5 %
    TCTAL VARIANCE ACCOUNTED FOR 45 %

DEFINITION OF PIASTRE SAIGON
                     CONSTANT =    1.25345     NORMALIZED   VARIANCE
    WINTER - SUMMER   LAG =  0    -0.00676      -0.38277     13 %
    NV PREFER NV ACT  LAG =  1     0.07444       0.51317     13 %
    NV PREFER NV ACT  LAG =  0     0.06120       0.41996     11 %
    CHRISTMAS - TET   LAG =  0    -0.09905      -0.43509      4 %
    NV PREFER OUTCM   LAG =  1    -0.05439      -0.22201      3 %
    NV PREFER NEGOT   LAG =  0     0.02705       0.18744      3 %
    TCTAL VARIANCE ACCOUNTED FOR 47 %
```

DEFINITION OF PIASTRE HONGKONG

			CONSTANT =	0.30794	NORMALIZED	VARIANCE
PIASTRE HONGKONG	LAG =	1		0.64413	0.65904	70 %
DELTA US SUPPORT	LAG =	0		-0.07894	-0.34814	6 %
ARVN CASUALTIES	LAG =	1		0.16857	0.25927	5 %
MILITARY INITIAT	LAG =	3		-0.03359	-0.20593	3 %
DEL US COMMITMNT	LAG =	5		-0.02252	-0.21446	3 %
DEL US COMMITMNT	LAG =	1		0.01666	0.16029	2 %

TOTAL VARIANCE ACCOUNTED FOR 89 %

DEFINITION OF PIASTRE HONGKONG

			CONSTANT =	1.36030	NORMALIZED	VARIANCE
WINTER - SUMMER	LAG =	0		-0.02013	-0.99885	19 %
US BOMBING OF NV	LAG =	0		-0.37886	-1.07574	14 %
US BOMBING OF NV	LAG =	5		0.31233	0.84304	13 %
US PREFER NEGOT	LAG =	1		-0.04036	-0.35209	5 %
US PERCEIVE NV	LAG =	1		0.04771	0.31182	7 %
AUGUST WEATHER	LAG =	0		0.03827	0.24436	4 %

TOTAL VARIANCE ACCOUNTED FOR 62 %

DEFINITION OF PIASTRE HONGKONG

			CONSTANT =	1.27950	NORMALIZED	VARIANCE
DEL NV+VC TROOPS	LAG =	0		0.07212	0.36618	22 %
WINTER - SUMMER	LAG =	0		-0.00184	-0.09130	11 %
DEL NV+VC TROOPS	LAG =	1		0.06986	0.37900	7 %
NV PERCEIVE US	LAG =	0		-0.08867	-0.37130	5 %
NV PREFER OUTCM	LAG =	1		-0.05904	-0.21119	4 %
AUGUST WEATHER	LAG =	0		0.02854	0.18223	2 %

TOTAL VARIANCE ACCOUNTED FOR 51 %

DEFINITION OF DEL US COMMITMNT

			CONSTANT =	3.22674	NORMALIZED	VARIANCE
US BOMBING OF NV	LAG =	1		-2.52377	-0.75268	17 %
DEL PIASTRE SAIG	LAG =	1		0.75524	0.37685	11 %
DEL NV+VC TROOPS	LAG =	1		-0.66791	-0.37150	10 %
DEL US COMMITMNT	LAG =	5		-0.30277	-0.29560	7 %
NV PREFER NV ACT	LAG =	1		-0.62978	-0.39006	8 %
DEL* BOMBING NV	LAG =	1		-0.11410	-0.25767	6 %

TOTAL VARIANCE ACCOUNTED FOR 59 %

DEFINITION OF DEL US COMMITMNT

			CONSTANT =	3.43241	NORMALIZED	VARIANCE
NV+VC ATTRITION	LAG =	1		-0.31091	-0.20693	18 %
DEL NV+VC TROOPS	LAG =	1		-0.75386	-0.41931	10 %
DEL PIASTRE SAIG	LAG =	1		0.68746	0.34303	10 %
US BOMBING OF NV	LAG =	1		-1.93853	-0.57814	7 %
NV PREFER NV ACT	LAG =	1		-0.44422	-0.27513	6 %
DEL US COMMITMNT	LAG =	5		-0.26902	-0.26265	6 %

TOTAL VARIANCE ACCOUNTED FOR 57 %

DEFINITION OF DEL US COMMITMNT

			CONSTANT =	0.87847	NORMALIZED	VARIANCE
NV PREFER NEGOT	LAG =	1		0.47091	0.28790	12 %
AUGUST WEATHER	LAG =	0		-0.50077	-0.32782	3 %
DEL NV+VC TROOPS	LAG =	3		0.35738	0.19795	3 %
WINTER - SUMMER	LAG =	0		-0.03856	-0.19616	2 %
NV PREFER OUTCM	LAG =	0		0.52060	0.18747	2 %
NV PREFER NV ACT	LAG =	0		-0.19574	-0.12068	1 %

TOTAL VARIANCE ACCOUNTED FOR 23 %

```
DEFINITION OF US CASUALTIES
                     CONSTANT =   -1.58034      NORMALIZED   VARIANCE
    US CASUALTIES    LAG =   1     0.46126        0.46951      69 %
    US BOMBING OF NV LAG =   5     2.40686        0.20804       5 %
    NV+VC DEFECTORS  LAG =   3    16.00336        0.34016       6 %
    DEL US COMMITMNT LAG =   3    -0.64398       -0.19928       3 %
    DEL US COMMITMNT LAG =   0     0.63771        0.19918       2 %
    MILITARY INITIAT LAG =   1     1.05547        0.18410       3 %
    TOTAL VARIANCE ACCOUNTED FOR 88 %

DEFINITION OF US CASUALTIES
                     CONSTANT =    1.43955      NORMALIZED   VARIANCE
    US BOMBING OF NV LAG =   5     7.85382        0.67885      54 %
    US BOMBING OF NV LAG =   0     9.30349        0.84592      10 %
    SPRING - FALL    LAG =   0     0.08077        0.13278      10 %
    AUGUST WEATHER   LAG =   0    -1.19261       -0.24386       2 %
    US BOMBING OF NV LAG =   3    -6.48338       -0.59872       2 %
    US PERCEIVE NV   LAG =   0     0.73323        0.15357       2 %
    TOTAL VARIANCE ACCOUNTED FOR 80 %

DEFINITION OF US CASUALTIES
                     CONSTANT =   11.16920      NORMALIZED   VARIANCE
    DEL NV+VC TROOPS LAG =   1    -3.80939       -0.66180      24 %
    DEL NV+VC TROOPS LAG =   3    -3.64543       -0.63066      30 %
    CHRISTMAS - TET  LAG =   0    -1.98099       -0.24419       9 %
    NV PREFER OUTCM  LAG =   1     0.97288        0.11144       1 %
    WINTER - SUMMER  LAG =   0    -0.07424       -0.11796       1 %
    NV PREFER NV ACT LAG =   0     0.46542        0.08962       1 %
    TOTAL VARIANCE ACCOUNTED FOR 66 %

DEFINITION OF MILITARY INITIAT
                     CONSTANT =    0.24330      NORMALIZED   VARIANCE
    MILITARY INITIAT LAG =   1     0.71690        0.77600      25 %
    DEL MIL INITIATE LAG =   1    -0.59859       -0.62246      11 %
    AUGUST WEATHER   LAG =   0     0.41440        0.52584      16 %
    DEL US COMMITMNT LAG =   5    -0.14802       -0.28013      10 %
    DEL US COMMITMNT LAG =   3     0.14827        0.28473       7 %
    DEL US COMMITMNT LAG =   0     0.12875        0.24956       5 %
    TOTAL VARIANCE ACCOUNTED FOR 74 %

DEFINITION OF MILITARY INITIAT
                     CONSTANT =    1.71200      NORMALIZED   VARIANCE
    SPRING - FALL    LAG =   0    -0.05080       -0.51827      25 %
    DEL US COMMITMNT LAG =   3     0.21329        0.40960      12 %
    DEL* BOMBING NV  LAG =   3    -0.06415       -0.31703       9 %
    US PERCEIVE NV   LAG =   0    -0.20819       -0.27060      10 %
    US PREFER OUTCM  LAG =   1    -0.18109       -0.28803       6 %
    AUGUST WEATHER   LAG =   0     0.17233        0.21867       4 %
    TOTAL VARIANCE ACCOUNTED FOR 66 %

DEFINITION OF MILITARY INITIAT
                     CONSTANT =    1.55905      NORMALIZED   VARIANCE
    SPRING - FALL    LAG =   0    -0.04397       -0.44859      25 %
    NV PREFER OUTCM  LAG =   1     0.26177        0.18608       5 %
    AUGUST WEATHER   LAG =   0     0.21642        0.27462       4 %
    DEL NV+VC TROOPS LAG =   1    -0.21754       -0.23454       5 %
    NV PREFER NV ACT LAG =   0    -0.18861       -0.22539       3 %
    CHRISTMAS - TET  LAG =   0     0.19920        0.15236       2 %
    TOTAL VARIANCE ACCOUNTED FOR 44 %
```

```
DEFINITION OF US BOMBING OF NV
                        CONSTANT =    0.52250     NORMALIZED   VARIANCE
   US BOMBING OF NV  LAG =   1       0.48282       0.49464      85 %
   US CASUALTIES     LAG =   1       0.03751       0.41992       3 %
   WINTER - SUMMER   LAG =   0      -0.00715      -0.12495       3 %
   ARVN CASUALTIES   LAG =   1      -0.37212      -0.20157       2 %
   AUGUST WEATHER    LAG =   0       0.06983       0.15703       1 %
   DEL NV+VC TROOPS  LAG =   1      -0.07402      -0.14143       1 %
   TOTAL VARIANCE ACCOUNTED FOR 95 %

DEFINITION OF US BOMBING OF NV
                        CONSTANT =    0.52250     NORMALIZED   VARIANCE
   US BOMBING OF NV  LAG =   1       0.48282       0.49464      85 %
   US CASUALTIES     LAG =   1       0.03751       0.41992       3 %
   WINTER - SUMMER   LAG =   0      -0.00715      -0.12495       3 %
   ARVN CASUALTIES   LAG =   1      -0.37212      -0.20157       2 %
   AUGUST WEATHER    LAG =   0       0.06983       0.15703       1 %
   DEL NV+VC TROOPS  LAG =   1      -0.07402      -0.14143       1 %
   TOTAL VARIANCE ACCOUNTED FOR 95 %

DEFINITION OF US BOMBING OF NV
                        CONSTANT =    0.94322     NORMALIZED   VARIANCE
   DEL NV+VC TROOPS  LAG =   1      -0.31266      -0.59739      17 %
   WINTER - SUMMER   LAG =   0      -0.03412      -0.59626      17 %
   DEL NV+VC TROOPS  LAG =   3      -0.28839      -0.54871      27 %
   SPRING - FALL     LAG =   0      -0.01215      -0.21967       9 %
   NV PREFER NEGOT   LAG =   1      -0.09045      -0.18996       3 %
   DEL NV+VC TROOPS  LAG =   0      -0.09124      -0.16316       2 %
   TOTAL VARIANCE ACCOUNTED FOR 75 %

DEFINITION OF DELTA US SUPPORT
                        CONSTANT =   -0.10719     NORMALIZED   VARIANCE
   DEL* SV CASULTY   LAG =   1       0.44686       0.81157      21 %
   DEL US COMMITMNT  LAG =   5      -0.22950      -0.49557      10 %
   US PREFER NEGOT   LAG =   1       0.09628       0.19045       7 %
   NV PERCEIVE US    LAG =   1       0.35156       0.33037       5 %
   DEL MIL INITIATE  LAG =   1      -0.24438      -0.28996       5 %
   DEL VC DEFECTORS  LAG =   1      -0.29106      -0.29824       7 %
   TOTAL VARIANCE ACCOUNTED FOR 55 %

DEFINITION OF DELTA US SUPPORT
                        CONSTANT =   -0.19756     NORMALIZED   VARIANCE
   AUGUST WEATHER    LAG =   0      -0.42818      -0.61994      23 %
   US PREFER US ACT  LAG =   0      -0.19855      -0.50010      19 %
   DEL US COMMITMNT  LAG =   1       0.19842       0.43288       6 %
   US PERCEIVE NV    LAG =   0       0.16929       0.25106       4 %
   US PREFER OUTCM   LAG =   0       0.13263       0.25855       5 %
   US PREFER NEGOT   LAG =   1       0.10409       0.20590       4 %
   TOTAL VARIANCE ACCOUNTED FOR 61 %

DEFINITION OF DELTA US SUPPORT
                        CONSTANT =   -0.09666     NORMALIZED   VARIANCE
   AUGUST WEATHER    LAG =   0      -0.39902      -0.57772      23 %
   NV PREFER NV ACT  LAG =   0       0.28814       0.39289      11 %
   NV PREFER NEGOT   LAG =   1      -0.12096      -0.16356       3 %
   NV PERCEIVE US    LAG =   0       0.27847       0.26441       3 %
   WINTER - SUMMER   LAG =   0      -0.02138      -0.24055       2 %
   DEL NV+VC TROOPS  LAG =   0      -0.14057      -0.16184       2 %
   TOTAL VARIANCE ACCOUNTED FOR 44 %
```

```
DEFINITION OF NV PREFER NV ACT
                    CONSTANT =   -0.78486      NORMALIZED   VARIANCE
    ARVN CASUALTIES   LAG =  1    1.79722        0.45968      19 %
    NV+VC ATTRITION   LAG =  3   -1.00643       -1.08274      10 %
    US BOMBING OF NV  LAG =  3    2.12872        1.02087      29 %
    DELTA US SUPPORT  LAG =  3    0.33777        0.22547       5 %
    DEL VC DEFECTORS  LAG =  1   -0.31098       -0.23370       4 %
    MILITARY INITIAT  LAG =  0   -0.25630       -0.21447       4 %
    TOTAL VARIANCE ACCOUNTED FOR 71 %

DEFINITION OF NV PREFER NV ACT
                    CONSTANT =   -0.26019      NORMALIZED   VARIANCE
    US PERCEIVE NV    LAG =  0    0.55470        0.60332      16 %
    DEL US COMMITMNT  LAG =  1    0.31491        0.50385      21 %
    DEL* BOMBING NV   LAG =  1    0.09954        0.36462       8 %
    CHRISTMAS - TET   LAG =  0    0.56911        0.36431       7 %
    US PREFER OUTCM   LAG =  1   -0.17778       -0.23662       7 %
    DEL US COMMITMNT  LAG =  3   -0.14990       -0.24089       5 %
    TOTAL VARIANCE ACCOUNTED FOR 64 %

DEFINITION OF NV PREFER NV ACT
                    CONSTANT =   -1.33845      NORMALIZED   VARIANCE
    ARVN CASUALTIES   LAG =  1    1.84514        0.47194      19 %
    NV+VC ATTRITION   LAG =  3   -0.96275       -1.03575      10 %
    US BOMBING OF NV  LAG =  3    2.03017        0.97360      29 %
    DELTA US SUPPORT  LAG =  3    0.31918        0.21306       5 %
    DEL VC DEFECTORS  LAG =  1   -0.31809       -0.23904       4 %
    DEL* BOMBING NV   LAG =  1    0.04825        0.17674       3 %
    TOTAL VARIANCE ACCOUNTED FOR 70 %

DEFINITION OF NV PERCEIVE US
                    CONSTANT =    2.71150      NORMALIZED   VARIANCE
    NV+VC DEFECTORS   LAG =  1   -3.49531       -0.52643      18 %
    US PREFER US ACT  LAG =  0   -0.14202       -0.37674       9 %
    US PREFER US ACT  LAG =  1    0.09287        0.24520       7 %
    PIASTRE SAIGON    LAG =  1   -1.29488       -0.27826       8 %
    DEL* BOMBING NV   LAG =  1   -0.05501       -0.28937       4 %
    DEL* NV ATTRITON  LAG =  1    0.11080        0.28081       7 %
    TOTAL VARIANCE ACCOUNTED FOR 53 %

DEFINITION OF NV PERCEIVE US
                    CONSTANT =    0.80469      NORMALIZED   VARIANCE
    US PREFER US ACT  LAG =  0   -0.18335       -0.48637      11 %
    US BOMBING OF NV  LAG =  0   -0.35429       -0.24024       9 %
    DEL* BOMBING NV   LAG =  1   -0.03859       -0.20299       8 %
    US PREFER OUTCM   LAG =  1    0.20421        0.39032       8 %
    US PREFER NEGOT   LAG =  1    0.19329        0.40268       8 %
    US BOMBING OF NV  LAG =  5   -0.43657       -0.28141       4 %
    TOTAL VARIANCE ACCOUNTED FOR 48 %

DEFINITION OF NV PERCEIVE US
                    CONSTANT =    1.47367      NORMALIZED   VARIANCE
    NV+VC DEFECTORS   LAG =  1   -2.13037       -0.32085      18 %
    DEL* US CASULTY   LAG =  1   -0.16225       -0.54398       9 %
    DEL* NV ATTRITON  LAG =  1    0.25244        0.63978      17 %
    CHRISTMAS - TET   LAG =  0    0.25270        0.23230       9 %
    DEL* BOMBING NV   LAG =  1   -0.04554       -0.23955       4 %
    KILL RATIO NV/US  LAG =  1   -0.01655       -0.25698       5 %
    TOTAL VARIANCE ACCOUNTED FOR 62 %
```

DEFINITION OF NV PREFER NEGOT

		CONSTANT =	-1.99907	NORMALIZED	VARIANCE
ARVN CASUALTIES	LAG =	3	1.67543	0.40126	15 %
CHRISTMAS − TET	LAG =	0	1.11489	0.70675	13 %
NV PREFER OUTCM	LAG =	0	-0.93831	-0.54272	11 %
SPRING − FALL	LAG =	0	0.03757	0.31762	8 %
DELTA KILL RATIO	LAG =	1	0.31735	0.28992	5 %
DEL US COMMITMNT	LAG =	3	-0.15996	-0.25455	5 %

TOTAL VARIANCE ACCOUNTED FOR 57 %

DEFINITION OF NV PREFER NEGOT

		CONSTANT =	-0.03701	NORMALIZED	VARIANCE
CHRISTMAS − TET	LAG =	0	0.35031	0.22207	11 %
US BOMBING OF NV	LAG =	0	-1.62471	-0.75971	4 %
US PREFER US ACT	LAG =	1	-0.13980	-0.25453	6 %
US PREFER NEGOT	LAG =	0	0.12385	0.17698	4 %
SPRING − FALL	LAG =	0	0.03282	0.27747	3 %
US BOMBING OF NV	LAG =	1	1.12998	0.54131	3 %

TOTAL VARIANCE ACCOUNTED FOR 31 %

DEFINITION OF NV PREFER NEGOT

		CONSTANT =	-1.99907	NORMALIZED	VARIANCE
ARVN CASUALTIES	LAG =	3	1.67543	0.40126	15 %
CHRISTMAS − TET	LAG =	0	1.11489	0.70675	13 %
NV PREFER OUTCM	LAG =	0	-0.93831	-0.54272	11 %
SPRING − FALL	LAG =	0	0.03757	0.31762	8 %
DELTA KILL RATIO	LAG =	1	0.31735	0.28992	5 %
DEL US COMMITMNT	LAG =	3	-0.15996	-0.25455	5 %

TOTAL VARIANCE ACCOUNTED FOR 57 %

DEFINITION OF NV PREFER OUTCM

		CONSTANT =	1.47677	NORMALIZED	VARIANCE
DEL* BOMBING NV	LAG =	3	-0.04286	-0.30346	19 %
NV PREFER NEGOT	LAG =	1	0.27974	0.47495	11 %
DEL US COMMITMNT	LAG =	5	-0.15650	-0.42432	10 %
PIASTRE SAIGON	LAG =	1	-0.94574	-0.24229	12 %
NV PERCEIVE US	LAG =	1	0.28961	0.34173	6 %
NV+VC DEFECTORS	LAG =	1	1.73117	0.31085	8 %

TOTAL VARIANCE ACCOUNTED FOR 66 %

DEFINITION OF NV PREFER OUTCM

		CONSTANT =	0.57261	NORMALIZED	VARIANCE
DEL* BOMBING NV	LAG =	3	-0.04829	-0.34191	19 %
SPRING − FALL	LAG =	0	0.02037	0.29774	9 %
US PERCEIVE NV	LAG =	1	0.10146	0.18880	7 %
DEL US COMMITMNT	LAG =	5	-0.08013	-0.21726	5 %
CHRISTMAS − TET	LAG =	0	0.20167	0.22102	3 %
DEL US COMMITMNT	LAG =	3	-0.06800	-0.18709	3 %

TOTAL VARIANCE ACCOUNTED FOR 46 %

DEFINITION OF NV PREFER OUTCM

		CONSTANT =	1.47677	NORMALIZED	VARIANCE
DEL* BOMBING NV	LAG =	3	-0.04286	-0.30346	19 %
NV PREFER NEGOT	LAG =	1	0.27974	0.47495	11 %
DEL US COMMITMNT	LAG =	5	-0.15650	-0.42432	10 %
PIASTRE SAIGON	LAG =	1	-0.94574	-0.24229	12 %
NV PERCEIVE US	LAG =	1	0.28961	0.34173	6 %
NV+VC DEFECTORS	LAG =	1	1.73117	0.31085	8 %

TOTAL VARIANCE ACCOUNTED FOR 66 %

```
DEFINITION OF US PERCEIVE NV
                        CONSTANT =  -1.32038      NORMALIZED   VARIANCE
    DEL US COMMITMNT  LAG =  1    -0.43067        -0.63354      30 %
    NV PREFER NV ACT  LAG =  0     0.58646         0.53920      24 %
    ARVN CASUALTIES   LAG =  1     1.64443         0.38671       7 %
    DEL* BOMBING NV   LAG =  1    -0.08158        -0.27475       4 %
    DELTA US SUPPORT  LAG =  1    -0.42425        -0.26080       4 %
    DELTA US SUPPORT  LAG =  0    -0.36892        -0.24876       5 %
    TOTAL VARIANCE ACCOUNTED FOR 74 %

DEFINITION OF US PERCEIVE NV
                        CONSTANT =  -2.37846      NORMALIZED   VARIANCE
    DEL US COMMITMNT  LAG =  1    -0.43409        -0.63857      30 %
    ARVN CASUALTIES   LAG =  1     2.46140         0.57883      19 %
    MILITARY INITIAT  LAG =  3     0.45601         0.42744       6 %
    NV+VC DEFECTORS   LAG =  1    -2.77869        -0.26794       5 %
    DELTA KILL RATIO  LAG =  1     0.25854         0.21929       3 %
    DEL* US CASULTY   LAG =  1    -0.07189        -0.15431       2 %
    TOTAL VARIANCE ACCCUNTED FOR 65 %

DEFINITION OF US PERCEIVE NV
                        CONSTANT =   0.62143      NORMALIZED   VARIANCE
    CHRISTMAS - TET   LAG =  0     0.47065         0.27700      18 %
    NV PREFER NV ACT  LAG =  0     0.35277         0.32434       6 %
    SPRING - FALL     LAG =  0    -0.03000        -0.23548       4 %
    DEL NV+VC TROOPS  LAG =  3    -0.34366        -0.28387       6 %
    NV PREFER OUTCM   LAG =  0    -0.39683        -0.21310       2 %
    NV PREFER NEGOT   LAG =  1     0.18358         0.16738       2 %
    TOTAL VARIANCE ACCOUNTED FOR 38 %

DEFINITION OF US PREFER US ACT
                        CONSTANT =  -0.46160      NORMALIZED   VARIANCE
    DEL NV+VC TROOPS  LAG =  3     1.10813         0.53895      19 %
    NV+VC DEFECTORS   LAG =  0     6.77398         0.37754      16 %
    NV PREFER OUTCM   LAG =  0    -0.97573        -0.30852      10 %
    DELTA US SUPPORT  LAG =  0    -1.21638        -0.48293       7 %
    AUGUST WEATHER    LAG =  0    -0.67559        -0.38835      11 %
    DEL VC DEFECTORS  LAG =  1     0.58238         0.23693       5 %
    TOTAL VARIANCE ACCCUNTED FOR 68 %

DEFINITION OF US PREFER US ACT
                        CONSTANT =   0.93237      NORMALIZED   VARIANCE
    DEL NV+VC TROOPS  LAG =  3     0.89282         0.43423      19 %
    NV PERCEIVE US    LAG =  1    -1.21284        -0.45251      10 %
    DEL VC DEFECTORS  LAG =  1     0.60958         0.24799      12 %
    DEL* BOMBING NV   LAG =  3     0.16865         0.37756       6 %
    WINTER - SUMMER   LAG =  0     0.10746         0.48003       6 %
    CHRISTMAS - TET   LAG =  0    -0.90822        -0.31473       6 %
    TOTAL VARIANCE ACCCUNTED FOR 59 %

DEFINITION OF US PREFER US ACT
                        CONSTANT =   0.94357      NORMALIZED   VARIANCE
    DEL NV+VC TROOPS  LAG =  3     1.35423         0.65864      19 %
    NV PERCEIVE US    LAG =  1    -1.69784        -0.63346      10 %
    DEL NV+VC TROOPS  LAG =  0    -1.00401        -0.45893       7 %
    DEL NV+VC TROOPS  LAG =  1     1.03904         0.50747      11 %
    WINTER - SUMMER   LAG =  0     0.09978         0.44572       7 %
    CHRISTMAS - TET   LAG =  0    -0.76727        -0.26589       5 %
    TOTAL VARIANCE ACCCUNTED FOR 59 %
```

```
DEFINITION OF US PREFER NEGOT
                     CONSTANT =  -0.13382     NORMALIZED   VARIANCE
   MILITARY INITIAT  LAG =  3     0.91490      0.64638      25 %
   DEL* BOMBING NV   LAG =  3     0.15539      0.44532      17 %
   US PREFER OUTCM   LAG =  0    -0.40071     -0.39700      10 %
   DEL US COMMITMNT  LAG =  5    -0.23000     -0.25241       9 %
   NV+VC DEFECTORS   LAG =  0    -4.71874     -0.33666       4 %
   US BOMBING OF NV  LAG =  5     0.88908      0.27656       5 %
   TOTAL VARIANCE ACCOUNTED FOR 70 %

DEFINITION OF US PREFER NEGOT
                     CONSTANT =  -0.66956     NORMALIZED   VARIANCE
   MILITARY INITIAT  LAG =  3     0.70328      0.49687      25 %
   DEL* BOMBING NV   LAG =  3     0.15516      0.44466      17 %
   US PREFER OUTCM   LAG =  0    -0.35601     -0.35271      10 %
   DEL US COMMITMNT  LAG =  5    -0.25289     -0.27753       9 %
   US PERCEIVE NV    LAG =  0     0.33164      0.24997       5 %
   US BOMBING OF NV  LAG =  1     0.53731      0.18012       3 %
   TOTAL VARIANCE ACCOUNTED FOR 69 %

DEFINITION OF US PREFER NEGOT
                     CONSTANT =   0.42921     NORMALIZED   VARIANCE
   CHRISTMAS - TET   LAG =  0     0.73961      0.32810      15 %
   NV PREFER NEGOT   LAG =  1    -0.40313     -0.27704       7 %
   AUGUST WEATHER    LAG =  0    -0.26714     -0.19657       5 %
   NV PREFER NV ACT  LAG =  1    -0.31736     -0.22094       4 %
   NV PREFER NEGOT   LAG =  0     0.29860      0.20896       2 %
   DEL NV+VC TROOPS  LAG =  1    -0.27730     -0.17337       3 %
   TOTAL VARIANCE ACCOUNTED FOR 36 %

DEFINITION OF US PREFER OUTCM
                     CONSTANT =  -3.18363     NORMALIZED   VARIANCE
   PIASTRE SAIGON    LAG =  3    10.40010      1.14850      16 %
   US CASUALTIES     LAG =  3     0.20616      0.77521      14 %
   PIASTRE SAIGON    LAG =  1    -8.31802     -0.87062      17 %
   DEL US COMMITMNT  LAG =  5    -0.38359     -0.42490      10 %
   US BOMBING OF NV  LAG =  5    -1.29515     -0.40664       5 %
   ARVN CASUALTIES   LAG =  0     1.16215      0.22409       4 %
   TOTAL VARIANCE ACCOUNTED FOR 66 %

DEFINITION OF US PREFER OUTCM
                     CONSTANT =  -4.97636     NORMALIZED   VARIANCE
   PIASTRE SAIGON    LAG =  3    10.45210      1.15424      16 %
   NV+VC ATTRITION   LAG =  1     0.86413      0.65251      16 %
   PIASTRE SAIGON    LAG =  1   -16.88180     -1.76697      14 %
   DEL* NV ATTRITON  LAG =  1    -0.34796     -0.42953      12 %
   PIASTRE HONGKONG  LAG =  1     9.32162      1.10938       7 %
   DEL PIASTRE SAIG  LAG =  1     0.59578      0.33729       5 %
   TOTAL VARIANCE ACCOUNTED FOR 70 %

DEFINITION OF US PREFER OUTCM
                     CONSTANT =   0.93054     NORMALIZED   VARIANCE
   DEL NV+VC TROOPS  LAG =  3     0.43244      0.27175       5 %
   NV PREFER OUTCM   LAG =  1    -0.72450     -0.30145       3 %
   NV PREFER NV ACT  LAG =  0    -0.37967     -0.26557       4 %
   NV PREFER OUTCM   LAG =  0     0.58779      0.24014       2 %
   NV PREFER NEGOT   LAG =  1    -0.23409     -0.16237       2 %
   DEL NV+VC TROOPS  LAG =  0    -0.18025     -0.10646       1 %
   TOTAL VARIANCE ACCOUNTED FOR 17 %
```

Produced for the publishers
by Ray Freiman & Company
and printed by The McQuiddy Printing Co.